The
Victorian
"Lives" of Jesus

The
Victorian
"Lives" of Jesus

DANIEL L. PALS

TRINITY UNIVERSITY MONOGRAPH SERIES
IN RELIGION   VOLUME VII

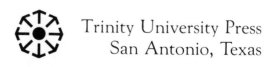

Trinity University Press
San Antonio, Texas

$\top U M S_R$ Trinity University Monograph
Series in Religion

A portion of chapter one (pages 39-50) is adapted from Pals' "Reception of *Ecce Homo*," March 1977 issue of the *Historical Magazine of the Protestant Episcopal Church* with permission.

CONTENTS

PREFACE

Study of the life of Jesus is an immense undertaking. Study of those who have studied the life of Jesus borders on the inconceivable. When the author of the Fourth Gospel mused that the world itself could not contain the books that might be written of Jesus' words and deeds, he could hardly have known that speculation would turn to prophecy. Over the twenty centuries of Christendom, myriads of books in scores of tongues have transformed the words of the Evangelist into a virtual truism. Scrawled on papyrus, etched in runes, bound in vellum tomes, spun off in thousands by the modern paperback press—books about Jesus have become so plentiful that one does indeed wonder if the globe can contain them.

While believers might well rejoice in such a phenomenon, the delight of the pious is in many ways the despair of the historian. On first looking into the literature one scarcely knows where to begin. Yet no task is so great that it cannot be subdivided and undertaken in parts. Precisely that has happened, moreover, in what the Germans describe—in their compound way—as *Leben-jesu-forschung:* the scholarly study of the life of Jesus. In the modern era there have in fact been any number of good books which have charted the trends and paths of inquiry, among them certainly one of the great scholarly achievements in our century: Albert Schweitzer's *Quest of the Historical Jesus.* The chief justification for gently edging this book into such prestigious company is appropriate to its aims, which are rather modest than grand. Alongside the German enterprise chronicled by Schweitzer, there arose in Great Britain an intriguing alternative form of inquiry into the life of Jesus. The essence of this tradition was embodied in Britain's "Lives," or biographies of Jesus. It should be stated with candor that as a rule these Lives did not provide the turning points of critical investigation. Many were predictable, derivative, obvious. Yet it would be a mistake to assume—as some critics apparently have—that Britain's Lives are for that reason trivial. They are not. They reveal too much about the intersecting currents of Victorian society, popular attitudes, religious thought, biblical study, and cultural change to be passed over so easily. Hence, the discussion that follows.

"Discussion," with its suggestion of several participants, is surely the appropriate word here. None knows better than the writer that a book is the product of many hands. This one is certainly no exception. Invisibly it owes much to three superb teaching scholars from college years and after: Professors Robert Otten, Henry Stob, and David Holwerda. It later began as a doctoral dissertation, proceeded by fits and starts through five years preoccupied with college teaching, and survived two full-scale uprootings of house and home. The largest debt from doctoral years is owed to Professor Martin E. Marty, dissertation advisor, gentleman, friend, and counselor during and after my years at the Divinity School of the University of Chicago. Included on the Chicago committee which supervised the project were Professors Langdon Gilkey, Leonard Krieger, Nathan A. Scott, and not least Norman Perrin, whose shift from scepticism to enthusiasm about this work makes personal the memory of a man still greatly missed by contemporary biblical study. In addition, the fruitful hours spent in discussion on the second floor of Swift Hall with Jerald C. Brauer make him a *de facto* sixth on the committee.

Others who early on corresponded and gave advice include Bishop Stephen Neill of Oxford University, Patrick Scott of Edinburgh, and James Barnes of Wabash College in Crawfordsville, Indiana, whose knowledge of backroads and byways through the Victorian book trade still astonishes. In Britain T. & T. Clark Publishers of Edinburgh and Mr. J. A. E. Higham of Longman Group Limited, Burnt Mill, Harlow, Essex furnished valuable information from their nineteenth-century records.

Financial support came from the German Academic Exchange Service, which during graduate years provided a stipend for German language study that was to prove useful for comparative aspects of the project; from the Faculty Development Committee of Centre College, Danville, Kentucky, which provided a summer study grant during 1978; and from the University of Miami, which provided a Max Orovitz summer award for July and August of 1981, when the project was brought to completion.

Fortune smiled in providing my overseers. Provost E. C. Reckard of Centre College and Dean Arthur Brown at the University of Miami may not know it, but they are kindred spirits who prove that learning flourishes when the soul of the humanist animates the flesh of the administrator. Alongside them, thanks must go to two sets of skilled colleagues, at Centre and Miami, whose thinking presence has been a whetstone for the critical intellect; to Ms. Carol Gillespie, Staff Coordinator of the Religion Department at Miami, who, mind of the absent-minded, handled without a grimace the unrewarding associated labors of correspondence, copying, and mailing; to Ms. Yolanda Crespo, who cheerfully took on the index; and especially to Editors John H. Hayes and Lois Boyd of the Trinity University Press. Their diligent red markings have cleansed the text, and their unseen labor forms an invisible footnote to every page.

Finally, if a first-time author is to be indulged a lapse into sentiment, two debts loom so large as to be finally unpayable: to my parents, Mr. and Mrs. Herbert Pals, and to my wife, Phyllis. During a long apprenticeship they understood—and paid the bills.

The
Victorian
"Lives" of Jesus

INTRODUCTION
THE LIFE OF JESUS IN THE
CONTEXT OF CHRISTENDOM

During the nineteenth century authors in Britain, as elsewhere in
Europe, developed a keen interest in the historical Life, or biography,
of Jesus. Especially after about 1860 Lives of Christ became in fact a
sort of vogue among the Victorians, to which every type of writer—
devotional, radical, clerical, or eccentric—was sooner or later
attracted. The books mirrored many facets of the Victorian mind.
They came in every shape and style and size, and they explored a
wealth of interpretations. Some were hostile, concerned to shatter the
conventional Christ and deliver a blow to the dogma of the churches.
Some were historical, or at least came near the modern critical
approach to ancient documents. A great many were purely practical,
designed for devotion or religious instruction. They ranged from the
important to the trivial, from the dull and sententious to the sweet and
sentimental. A Life of Christ might appear as a Sunday school handbook, or among parish materials; it might originate in a series of
lengthy sermons or an encyclopedia article; it might be the simple
effusion of an ordinary believer with a facile pen or the mature fruit of
long labors by a churchman-scholar. Useful for their ends, most of
these works claimed neither literary nor critical distinction; they commanded little notice beyond the circle for which they were intended.
They had their moment and have now vanished.

Within this vast literature, however, there also appeared works of
real cultural significance, and those books are the chief concern of the
present study. There were two ways in which a Life of Christ might
become important. Either it was critically decisive, introducing a new
scholarly approach; or it was a popular success, exercising a deep
effect on the mind of the religious community. The first instinct of the
historian is to sever these two forms and discuss them separately. But
while that procedure might apply well to other times and places, it will
not work here; for in Victorian Britain the fate of scholarship is closely
linked to the larger climate of religious opinion. The one cannot be
understood without the other. Our understanding of this will be clear-
est if we first establish a context, and the context must be a large one.
We need first to observe how over the long span the Christian tradition has seen and studied the life of Christ.

From its earliest days, Christian belief has centered upon the pattern of Jesus' life, death, and resurrection. While looking back to the
law and prophets, the preaching of the first apostles did not hesitate to

make Hebrew history the preface to God's central act, the Messianic appearance of Christ. Contemporary scholarship has shown us how this early message was at the start preserved orally for the worship and instruction of the tiny Christian communities. Then, as the first converts began to pass away and the oral record grew faint, written versions began to appear in the shape of the documents now called gospels, a literary form some see as without precedent in the ancient world.[1] On the surface, the aim of these gospels seems clear enough: to record the crucial events or teachings (or both) in Jesus' life. But the deeper one looks, the more clouded the picture. We know today more than ever that there were many such "gospels" in the first Christian centuries, and by no means did they all have the same purpose. Recovered manuscript fragments and other sources have disclosed a welter of such gospel literature arising from various regions and groups in the Greco-Roman world. In addition to the four biblical gospels, there are others which resemble them, associated with special sects. There are also gnostic gospels, filled with the arcane wisdom by which one escapes the material world and enters the realm of spirit, and infancy gospels, which freely mixed legend and pious imagination.[2] The process by which Christian leaders filtered out all gospels but the four recognized today as scripture is a complex one, known in broad outline but puzzling in many details. Equally vexing, especially to theologians, is the question of the motive behind their composition. Since early in our century, Rudolph Bultmann and some of his disciples have contended that the concerns of gospel writers were almost wholly religious or, to use the philosophical term, "existential." In such writings, historical recollection was unimportant—and usually inaccurate.[3] Others insist that genuine historical reminiscence, much of it accurate, was crucial to the mind of the compilers.[4]

The theological dispute can be laid aside for the moment, though it will emerge again upon examination of the forces which affected the Victorians who wrote Lives of Jesus. We do know that by about 200 A.D. Christian leaders had decided on the four biblical gospels as canonical.[5] Others survived; new ones still appeared. But none earned a similar consensus.

With the establishment of the sacred canon, interest in the life of Jesus took a new form. The biblical gospels became the basis of secondary endeavors aimed at reconstructing the sequence of Christ's deeds and retelling his story. Here in a sense is the real beginning of the Lives of Jesus, for with the establishment of the scriptural sources it fell to each new generation of Christians to make the story its own—by rereading, which was insured by the use of the Bible in worship, but also by analysis, meditation, commentary, or even fresh retelling of the tale. It should be clear that from the start this enterprise was strongly marked by two different impulses, or motives. The one may be called technical or analytical. It notices first that there is in the gospels an intellectual riddle, that certain conflicts in the narratives need to be resolved, that certain criticisms likely to be launched by opponents must be answered. Those who took this approach did not do so to the exclusion of all other concerns, but the intellectual problems do seem to have been uppermost in their minds. The other major style may be described as practical, or religious, or even popular. The first concern of writers in this vein is not solving problems or defending the scriptural record, but simply retelling the story of Jesus for the Christian community in a way that is fresh, or compelling, or dramatically inspirational. It will become clear that both styles persist throughout the history of Christianity, though at different times and places one or the other may predominate. In general, the two styles have tended to travel separate paths. Yet one of the intriguing things about Victorian Britain, especially in the last quarter of the nineteenth century, is that here the two traditions merged in a unique, if temporary, synthesis.

Understandably the analytical style made its appearance first, while the debate over the canon was still in progress. A first instance, certainly, is Tatian's *Diatessaron*, a harmony of the biblical gospels drawn up in the second century by interweaving the four into a single narrative.[6] As Oscar Cullmann has pointed out, the plurality of the four gospels, which differed in their records of Jesus, created a theological problem for early Christians, and Tatian's work was one attempt to solve it.[7] In order to integrate the four accounts, Tatian conceded that the evangelists might have made minor errors that needed correction. He sometimes reduced to one the multiple narratives which seemed to describe the same event with different particulars.[8] In fact, says Robert Grant, he made judgments not unlike those of a modern historical critic.[9] Nor was he alone. Origen in the third century applied Greek methods of historical and literary study to the gospel problems.[10] Still later Augustine, feeling the force of pagan objections that "the evangelists are not in harmony with each other," composed his *De Consensu Evangelistarum* (ca. 400) in defense of the biblical gospels.[11] This work was to have great influence in the Middle Ages. Particularly important was his idea that the order of recollection in the gospels often differs from the order of occurrence of events in the life of Jesus. It is apparent that despite his wholly supernatural view of the Bible, Augustine too felt the need, however reluctantly, to amend the narratives or account for discrepancies.

After Augustine and throughout the medieval period true representatives of the analytical tradition are hard to find. Victor of Capua, a sixth-century Latin imitator of Tatian, and Clement of Llanthony, author of the twelfth-century harmony *Unum ex Quattuor,* might be cited. But in the absence of new methods and in the shadow of the achievements of Tatian and Augustine, medieval writers generally avoided harmonization.[12] They turned with much greater interest to interpretation under the fourfold scheme, which placed the literal sense of the text well below its moral, allegorical, and anagogical applications in order of importance.[13]

What we do find in the Middle Ages is a flourishing literature inspired by the second style, the retelling of the gospel tale to inspire or instruct. This devotional impulse, like the analytical, can be discerned well before the medieval period. It certainly is evident in the early infancy gospels, which sought in ways that were sometimes charming, sometimes grotesque, to satisfy the curiosity of simple believers about the empty spaces left by the gospels in the life of Jesus.[14] To some extent it is apparent even in the biblical gospels, where Matthew and Luke preserve tales of Christ's infancy and childhood. We see it later in the early period, when the appeal of old and new apocryphal gospels is so strong that even papal condemnations fail to stop the use of them.[15] It appears vividly in several early efforts at Christian epic poetry: Juvencus' *Evangeliorum Libri Quattuor* (330) written in imitation of Vergil; Proba's *Cento* (ca. 350); and Sedulius's *Carmen Paschale* and prose *Opus* composed in the fifth century.[16]

From these beginnings the tradition gained greater momentum throughout the medieval Latin West. It drew its core of incident and discourse not only from the biblical gospels, but from the infancy gospels, other legends, and even older works in the analytical style, such as Tatian's *Diatessaron.*[17] In the Dark Age poems like Cynewulf's *Christ,* the Anglo-Saxon *Heliand,* Otfrid of Weissenburg's *Evangelienbuch,* and Ezzo von Bamberg's *Cantilena* plainly reflect this approach. In a troubled, unsettled epoch of minimum civilization, they served as vehicles for the inculcation of Christian sentiments in the newly converted peoples of Northern Europe. Just how strongly popular needs were felt in these works can be seen in new tones and settings the life of Jesus acquired. Consider the *Heliand's* account of the disciples:

> Then they stepped nearer to All-Saving Christ,
> Such disciples, as He had chosen Himself,
> The Wielder amid His vassals there. And the wise men
> The heroes, stood all gladly about God's son,
> The war-men most willingly; they awaited His word,
> Thought and were silent, longing to hear what the Lord of the Land-folk
> The Wielder Himself, would make known with His Words
> For love of the land-folk.[18]

Passages like these are not without an intriguing, rugged charm, and they illustrate clearly how popular needs could give the story a dramatic, heroic, or romantic turn. In the feudal age Christ becomes a Saxon lord.

With the advent of the crusades, the coming of Franciscan spirituality, and the spread of a more contemplative piety in the high Middle Ages, new forces came into play. Dramatic and heroic portraits gave way to what Elizabeth Salter has called meditation on the sacred humanity of Christ.[19] The *Meditationes Vitae Christi* of the late thirteenth century, once attributed to St. Bonaventure, patently expressed these ideals. Widely circulated and often translated, it "proceeded on the basis of an imaginative recapitulation of the actual scenes in the life of Christ."[20] In Britain the most popular version was Nicholas Love's *Myrrour of the Blessed Lyf of Jesus Christ,* a most effective translation and reworking of the Latin original.[21] In a similar vein was another work, Simone Fidati's massive *De Gestis Domini Salvatoris;* topically arranged, it was popular both in the original and an Italian version by John of Salerno.[22] Devotional realization of the life of Christ reached its apex, however, in Ludolph the Carthusian's extraordinarily successful *Vita Christi* (ca. 1350), which appeared after the author's death and circulated in countless editions and translations. Carrying the style of the *Meditationes* to even greater lengths, Ludolph produced a treasury for the meditative soul. He began his discussions with the literal gospel texts, then accumulated commentary from numerous early fathers, roamed frequently into moral and allegorical interpretations, included homilies on the evangelical counsels, cardinal virtues, or other set themes, and concluded each section with a devotional prayer. The *Vita* was not meant for people in a hurry. To assist his readers in meditation Ludolph drew from Burchardus of Mount Zion's eyewitness descriptions of the sacred sites.[23] This literary device was an intriguing anticipation of the Victorian writers, who were to adopt the practice with great enthusiasm. In Ludolph, the technical concerns of gospel harmonization are not wholly absent, any more than in other medieval devotionalists, but they are not his metier. He observes no consistent harmonic principles in using his sources. John and Matthew are usually, but not always, his chronological guides. Rather arbitrarily he sometimes applies the multiple gospel traditions to one occurrence, sometimes to several. That is because devotion and meditation are his interests, not the solving of textual problems.[24]

In the Eastern church of the Middle Ages there was a similar reticence to engage in the analytical work of the harmonist, though apparently for different reasons. Early on the school of Antioch, which advocated literal historical study of the scriptures, had been over-shadowed by the Alexandrian school, where speculative theology reigned supreme.[25] In the process the theology of the divine Christ overwhelmed most feeling for the historical, human Jesus. Later, in the fifth century, the Council of Chalcedon reached a compromise which placed equal stress on Christ's humanity and divinity. But in subsequent centuries the Eastern church found itself laboring instead to accommodate the Monophysite faction, which held fanatically to the dogma of one divine nature of Christ.[26] The result was that the historical sensibility, whenever it might appear, struggled against a huge theological framework structured against it.[27] As in the icon and mosaic, the Eastern Christ assumed the persona of timeless, motionless divinity, not the striding, eating, speaking, weeping, quarreling human figure one expects to find in a Life of Christ.

Returning now to the West at the end of the medieval era, we suddenly discover that the pendulum has swung back. The late fifteenth and entire sixteenth centuries were marked by a striking resurgence of the analytical style and a flurry of new gospel harmonies. The reasons for this development are not entirely clear. Some insist that growing awareness of the non-Christian world rekindled the apologetic spirit of the early church.[28] Certainly the emphasis of the reformers on the Bible played a part, for it drew both Catholic and Protestant into intense scriptural study. Even more important, it would seem, is an occurrence known to students of humanism: the reinvigorated study of ancient languages and texts which occurred with the Renaissance. Lorenzo Valla's celebrated study of the Vulgate, the new translations of the ancients and the scriptures, and Erasmus's new edition of the Greek New Testament undoubtedly provided a strong stimulus toward a renewed and serious technical study of the biblical documents. Whatever the precise cause, harmonies flowered in the sixteenth century. Their importance may be gleaned partly from the prestigious names of those who composed them, many of whom were major scholars of the Reformation age: Bucer, Osiander, Jansen, Calvin, Flacius, Baronius, Salmeron, Chemnitz, and others. We shall return to the harmonists briefly at the outset of the next chapter. For the present, one significant innovation in these works is worthy of note: the arrangement of gospel texts in parallel columns as well as in the integrated narrative of Tatian and Augustine. This device clearly signals the return to the arena of scholarship rather than popular presentations. Where the medieval author faced problems of harmonization, he solved them as best he could, left them behind, and passed the finished treatise on to his readers. Discussion of difficulties was not his aim. The parallel-column harmony of the Reformation age is on the contrary an invitation to dialogue; it sets out difficulties in the collegial mode of the academy. As Harvey McArthur has noted, the parallel harmony "allowed the reader to evaluate the problems of order and the proposals of the harmonists."[29]

In the aftermath of the Reformation age both harmonies and works of devotion continued to appear.[30] Interest ebbed and flowed, but the two paths first charted in the early days of Christianity were still discernible. From the second century to the seventeenth students of the life of Christ contented themselves with either a harmony or a work of devotion. But it would not remain so for long. The seventeenth century also saw the first stirring of something entirely new: the modern critical study of the scriptures. It began almost invisibly among outcast thinkers, Hobbes in England, Spinoza in the Netherlands, Simon and later Astruc in France. Scarcely crusaders, they began by applying to the scriptures the same literary canons and philological analyses that were used with other ancient texts. By the middle of the eighteenth century the literary, linguistic, and historical questions combined with the philosophical scepticism of the Enlightenment to produce a powerful solvent, which for some seemed capable of eroding orthodox beliefs. Its effects were felt everywhere, but the historical application was most evident in Germany, where thinkers like Lessing, Semler, Reimarus, and others jettisoned supernatural beliefs and claimed to find distortion, superstition, and forgery in the scriptures.

These attitudes were only a beginning. The full consequence of the new historical studies was not to be felt until the nineteenth century, and here again the foremost site of impact was Germany. In a variety of disciplines German scholars mounted a revolution in the study of ancient documents. Their work on both classical and biblical materials was dense with detail, minutely attentive to subtle linguistic differences in the texts, exhaustive in the range of sources consulted, searching in its scepticism of supernatural dogmas. In gospel studies the German critics disdained the credulous speculations of the old devotional Lives, then turned their analyses against the archaic methods and forced readings of the harmonists. Their rigorous frontal assault on the old styles achieved nothing less than the establishment of a third tradition in biblical study, the critical style, which came very near to a total victory over the old ways. The story of these remarkable changes, particularly as they affected study of the life of Christ, has already been told with inimitable skill and perception by Albert Schweitzer in his great survey of criticism from Reimarus to Wrede, *The Quest of the Historical Jesus* (1906).[31]

It was during this same era that Great Britain also witnessed a resurgence of interest in the life of Christ. Yet on Britain's quest neither

Schweitzer, his successors in the field of biblical study,[32] nor the students of Victorian thought and culture[33] have had much to say. Except for Owen Chadwick, who has partly corrected the oversight in a recent work, *The Victorian Church,* the distinctively British Lives of Jesus written during the Victorian era remain unexamined and, indeed, almost unnoticed.[34] This gap the present study is at least partly designed to fill. One of its chief aims is to examine the form which literature on the life of Christ assumed during an age in which it flourished immensely and exercised great influence on religious opinion. Although a number of earlier developments of necessity will have to be taken up, the half century which requires most of our attention extends from about 1860 to 1910. It was not until this era, when students of the subject were presented with opportunities for extensive travel in the Near East, a vast increase of archaeological data from the lands and locales of antiquity, striking new developments in historical criticism, and a rapidly expanding market for instructive religious books, that scholars and populace alike became captivated by the search for the historical Jesus.

This period and the works which appeared in it require some preliminary comments. British Lives were quite different from the continental literature examined by Schweitzer in the *Quest.* The reasons for this will be explored in chapter four. At this point we can simply assert that German critics came nearer achieving a tradition of pure scholarship. In contrast, the typical British Life of Christ, even when unorthodox, sought to turn scholarship into public literature. It endeavored to bridge the inevitable gap between cloistered scholar and common reader. Many of the authors were active churchmen writing for interested churchgoers, and they frequently opted for literary indulgences the purist would disdain. Nevertheless, those writers who followed this plan received their reward—as is plain in the enormous total of sales they could sometimes ring to their credit. At the same time, the pressures to popularize never shook the Victorians from the strong conviction that they were composing sound, accurate, and scientifically credible Lives of Jesus. Throughout most of the period under consideration here, they labored in the firm belief that the claims of genuine biblical science, orthodox faith, and popular religious edification could be united without strain or sacrifice. In light of what has been observed in previous ages, this should be recognized as an extraordinarily ambitious enterprise. Even before the rise of the modern critical style in Germany, it must be remembered, the analytical style of the harmonist and the popular approach of the devotionist had traveled largely separate paths. Only in the rarest instances did they ever come close to converging. British authors now set about the even more difficult task of blending popular concerns not with the ways of the harmonist but with the foreboding new techniques of the modern historian. Despite the risks, it was a venture that, in the context of Victorian religious attitudes, must be counted at least a partial success. This study will examine how it unfolded.

Whatever the underlying aims, the Victorians succeeded in producing a very large literature on our topic. Britain's Lives of Jesus encompass a much larger landscape than even the numerous works cited in this study would lead the reader to believe. One need only peruse Samuel Ayres's spacious (but still incomplete) bibliography of Lives and related works in English to see how large the tally is.[35] Given this circumstance, the historian is compelled to make choices. One must learn from the artist to look for the distinctive line, the crucial lights and shades. I have tried to follow that policy here. First to be excluded are the innumerable partial studies, which center upon phases, discourses, or single episodes of Christ's life; theological treatises on Jesus' person and work; and exegetical monographs limited to parables or miracles or a single gospel. Unless such works bear directly on the task of putting the entire life into a single, connected narrative, they are not relevant to this study and have been rigorously shunted aside. They are certainly worth being aware of, if only as further testimony to the keen interest generated by the life of Christ. But there is no room for them here.

Among the Lives themselves it has also been necessary to select, to separate the two kinds of books important for this study from the more ephemeral pieces. Choosing the works of critical importance presents little difficulty in the British context. One has only to follow the central current of religious discussion to recognize that Strauss and *Ecce Homo* and Sanday's *Outlines* marked turning points in the Victorian encounter with criticism. Isolating the most important popular works is a more hazardous task, for one is tempted to make purely impressionistic selections. It seemed wise, therefore, to reduce subjectivity as much as possible by allowing the Victorians themselves to make most of the selections. On this principle I have consulted a wide spectrum of contemporary periodicals, religious and secular, closely attending to mere notices of Lives as well as full-length reviews, in order to discover which books merited comment. Religious quarterlies and monthlies such as the *London Quarterly, British Quarterly,* and *British and Foreign Evangelical Review;* the Anglican *Christian Observer, Christian Remembrancer,* and *Church Quarterly Review;* the Catholic *Month* and *Dublin Review;* the liberal *Hibbert Journal;* and the more explicitly secular organs like the *Edinburgh* and *Quarterly Reviews,* the *Contemporary* and *Westminster Reviews,* and the *Nine-*

teenth Century have all been scanned for notices and often consulted in depth. In addition some attention has been paid to fortnightlies like the Anglican *Literary Churchman* and the rationalist *Fortnightly Review;* to prominent weeklies such as the *Guardian, Spectator,* and *British Weekly,* which gave considerable space to religious subjects; and to cultivated literary weeklies like the *Athenaeum* and *Saturday Review.* Emphasis has been placed primarily on the quarterly reviews, where the limitations of the format compelled editors to be selective about the books that received notice.

That this method has weaknesses none can deny. As is natural in journalism, editors of Victorian periodicals had views to state, causes to promote. In the process of being advocates they were likely to ignore important books which ran counter to their favorite opinions, while giving extended, even exaggerated notice to lesser works merely because an author had arrived at more agreeable conclusions.[36] Consciously or not, such motives were plainly at work in the treatment which the religious press, for example, gave (or rather failed to give) Lives of Christ written by rationalists. One such ignored freethinker was Thomas Scott, author of *The English Life of Jesus,* who prefaced his work with a lament that religious journalists had refused even to notice his writings.[37] The same charge may on the other side be brought against rationalist and secular periodicals, which were often inclined to ignore, or treat with patronizing brevity, significant conservative books like Alfred Edersheim's *Life and Times of Jesus the Messiah.* So too among the organs of church party or denomination. Catholics tended to notice Catholic Lives; Protestants, Protestant works; dissenters, dissenting products, and so forth according to natural biases and leanings.

To reduce the effect of such distortions I have worked from a broad cross-section of the periodicals and selected for consideration only such Lives as were able to secure a fairly wide spread of notices whether favorable or unfavorable. An obvious choice on this method would be John Seeley's *Ecce Homo,* which dominated religious discussion through the first half of 1866 and drew comment from almost every leading periodical. It was applauded by some, loathed by others. In selecting the book, however, we need not concern ourselves with praise or blame, but only with the extent to which both are a measure of the book's importance in the contemporary culture. No Life after *Ecce Homo* ever received such universal attention in the press; but many were noticed or reviewed sufficiently to make the present method workable. A single notice in a journal already disposed to the author's viewpoint, therefore, will not earn a Life a place in this survey. Several notices, especially if combined with evidence that the book went beyond a first edition, more than likely will.

This system I have had to apply flexibly, in particular for rationalist works, but it does seem to have achieved a fair selection of the most important Lives from the standpoints of both critical importance and popular influence. And if that is so, there is no need for alarm at the charge most likely to turn historians pale with fear: that this or that "primary source" has been overlooked. In a work of this sort, certain primary sources *must* be overlooked if it is to be done at all. There is no harm in passing over a minor source unless it is of such a nature as to alter sharply the generalizations drawn from the more important Lives which *have* come into the discussion. I am confident that such a thing has not happened.

In what follows, chapter one will trace the earlier tradition in Britain from the harmonies and devotional works of the post-Reformation era through the pre-Victorian years to the decades of Britain's reaction to Strauss's infamous *Leben Jesu* and other controversial works of later decades. Chapter two focuses upon the important decade between 1865 and 1874 when the elements of a definitive Life began to emerge but were not blended successfully until F. W. Farrar's extraordinarily popular *Life of Christ*. Chapter three measures the impact of Farrar through a succession of sequels and rivals which shaped Victorian attitudes on this topic to the end of the century. Chapter four explores the causes and circumstances which gave shape to this literature and the influence which the Lives, in turn, exerted on the Victorian religious mind. Chapter five, finally, examines the dissolution of those elements which made up the Lives under the pressure of the new critical and social climate which emerged after 1900.

NOTES

1. Wilhelm Schneemelcher, "Gospels: Non-biblical Material about Jesus," in Edgar Hennecke and Wilhelm Schneemelcher, *New Testament Apocrypha* (hereafter Hennecke, *Apocrypha*), tr. R. McL. Wilson, vol. 1: *Gospels and Related Writings* (Philadelphia: Westminster Press, 1963) 76.

2. The best comprehensive discussion of these developments is to be found in Wilhelm Schneemelcher, "General Introduction," in Hennecke, *Apocrypha,* 1:19-80. The essays by various scholars on specific categories of gospel literature are most instructive, particularly so for H.-Ch. Puech's introduction to the gnostic gospels, which are becoming much better understood as a result of evidence recently discovered at Nag Hammadi in Egypt.

3. The most aggressive advocates of this view in our century have been certain neo-orthodox theologians and of course Rudolph Bultmann, whose distinction between history and myth is now a fixture of modern theological discussion. There are ancient precedents; see R. M. Grant, *The Earliest Lives of Jesus* (London: S.P.C.K., 1961) 116-17, on Origen.

4. Fundamentalist and evangelical theologians are an extreme recent instance; Harold Lindsell, *The Battle for the Bible* (Grand Rapids: Zondervan, 1978) upholds the view that the gospels are wholly or chiefly historical records. It is difficult to deny that the historical motive, including a lively curiosity, is at least partly to account for the gospel literature. See the perceptive comments by Oscar Cullmann, "Infancy Gospels," in Hennecke, *Apocrypha,* 1:363-69.

5. On the development of the canon there is an extensive literature, but for a useful survey with special emphasis on disentangling the canonical from apocryphal gospels, see Schneemelcher, "General Introduction," in Hennecke, *Apocrypha,* 1:19-64.

6. On the *Diatessaron,* see Grant, *Earliest Lives,* 23-28; also Harvey K. McArthur, *The Quest through the Centuries* (Philadelphia: Fortress Press, 1966) 38-44.

7. Oscar Cullman, "The Plurality of the Gospels as a Theological Problem in Antiquity," in his *The Early Church: Studies in Early Church History and Theology* (Philadelphia: Westminster Press, 1956) 39-54.

8. On Tatian, see Grant, *Earliest Lives,* ibid. and McArthur, *Quest,* ibid.

9. Grant, *Earliest Lives,* 26-27.

10. Ibid., 50-110.

11. Quoted in McArthur, *Quest,* 50, where there is a brief discussion of Augustine's harmonic principles and their impact.

12. Elizabeth Salter, *Nicholas Love's "Myrrour of the Blessed Lyf of Jesu Christ"* (Salzburg: Institut für Englische Sprache und Literatur, 1974), is useful in this connection. Of the works she cites (pp. 73-77), three show signs of a more scholarly approach to the subject, but their aims are fundamentally devotional, dramatic, or simply instructional.

13. Discussion of these matters may be found in the work that is still a classic on this subject, Beryl Smalley, *The Study of the Bible in the Middle Ages* (Oxford: Clarendon Press, 1941).

14. Schneemelcher, "General Introduction," in Hennecke, *Apocrypha,* 1:41.

15. Ibid., p. 62.

16. On these early efforts see McArthur, *Quest,* 60-61 and *The New Catholic Encyclopedia,* s.v. "Jesus Christ, Biographical Studies."

17. See McArthur, *Quest,* 62; also Schneemelcher, "Gospels: Non-biblical Material about Jesus."

18. *The Heliand,* tr. Mariana Scot (Chapel Hill: University of North Carolina Press, n.d.) 42.

19. *Nicholas Love's "Myrrour,"* 119-78, where there is a chronicle of changes in the medieval sensibility concerning the figure of Jesus.

20. McArthur, *Quest,* 64.

21. See Salter, *Nicholas Love's "Myrrour,"* especially the survey "Medieval Lives of Christ," 55-118.

22. McArthur, *Quest,* 72-78.

23. Sister Mary Immaculate Bodenstedt, *The* Vita Christi *of Ludolphus the Carthusian* (Washington: The Catholic University Press, 1944) 27.

24. Ibid., 78-83.

25. John Meyendorff, *Christ in Eastern Christian Thought,* t. Yves Dubois, rev. ed. (Crestwood, New York: St. Vladmir's Seminary Press, 1975) 16.

26. Ibid., 80-83.

27. An exception of sorts was the Patriarch Nicephorus (ca. 800), who "stressed the human reality of Jesus, his experience of tiredness, of hunger, of thirst, and of human ignorance," ibid., 186; a much more forcible advocate of this view was John of Damascus, ibid., 168. Salter, *Nicholas Love's "Myrrour,"* 121-23, argues that the East did show sensitivity to the humanity of Christ and that in fact the sentiment originated there. In support she cites Émile Mâle's conclusion that Italian artists were guided by Greek masters in their pictorial representations of the passion of Christ; she then argues that "it is not impossible that in literature too Western devotion to the Humanity owed something to Eastern Christian sources." But the literary evidence she cites consists of two treatises devoted to the Virgin, not Christ. Mâle's discussion, moreover, focuses upon artistic portrayals of the *passion,* not the entire life of Christ. Iconic depictions of the suffering of the savior in the East would perhaps better be associated not with a historical feeling for the human Jesus, but with the Eastern affinity for the paradox of the divine Christ subject to human constraints, a theme given classic expression in the *Divine Liturgy* of Chrysostom. In literature as in art, the East seems rarely to have lost sight of the transcendent Christ, even where he is depicted amid human circumstances.

28. McArthur, *Quest,* 87-88, but the argument, citing a seventeenth-century harmonist who offered his work as a defense against "Jews and Turks," is a weak one; Judaism and Islam were recognized adversaries of Christendom long before the age of the Reformation.

29. Ibid., 91-92.

30. Ibid., 93.

31. Originally published as *Von Reimarus zu Wrede,* Schweitzer's book was translated into English in 1910 at the instigation of the Cambridge critic F. C. Burkitt, who also furnished an introduction. The translator, W. Montgomery, seems to have been responsible for the illuminating English title. For an anecdotal sketch of both the composition of the *Quest* and the role of its translator, see Stephen Neill, *The Interpretation of the New Testament 1861-1961* (New York: Galaxy Books, 1966) 192 and n. 1.

32. Among the historians of biblical criticism who touch briefly on the subject are Chester Charlton McCown, *The Search for the Real Jesus: A Century of Historical Study* (New York: Charles Scribner's Sons, 1940), who gives most space to twentieth-century developments; Norman Perrin, *The Kingdom of God in the Teaching of Jesus* (Philadelphia: Westminster Press, 1963), which is primarily an essay in gospel criticism but provides in the opening historical sketch a useful survey of attitudes after 1899; and Neill, *Interpretation,* 114 n. 1 and 294-95, where the author makes brief mention of a few of the more important Victorian Lives. Schweitzer virtually ignored the British Lives except for passing references to two rationalists and to the converted Jew Alfred Edersheim. So too Werner Kümmel more recently in *The New Testament: The History of the Investigation of its Problems,* tr. S. MacClean Gilmour and Howard C. Kee (Nashville: Abingdon Press, 1972), where British critics do not assume much of a place in the discussion until the twentieth century. The same holds for a rather general recent survey by Dennis Duling, *Jesus Christ Through History* (New York: Harcourt Brace Jovanovich, Inc., 1979).

Historians of religious thought have given some attention to Lives in Britain, but their comments have been confined chiefly to J. R. Seeley's anonymous *Ecce Homo,* which stirred up a controversy in 1865-66. In earlier generations scholars who touched on the subject included D. C. Somervell, *English Thought in the Nineteenth Century* (London: Methuen & Co., 1929) 119-20; John Dickie, *Fifty Years of British Theology* (Edinburgh: T. & T. Clark, 1937) 42-61, 82-102; J. K. Mozley, *Some Tendencies in British Theology* (London: S.P.C.K., 1951) 10-46; L. E. Elliott-Binns, *The Development of English Theology in the Later Nineteenth Century* (London: Longmans, Green & Co., 1952) 73-76; and idem., *English Thought: The Theological Aspect* (London: Longmans, Green & Co., 1956) 157-58. There is no notice of Lives in C. C. J. Webb, *A Study of Religious Thought in England from 1850* (Oxford: Clarendon Press, 1933); little in either of Basil Willey's two works, *Nineteenth Century Studies* (New York: Columbia University Press, 1949) and *More Nineteenth Century Studies* (New York: Harper Torchbooks, 1966); and nothing again in A. O. J. Cockshut, *Anglican*

Attitudes: A Study of Victorian Religious Controversies (London: Collins, 1959). More recently M. A. Crowther, *Church Embattled: Religious Controversy in Mid-Victorian England* (Hamden, Connecticut: Archon Books, 1970), and B. M. G. Reardon, *From Coleridge to Gore: A Century of Religious Thought in Britain* (London: Longman Group Ltd., 1971) consider the rise of biblical criticism, but except for *Ecce Homo,* which receives a sentence in each, Lives of Christ go unmentioned.

33. Among the innumerable studies of Victorian literature and society, few have ventured far into the vast and uninviting terrain formed by books of religious instruction and devotion. Literary histories from Oliver Elton's magisterial *Survey of English Literature, 1830-1880,* 2 vols. (New York: Macmillan & Co., 1920) to the present-day serial efforts by multiple authors have been drawn invariably to the cultural elite, leaving little space for those in the second rank, where many authors of Lives are to be found. Even works designed with broader aims fail to touch on this literature except with the faintest strokes; see, for example, F. E. Hutchinson, "The Growth of Liberal Theology," in *The Nineteenth Century,* vol. 12 of *The Cambridge History of English Literature,* ed. A. W. Ward and A. R. Wallace (New York: G. P. Putnam's Sons, 1916), where only one Life, *Ecce Homo,* figures in the sketch, and merely as an illustration of a theological trend. Boris Ford, ed., *From Dickens to Hardy,* The Pelican Guide to English Literature, vol. 6 (Baltimore: Penguin Books, 1958) is typical of more recent surveys which confine themselves to higher fiction and fail to mention even the religious novel, a genre which, however unpalatable to some present-day tastes, the Victorians found quite to their liking. Full-dress histories of the era which address religious and intellectual developments include the later volumes of Elie Halévy's important *History of the English People in the Nineteenth Century,* 6 vols. (New York: Barnes & Noble, 1924-1951); R. C. K. Ensor, *England: 1870-1914* (Oxford: Clarendon Press, 1936), and R. K. Webb's recent *Modern England: From the Eighteenth Century to the Present,* 2d ed. (New York: Harper & Row, 1980); yet except for a few passages in Halévy, their broad scope affords them no more than a passing glance at the world of religious books.

Studies of the book trade and publishing have been more helpful on this score; they include Amy Cruse, *The Victorians and Their Reading* (New York: Houghton, Mifflin Company, 1935) and *After the Victorians* (1938; St. Claire Shores, MI: Scholarly Press, Inc., 1971); Richard Altick, *The English Common Reader: A Social History of the Mass Reading Public 1800-1900* (Chicago: University of Chicago Press, 1957); R. K. Webb, "The Victorian Reading Public," *From Dickens to Hardy,* 205-26; Patrick Scott, "The Business of Belief: The Emergence of 'Religious' Publishing," in *Sanctity and Secularity: The Church and the World,* ed. Derek Baker (Oxford: Basil Blackwell, 1973) 213-24.

Social history addressed in part to religious concerns has flourished in the last decade. Better efforts include Geoffrey Best, *Mid-Victorian Britain 1851-1875* (New York: Schocken Books, 1972); Hugh McLeod, *Class and Religion in the Late Victorian City* (Hamden, CT: Archon Books, 1974); and

A. D. Gilbert, *Religion and Society in Industrial England* (London: Longman, 1976). Such works refer in general to the importance of religious literature, but not to specific forms such as Lives of Christ.

Useful also are thematic studies and intellectual histories broadly or narrowly defined, such as Owen Chadwick, *The Secularization of the European Mind in the Nineteenth Century* (Cambridge: University Press, 1975); Robert Wolff, *Gains and Losses: Novels of Faith and Doubt in Victorian England* (London: John Murray, 1977); and George P. Landow, *Victorian Types, Victorian Shadows: Biblical Typology in Victorian Literature and Thought* (London: Routledge and Kegan Paul, 1980). Yet enlightening as such works are on crucial issues of background, they offer no discussion of either the scholarly quest or the popular understanding of the historical Jesus.

34. Chadwick's treatment of the subject is quite extensive, given the limits imposed by the format of a large survey work. See *The Victorian Church,* 2 vols. (New York: Oxford University Press, 1966, 1970) 2:60-68.

35. See Samuel Ayres, *Jesus Christ Our Lord* (New York: A. C. Armstrong & Son, 1906), a remarkable compilation which embraces over 5,000 English titles.

36. A classic example of such unofficial censorship, in rather uninhibited form, was H. H. Milman's comment in the *Quarterly Review* that an article on Strauss's *Leben Jesu* would not be prudent. The editors evidently agreed, for none was published; see Crowther, *Church Embattled,* 53.

37. Thomas Scott, *The English Life of Jesus* (London: Trübner & Co., 1872) xi.

1 THE EARLIER TRADITION IN BRITAIN
LIVES FROM THE REFORMATION TO THE 1860s

Jesus of Nazareth, our divinest symbol! . . . A symbol of quite perennial, infinite character, whose significance will ever demand to be anew inquired into, and anew made manifest.

Thomas Carlyle

In Britain between the age of the reformers and the age of the Victorians, gospel study followed well-worn ancient paths. There were new harmonies, and there were new works of devotion. Neither the revolutionary social upheavals of the seventeenth century nor the Deist assault of the eighteenth greatly altered the scene. Since rationalists preferred philosophical weapons to historical, the scriptures figured somewhat obliquely in the great controversies between the Enlightenment and orthodoxy. The devotional Lives of this era are tinged a bit more heavily with the apologetic motif, but there are no new departures. The momentous scholarly revolution just breaking in the German universities had no parallel in British learning. The churches were content with a modestly educated clergy. In the Church of England the obligations of parish, cathedral, or the social calendar took precedence, and scholarship placed low on the agenda of cleric or don. Among Catholics and dissenters, pastoral needs and limited resources for higher religious training virtually ruled out the requisite opportunities. Serious biblical scholarship required a difficult novitiate in ancient languages which their seminaries and academies simply could not provide. So it is hardly surprising that the new critical approach was slow to arrive. In fact it did not draw any real interest until the first Victorian years, when David Strauss's infamous *Leben Jesu* (1835-36) began to trouble the biblical waters. From that point began a renewed, if defensive, interest in Lives of Jesus. Thoughtful minds began then to look for a new kind of book, an account of Christ unmarked by the old patterns.

In this chapter we shall trace the shifts in this changing scene through the three centuries they spanned. After marking the lineage of the harmonists in a few of its major representatives, the same will be done for devotional Lives. Then follows a look at the Deist attack, the impact of Strauss and the unsettlement he brought in his wake, and finally an account of two major works, Renan's *Vie de Jesus* and the anonymous *Ecce Homo,* which provided both excitement and clues of coming change when they appeared in the 1860s.

1. Harmonies of the Gospels

The Reformation was the great age of the harmonist. Not only did it witness the advent of the parallel-column harmony, which notably advanced the comparative study of the gospels, but there were other innovations as well. Andreas Osiander's 1537 *Harmoniae evangelicae libri quattuor* is regarded by some as the origin of the modern gospel harmony. In this lengthy work he enunciated two principles of importance to later scholars. Each gospel, he insisted, should be presented in its own sequence; and differing details in parallel passages must be taken to prove that behind them were several events, not multiple versions of the same event. The irony of these two axioms is that while the second is a backward step by modern criteria, the first is quite progressive. The second leads to absurdities—such as Osiander's bizarre conclusion that Peter nine times denied his Lord.[1] The first encourages one to treat each gospel as a unique narrative compiled and disposed to suit the theological agenda of its author; it leads, in fact, to the very destruction of the idea of a harmony. Unfortunately Osiander's successors in Britain were inclined to follow the less progressive of his *dicta,* and their work was accordingly thin on creative approaches. A more flexible work, with notable influence in Britain, was John Calvin's set of *Commentaries* on the harmony of Matthew, Mark, and Luke (1555). His decision to lay aside the Fourth Gospel provided a revealing anticipation of the verdict reached by modern criticism. He was also more inclined to see behind parallels only single events. Three denials by Peter were sufficient. He further divided his texts into small sections which were then recombined so as to present the life of Christ in a single chronological sequence. Already in the sixteenth century there was an English translation of Calvin's work.[2] It reached a second edition and was soon followed by other harmonies, in Greek, Latin, and English.

In 1644 John Lightfoot, a divine learned in the Talmud and Oriental languages, attempted a new sort of parallel-column harmony which cleared away certain difficulties by applying insights drawn from Hebrew literature outside the canon.[3] This was a work of some importance, not for its harmonistic solutions, but for its original use of the Talmud and Jewish books of antiquity. Schweitzer later pointed out that in this respect Lightfoot's work was not to be surpassed for two centuries.[4] His skills were unique, but his example was not followed. Subsequent efforts in Britain showed no evidence of attempts to build on his foundation, no matter how adroit the harmonist. As examples one might adduce early harmonies like those of Samuel Craddock in 1668, John Austin in 1705, or Matthew Hale in 1720. The works of this era tend to be wholly conventional. There is, usually, a strict adherence to the literal truth of the gospel texts, a determination to explain away all inconsistencies, a tendency to find separate incidents behind the several gospel accounts rather than multiple traditions of the same event, and a transposition of chronological sequences only where it is absolutely necessary to do so. To accomplish all of this the more diligent harmonists often provided an extensive commentary aimed at eluding anachronisms and resolving contradictions. Throughout the eighteenth century this format continued to hold its shape. A mid-century instance is James MacKnight's *Harmony of the Four Gospels* (1756), a work accompanied by a paraphrase, notes, and a few refinements, but basically constructed along the lines charted earlier. There were others as well.[5]

2. Devotional Lives

Turning now to devotional Lives since the Reformation, one finds that here too the familiar pattern recurs. A popular devotional author early on was Joseph Hall, the learned, pious Bishop of Norwich, who dealt with the life of Christ in the course of his *Contemplations upon the Principal Passages of the Holy Story.*[6] This multi-volume work arose from a series of devotional studies of the scriptures which was more than twenty years in the making (1612-33) and eventually embraced the whole of the Bible. On the bookshelves of many clerics, it became a standard companion to the scriptures.[7] The *Contemplations* were sermonic in origin and in a number of ways akin to the medieval works of devotion. In size and style the book resembled Ludolph's late-medieval *Vita Christi.* The bishop's purpose was to meditate and uplift, not to reconcile discrepancies in the manner of the harmonists. Whereas harmonists might have labored long on the chronology of Peter's denials, Bishop Hall preferred to hold before his readers more edifying matters. Peter's misfortunes were put to better use as a moral lesson for believers from the life of the man who was surely "the best saint on earth." In the *Contemplations* such scriptural passages were to be treated not as conundrums, but as stepping-stones to reflection, as reasons to think on the enduring truths of the faith. Indeed, there was in the work even less "scholarship" than one could find in some medieval Lives. At best there were quotations from fathers like Augustine and Chrysostom and a very rare note from, say, Josephus, or Hebrew literature outside the biblical canon.

In 1649 Jeremy Taylor, by then Chaplain in Ordinary to the King, published what his biographer has called "the first life of Christ ever to be written in English."[8] The assertion is questionable, but the *Great Exemplar,* subtitled a history of the life of Christ, was doubtless a splendid product of early Anglican divinity and survives today as a classic of seventeenth-century spiritual literature. A long, literate treatise of both theological subtlety and moral wisdom, it too was cast in the devotional mold. Somewhat in the manner of the *Contemplations,* it was an extended homiletic treatise which sought to build up the faith of believers by furnishing moral examples from scripture. "I have chosen to serve the purposes of religion by doing assistance to that part of theology which is wholly practical," wrote Taylor in the dedication, indicating, like other devotional writers, that he had small interest in the past for its own sake, but a real desire to use it for the sake of spiritual life in the present.[9] The very structure of the book bore a resemblance, again, to Ludolph's *Vita Christi. The Great Exemplar* was not arranged in a continuous narrative, but in brief sections of gospel history which were followed by extended passages of reflection or discourse and concluded with a prayer.

In the wake of Taylor's classic there appeared other devotional works. Throughout the later seventeenth and eighteenth centuries, clergy or laity with a measure of literary skill offered new Lives designed to satisfy the needs for inspiration or instruction. There were, for instance, Abraham Woodhead's *Historical Narrative of our Lord* (1685), Edmund Law's *Discourse on the Character of Christ* (1749), George Benson's *History of the Life of Jesus Christ* (1764), and John Fleetwood's *Life of Our Lord* (1767).[10]

A glance at one of these works will indicate again the essential features of the genre and reveal how little it changed over the years. John Fleetwood's *Life of Our Lord* was first published in 1767 and survived through reprints and frequent new editions till well into the mid-Victorian years.[11] Fleetwood was less sermonic than Hall, less literary than Taylor; yet his methods and aims remained the same. His *Life* combined an apologetic motif with a faithfulness to the gospel accounts so strict as to give the effect of a harmony written in the author's own prose. His favorite device was the extended paraphrase, which mingled Jesus' words with his own narrative of situations and events. He denounced rationalizations of the biblical story. The temptation of Christ was not a mental struggle with self-doubt, but a real meeting with the devil. Demoniacs were not mentally ill, but quite literally possessed. Fleetwood introduced his work with a strong defense of the evangelists as trustworthy men. This strategy was typical of the age. In popular debates over the Bible in the Enlightenment era, historical discussion ·rarely moved beyond a rather simplistic dilemma: either the apostles were deceivers whose story of Christ was a clever hoax, or they were "twelve good men" whose gospel was a credible account worthy of the believer's trust. Fleetwood rested his case with the latter. "If the testimony of the apostles is false," he wrote, "they must have acted as detestable and villainous a part as anyone can conceive."[12] Effective as it may have been in its day, such an argument scarcely signals any historical advance. Real sensitivity to the mind of antiquity, when men might not have been simply deceitful or truthful but governed by a mentality which made this distinction irrelevant, was only beginning to dawn at this time and chiefly in Germany. In Britain, it lay well in the future. Writing more than a century after Taylor and Hall, Fleetwood demonstrates virtually no advance over these older divines. His *Life* emerged, somewhat woodenly, from the Bible and a few references to Josephus.

3. Deist Disputes

The reason for this stagnancy is to be found less in the authors themselves than the context given them. The eighteenth century was an age of polemics. For at least the first half of the century Deists captured public attention with their assault on Christian orthodoxy. They appealed to reason to show that anything beyond a religion of simple theism was superstition. They appealed to natural law to argue that a genteel morality of decent behavior was the essence of religion. Whatever religion embraced beyond these was crude and primitive folly; it testified to the imbecility of the race.

Among Christian teachings, miracles, prophecy, and morals became special targets of Deist sarcasm. Thomas Woolston, most acerbic of the lot, worked sequentially through the more notable miracles of Jesus, the changing of water to wine, the transfiguration, the feeding of 5,000, the curse of the fig-tree, the resurrection of Lazarus, holding each in its turn up to heavy-handed ridicule.[13] So too Anthony Collins: his *Ground and Reason of the Christian Religion* detected pious frauds in scripture, discerned the supposed gullibility of early Christians, and lamented the "roguery and folly of bishops and churchmen."[14] Judaism he saw as a religion corrupted by the Egyptians; and he resurrected the ghosts of Celsus and Porphyry to support his claim that any literal fulfillment of Old Testament prophecy in the New is absurd. Charles Blount put the case against biblical morals. Abraham and Moses were tricksters, Elisha a vindictive buffoon, David a scheming traitor whom Blount devilishly described as "the man after God's own heart."[15] Thomas Morgan, a later Deist, took a kind of perverse pleasure in turning the moral tables. Disparaging Joseph, Samuel, and David, he praised Solomon and Ahab for their tolerance of idols.[16]

Amid all of this well-vented animosity the Deists occasionally hit upon issues of real importance to the historian. Blount and others correctly discerned the presence of mythology in the early chapters of

Genesis.[17] Collins pointed to variant readings and obvious corruptions in the Old Testament text.[18] However crudely put, the frequent refrain of Judaism corrupted by the Egyptians suggested something of the historian's sensitivity to contexts and cultural borrowings. The Deist obsession with refuting miracles and fulfilled prophecy was in its way a prescient anticipation of the very approach taken by David Strauss in the epoch-making *Leben Jesu* almost a century later. Strauss in fact recognized that both he and Reimarus owed a debt to English Deism.[19]

In the end, though, Deists did little to stimulate fresh and genuinely historical inquiry into the life of Jesus. In most of their polemics the occasional flower of historical insight blossomed alone in a weedbed of ridicule, sneering, bigotry, and laughter. With contemporary quarrels intruding so heavily upon study of the texts, the delicate historical impulse could not be kept in balance. At times, thinking even seemed to move backward. Collins suggested, apparently without irony, that the best method of explaining prophetic texts would be a return to allegory.[20] In sheer force of prejudice, Deist disbelief was a virtual match for the credulity of the orthodox. By the second half of the century, the Deist tide itself had begun to ebb. From writers like Richard Bentley, Joseph Butler, and David Hume, it was exposed to strong, sometimes scathing, counterattacks on both its flanks. The topics grew stale, the humor trite. Perhaps most important, the movement was simply swept aside by the great wave of revival which flowed over Britain in the wake of Wesley and Whitefield.[21]

The revivalists had a simple answer to Deism; they ignored it. But while in certain respects that may have caused no great loss, in others it was unfortunate. The glimmerings of critical insight and historical sensitivity which belonged to the Deist legacy soon vanished in Britain. The further Deism receded, the easier it became for some to deal with it as a strange aberration in the course of religious thought. "Who reads them now?" was Burke's comment on Tindal, Toland, and their company near the end of the century.[22]

Among students of the gospels and biblical literature, that sentiment certainly applied. From studies of the life of Christ, one would never guess that Deism had once been a major force in religious thought. The harmonies of Robert Willan in 1782 and James White in 1799 were for all practical purposes indistinguishable from works of a century or more earlier. Even when we move past the turn of the century, to Robert Fellowes in 1804 or to Edward Greswell in 1830, the pattern persists unbroken. Greswell's *Dissertations upon the Principles and Arrangements of an Harmony of the Gospels,* published along with his harmony in 1830, might in fact be taken as the last word in the harmonist's technique.[23] It was a long, laborious work in which all the manifold problems of the art—from the duplicate traditions of Matthew and Mark to the date of the Eastern star and the length of a day's journey—were catalogued and given the most careful consideration. The tradition of devotional Lives showed the very same constancy. Newer works like Edward Harwood's *Delineation of the Life and Character of Jesus* (1772), James Sibbald's *Record of the Public Ministry of Jesus Christ* (1798), and Henry Rutter's *History of Christ* (1803) were virtually interchangeable with devotional works written before the age of Enlightenment had ever arrived. In the end the mark left by Deism turned out to be very nearly invisible. In writing of Jesus the two time-honored styles of Christendom remained comfortably intact.

4. The *Leben Jesu*

It was in the first Victorian decade, while harmonies and old-style works of devotion still held the field in Britain, that a new and menacing figure emerged on the continental horizon. In 1835-36 David Friedrich Strauss published his celebrated *Leben Jesu,* the book that was to change the shape of biblical study of the gospels on the continent and open paths of inquiry not fully charted till the end of the century. At the time of its publication, the *Leben Jesu* also managed to provoke one of the most legendary controversies in the history of Christian thought.[24] During the years immediately after 1835, theological and literary forums in Germany rang with charges, countercharges, harangues, accusations, and even an occasional defense, all brought forth by Strauss's unprecedented work. By the end of the struggle hardly a weapon or shell in the arsenal of Christian apologetic was left unused. Moreover, the intellectual struggle, not always conducted on the highest level, was mirrored in the personal fate of Strauss himself. He was deposed from one position, prevented by popular outrage from obtaining another, and emerged from the furor a pathetic figure, broken by professional intolerance, misguided religious zeal, and his own inastute judgments.[25]

In the later 1830s at least one English periodical took note of this controversy and attempted, however sketchily, to explain the issues at stake.[26] But it was not actually until the early 1840s that the *Leben Jesu* began to take effect in Britain. German was not widely read, even among the theologically educated, so the full impact of Strauss waited upon suitable translations. At first the publishers seemed to fear the blasphemy laws. Then, in 1841, there appeared a summary of the *Leben Jesu's* arguments.[27] At about the same time the firm of Heatherington put out in penny numbers a poor, piecemeal translation taken from the French of Littré and designed for circulation among the working classes.[28] A complete English version did not appear until 1846, when it was finished by Marian Evans (the novelist George Eliot).[29]

Nothing could be more typical of the state of biblical science at the time than the peculiar reverse fashion by which the *Leben Jesu* came into English. The answers appeared well ahead of the book itself. W. H. Mill devoted four successive years of the Christian Advocate Lectures at Cambridge, from 1840 to 1844, to a learned refutation of Strauss.[30] Although J. R. Beard regretted that by 1845 there was still no "scholar-like" translation, he himself avoided the task, preferring to edit another response under the title *Voices of the Church in Reply to Dr. D. F. Strauss.*[31]

The argument of the *Leben Jesu* is perhaps familiar enough not to require extensive restatement here. Leaning on the newly fashionable idealist philosophy of Hegel, Strauss claimed to have cut through the stalemate which divided theologians into the two camps of rationalism and supernaturalism. The life of Christ, he argued, did not consist of the almost uninterrupted chain of miracles and fulfilled prophecies recorded by the New Testament evangelists and so ardently defended by orthodox supernaturalists; neither did it consist of purely natural events which the gospel writers by mistake or deception perceived as miraculous, as was held by naturalist thinkers like H. E. G. Paulus. The gospels quite simply were "myth"—a form of primitive religious literature in which historical events are frequently created or enlarged to fit certain ideal conceptions found in religious belief. Since the synoptic gospels, for example, were governed by Jewish religious conceptions, they portrayed Jesus as Judaism's promised Messiah. To fulfill Hebrew prophecies he was given a virgin mother, a royal lineage, a birthplace in Bethlehem, though in fact he possessed none of these. Since the Fourth Gospel was controlled by Greek conceptions, Jesus was there identified with the Hellenistic *logos;* he was the Word made flesh. All of this developed quite naturally, moreover, because the gospels were not accounts drawn up by eyewitnesses shortly after the events they describe. They arose slowly by a century-long process which issued in a tangled web of vague reminiscence, pious legend, and religious speculation.

From all of this there could be little doubt on which fronts Strauss was most offensive and most threatening. His denial of miracles and attack upon the reliability of the evangelists alarmed British theologians as much as the evangelical churchmen of Germany. On both points there were counterattacks. W. H. Mill was one of several who came to the defense:

> The most philosophical Christian has ever, without difficulty, traced
> . . . in the miracles of Christ most of all, the present power and majesty
> and restoring goodness of God. . . . A new race of men has however
> arisen,—the Spinozas and Strausses of these last times,—who tell us
> that all this is wrong and unphilosophical: that God has no personal
> existence or agency upon or above the world. . . . The ever repeated
> axiom of their philosophy, that the subjective thought is the very
> essence of things, leads them, as they imagine, demonstrably to this
> which all Christians, and all Theists, must deem most absurd as well as
> impious.[32]

Others came to the aid of the evangelists:

> The supposition that the gospels arose spontaneously in the minds of
> thousands in Judea, as the embodiment of the common feeling and
> views of the nation, is utterly absurd.[33]

These were the more dispassionate critics. There were others, like the
critic in the *Edinburgh Review,* who simply despaired of understanding a work which "lies as far beyond the visible diurnal sphere of English comprehension as the philosophy of Hegel."[34]

There was one noteworthy English writer who at about the same
time made an approach to the life of Jesus somewhat in the manner of
Strauss. Charles Hennell, freethinker and close friend of George
Eliot, published the *Inquiry Concerning the Origin of Christianity* in
1838. Though at the time of composition Hennell was unaware of
Strauss's book, his work showed intimations of the theory of myth,
even while it shared some qualities of the naturalistic Lives which were
ridiculed in the *Leben Jesu.* At any rate Strauss, on coming into contact with the *Inquiry,* was sufficiently impressed to furnish a preface
to the German translation. In Britain, its fate quietly foreshadowed
what was to happen to other Lives by native freethinkers throughout
the century: it created hardly a ripple of disturbance. This curious
slight testifies to the great reputation for profound and unorthodox
learning which German scholarship enjoyed in British opinion. Hennell and other freethinkers after him coveted, even expected, a *succès
de scandal* from their rationalist verdicts on Jesus. More often than
not native religious opinion cheated them of their wish and gave the
palm of infamy to the Germans, most of whose works were never even
read. In Hennell's case, however, the oversight may have been
deserved. His book did not accommodate the ordinary reader, and
despite the surface similarities to the *Leben Jesu,* it was not a work of
the same significance.[35]

It was Strauss, therefore, and not Hennell who became the symbolic
infidel of the 1840s. The orthodox recoiled in horror from this learned
German, and the effect of the *Leben Jesu,* initially at least, was not to

draw from British churchmen a creative response, but to throw them back upon the old ways. Even the historian H. H. Milman, by no means an obscurantist, could think of nothing better than another harmony:

> The best answer to Strauss is to show that a clear, consistent, and prob-
> able narrative can be formed out of that of the four Gospels, without
> more violence . . . than any historian ever found necessary to harmonise
> four contemporary chronicles of the same events.[36]

Many felt there was a need for conservative works on the gospels, both British and foreign, which would be able to comfort and reassure. The publishing firm of T. & T. Clark in Edinburgh began to supply translations from evangelical German divines like Olshausen, Stier, and Hengstenberg, and from mediating theologians like Tholuck and Neander. Many of these were published in Clark's two translation series, the "Biblical Cabinet," which came out between 1835 and 1841, and the "Foreign Theological Library," which began in the 1850s and continued until late in the century. The surest sign of this new need could perhaps be found in the decisions of H. G. Bohn, a London publisher who specialized in printing translations of German philosophy and literature. A shrewd observer of market demand, Bohn introduced in 1851 an "Ecclesiastical Library" which offered a translation of the revered Neander's *Life of Christ,* a conservative work written in response to Strauss.[37]

This search for reassuring books can perhaps be traced to a public concern that Strauss had gained influence over a number of leading English intellectuals. In an 1848 article in the *English Review,* Tractarian William Palmer claimed there existed in England a band of secret Straussians.[38] What he had actually seized upon was the Sterling Club, a group of scholars, literati, and theologians who met on a regular basis to discuss matters of philosophy and religion. Several of the thinkers in this group—among them Thomas Carlyle, J. C. Hare, F. W. Newman, and Connop Thirlwall—were without peer in Britain, but among them there was little unanimity of opinion. To suppose that these were all covert followers of Strauss was about as ridiculous as to suppose that thinkers like Samuel Wilberforce, F. D. Maurice, and John Stuart Mill, who also belonged, could have any more in common than the taste for intelligent discussion. The extent of Palmer's confusion could be measured in his equally absurd judgment of the Germans, which placed devout, conservative scholars like Neander and Olshausen on the same footing with Strauss. However that may be, discussion was polarized. The *Leben Jesu* seemed dangerous to many, who were suspicious alike of the Germans, their "neology,"[39] and generally the new critical and historical approach to the scriptures. As late as 1856 the nonconformist *British and Foreign Evangelical Review,* with eyes trained warily on the Germans, welcomed a new set of harmonies as providing a "grand and comforting impression of the church's strong faith."[40] In 1862 a critic in the *Westminster Review* noted with wry amusement, "The name of Strauss has long been a bugbear in the English religious world. High Churchmen and Low Churchmen . . . hush naughty children with the name of Strauss."[41]

This sort of backward stance, with feet fixed against change, could not continue as the only response. Already in the 1830s, when Strauss was barely more than a strange name, there were hints of a new approach and traces of dissatisfaction with harmonies and devotional works in the old style. In 1838, for example, a Unitarian pastor, the Reverend Lant Carpenter, added what on first sight appeared to be another clone to the shelf of older harmonies. Considered strictly as such, his *Apostolical Harmony* offered little that was different from earlier efforts. Yet in the introductory dissertations he produced an extensive essay on the geography and political state of Palestine at the time of Christ. To give the sketch added realism he employed the reminiscences of Near Eastern travelers, hoping thereby to convey something of the social customs and the landscape that formed the background of Jesus' life and ministry. He himself regarded this as an enterprise "probably unique" among harmonists and explained that he was careful to choose from these memoirs "such passages only as afford a distinct and vivid conception of scenery in which the heart must ever feel a holy interest."[42]

The travelogues from which Carpenter took his material had been written by visitors to the Orient who were amateur observers at best. But they may be taken as the clue to a new approach, a new sensibility about to invade biblical studies. It was in the same decade that the American archaeologist Edward Robinson began his pioneer researches in biblical lands.[43] And it was not long before an army of scholars from both Europe and America would be mounting a sort of miniature invasion of the Near East, hoping to chart every Palestinian hill, every crevice, stream, cave, city, and village of the sacred countryside. By 1856 A. P. Stanley would be able to make a considerable success of his essay in historical geography, *Sinai and Palestine.* By 1865 there was sufficient patronage to establish the Palestine Exploration Fund.[44] By the later decades of the century, as we shall see, the landscape had been charted with scientific accuracy, so that it assumed a permanent place in the Victorian version of the gospel story.

In the 1830s of course this attitude was very much a novelty, but it blended well with an idea that was in the air among certain literary historians. Consider H. H. Milman, who in other moods was capable of more progressive thinking than is indicated by his reactionary remarks on Strauss. In his *History of Christianity* he wrote of the inquiry centering upon the life of Christ:

> Many Lives have been composed with a devotional, none at least to my knowledge, in this country, with an historic design; none in which the author has endeavoured to throw himself completely back into the age, when Jesus of Nazareth began to travel as the teacher of a new religion through the villages of Galilee; none which has attempted to keep up a perpetual reference to the circumstances of the times, the habits and national character of the people, and the state of public feeling; and thus, identifying itself with the past, to show the origin and progress of the new faith.[45]

Milman's context reveals almost as much as his remark. He belonged to a group of Anglican scholars who, under the influence of German examples, were beginning to change the shape of historical writing in England. Like Thomas Arnold, A. P. Stanley, and others, Milman was moved by what has been called the "liberal Anglican idea of history." He was concerned not only to make historical study more scientific, but to write it in a manner that conveyed an authentic sense of time and place.[46] In early Victorian England there was much to commend this search for an authentic picture of the past. The romantic spirit pressed various authors to recapture the customs, clothing, landscape, and inner spirit of historical subjects. Thomas Carlyle, T. B. Macaulay, and J. A. Froude, Britain's historical "portrait painters," were selling their volumes with a success almost equal to that of Walter Scott, whose historical novels conveyed the same effect to an ever widening circle of readers.[47]

To Milman in his better moments, and to others as well, it was becoming apparent that there must be a new, more sensitively historical way to look at the life of Jesus, one which could avoid the disintegrating scepticism of Strauss, yet reach a portrait of Christ more vivid, human, and authentically Jewish than the pasteboard figure who so often emerged from harmonies and works of devotion. In his earlier *History of the Jews* Milman had struck a similar note when he argued, "Superior in one respect alone [as the vehicle of certain great religious truths], the ancestors of the Jews and the Jews themselves were not beyond their age or country in acquirements, in knowledge, or even in morals."[48] This sort of approach, which sought to penetrate the sacred stories by means of the same sensibility applied to secular history, was the occasion of controversy when Milman first applied it to the Old Testament. Still, a few at least were convinced of its value and believed it might help to recover the Jesus of history.[49]

5. Responses; Renan

The liberal Anglican school applied its ideas to general histories—Arnold to Rome, Milman to the Jews, Stanley to Latin Christianity. But what of the life of Christ? What was to be done with the
gospels? One expedient, as we have seen, was to translate German
Lives, particularly if they were written by conservative or mediating
thinkers opposed to Strauss. But this was not altogether satisfactory,
since no German work was entirely free of suspicion. Some were long
and laborious, and (a factor which already seems to be separating the
British scene from the German) none employed the kind of literary
style or historical romance that might appeal to a general audience.[50]
What was needed was a native British attempt, a work built upon
respectable scholarship, conservative theology, and realistic history—
sensitive, that is, to the place, time and manners of first-century
Palestine. Scattered churchmen and scholars were the first to discern
what was missing. As they did, they began to disengage themselves
from the old alternatives of harmonies or works of devotion, and they
edged, uncomfortably perhaps, toward the newer critical tradition of
the Germans.

That uneasy shift seems at least partly present in C. J. Ellicott's
Historical Lectures on the Life of Christ. In these, the Hulsean Lectures for 1859, Ellicott sensed the need for scholarship that passed
beyond the weaknesses of the older harmonies.[51] He was acquainted
with the leading continental works, acknowledged readily his debt to
German philology and exegetical science, and made use of
geographical detail furnished in recent works on travel in Palestine.
All of this Ellicott brought to bear on his subject in the hope of
reaching both the scholar and the general reader. The achievement,
however, fell rather short of its ambitions. The *Historical Lectures*
sprang from what was at best a half-way commitment to the new style
in historical writing. However much he disapproved of the harmonists, Ellicott insisted that "it is not only possible, but our very
duty to endeavor judiciously to combine" the gospel narratives. "Let
us remember," he continued, "that we have four holy pictures, limned
by four loving hands, of Him who was 'fairer than the children of
men,' and that these have been vouchsafed to us, that by varying our
postures we may catch fresh beauties and fresh glories."[52] This was
inspiring rhetoric perhaps, but it was not the accent of the historian.

Elsewhere Ellicott asserted,

> It is the history of the Redeemer of our race that the Gospels present to
> us; the history, not of Jesus of Nazareth, but of the Savior of the world.
> . . . he who would presume to trace out that blessed history, without
> being influenced by this remembrance . . . must be prepared to find

himself adding one more unhonored name to the melancholy list of
those who have presumed to treat of these mysteries, with the eclectic
and critical spirit of the so-called biographer,—the biographer (O,
strangely inappropriate and unbecoming word) of Him in whom dwelt
the whole fulness of the Godhead.[53]

A Life of Christ which struggled into existence against dogmatic convictions this strong simply could not be historical enough to break new
ground. It hinted at new methods and a new flexibility, but failed to
deliver on its promise. It fell somewhere between a harmony and old-
style work of devotion without managing to be anything truly new.
There was, moreover, a difference between the lectures as delivered at
Cambridge and their publication in book form with a complete appar-
atus of notes. "A work which is so loaded with foot-notes," wrote
Scottish critic Marcus Dods, "is in great danger of being unpopular.
The narrative flows along the top of the pages easily enough, but one
is always forgetting, and ignoring its intrinsic value, and counting it
merely as a row of pegs to hang the notes upon."[54] As a footnote of
our own to Dods's comment, we ought to observe how the criterion of
general appeal figures in his assessment. Unlike the German version,
British scholarship was expected to exhibit a concern for a wider public of non-specialized readers. The expectation was to assert itself
again as the century wore on.

That the *Lectures* reached six editions by 1876 is evidence their format may not have been so forbidding as Dods seemed to think.[55] But
if reviews are any clue, it is true enough that Ellicott excited no widespread public interest.

The same cannot be said of yet another foreign Life which exploded
upon the British scene but a few years after Ellicott's sober lectures
and raised a fire of controversy perhaps as fierce as that created by
Strauss. The book was Ernest Renan's celebrated *Vie de Jesus*. It
appeared in France in the middle of 1863, scored an astounding
popular success, was translated immediately into the neighboring
languages, and came out in Britain before the end of the year. The *Vie*
was unquestionably a work of literary genius. Its sentimental charm
and imaginative effects captivated the reading public, if not the
scholarly community, of Europe. It passed swiftly through countless
editions and new printings, earned its author celebrity status, and
became beyond its age a literary classic, a book that, in the words of
Stephen Neill, "will have readers until the world's end."[56] The
author, Joseph Ernest Renan, was an Orientalist at the College de
France who once intended to be a priest but lost his faith by reading
German critical theology.[57] He was one of those rare men whose
natural gifts included both the aptitude for patient, tedious scholarly

investigation and the ability to put the results of his study into lucid, elegant, expressive prose. A biography of Christ aimed at the masses was the perfect showcase for such talents, and Renan applied them brilliantly to produce his alluring and unsettling book.

A sceptic and elitist, Renan held aloof from conventional beliefs and dismissed out of hand the traditional supernaturalist view of the scriptures. Like Strauss he believed that miracles did not occur; he felt the New Testament evangelists were not exempt from error, confusion, and the limitations of the age in which they lived. If they were inspired, this was only in the sense that the breath of genius has fallen on other human writers both before and after them. Thus, although it was certainly not errorless, the gospel record was in a real measure historical. Unlike Strauss, who reduced the substrate of fact in the gospels to a bare minimum, Renan believed the historian could recover a good deal of authentic data on the life of Christ. One could detect the basic thread of his ministry, his personal and religious motives, something of his travels and confrontations, and certainly the rare spiritual impact he made on those he met.

Jesus of Nazareth was born to poor parents who, despite the legends later associated with them, had no connection with the royal line of David. As a boy he was raised in the idyllic province of Galilee in the North, a region whose natural beauties contributed much to his disposition. He knew little of the Greeks and Romans, of Jewish sects, or the world outside his native province, though he had studied the Old Testament, especially the Psalms and the book of Daniel, and was acquainted with the maxims of the rabbi Hillel. His temperament was religious. Conscious of a close relation to God, he began as a young man to move about Galilee preaching a simple message of piety and love. He taught that men must understand God as Father and treat others as they would themselves. He spoke often of charity, and of the Galilean landscape, whose every hill and flower seemed to him a revelation of God's design. Men were moved by such words coming from the lips of a young, gentle, winning teacher. Jesus acquired a band of devoted followers.

But shortly he fell under the influence of John the Baptist—a more ascetic teacher who preached a message of judgment, repentance, and imminent world catastrophe. John drew Jesus into the steaming world of Jewish politico-religious passions. Although he at first sought to combine his gentler ideas with John's, Jesus' thinking came gradually to be dominated by the new and harsher conceptions. He meditated on the apocalypse. He began to think of himself as Judaism's long-awaited Messiah, the Son of God who at his final coming would signal the destruction of the present world and the advent of a

new one. He came to Jerusalem with these ideas and was not well
received, a turn of events which left him disillusioned with Jewish
tradition and convinced that the law must be abolished. He then began
to entertain the idea of self-sacrifice: the Messiah must be a suffering
servant who by his death might bring about the sudden convulsion of
the world and the end of days. Almost in spite of himself, Jesus was
becoming a fanatic. He encouraged the credulous to believe he worked
miracles, and he bitterly attacked the traditions of temple and law.
When at length he came again to Jerusalem, his doom was imminent.
The rulers had decided it better that he die than that the masses succumb to his delusions. During Passover week they had him seized by
night in his favorite garden and carried off to a secret trial. Condemned
to death for blasphemy, he was brought to the Roman governor who,
alarmed by the crowd and the fanatical hatreds Jesus aroused, allowed
him to be executed. He was crucified outside the city, a martyr to the
fabrications of his own restless, ever more fanatical mind. His
pathetic cry, "My God, my God, why hast thou forsaken me?," fell
from the cross unanswered, a sad witness to the fate of a gentle
teacher betrayed by the cruelty of men and his own overexcited
dreams.

Such were the life and death of Christ. As for the resurrection and
rise of Christianity, Renan left these for another work, though not
without hinting at the explanation to come.

> Let us say, however, that the vivid imagination of Mary Magdalen
> played in this circumstance an essential part. Divine power of love!
> Sacred moments, in which the illusion of an impassioned woman gave to
> the world a deity risen from the grave![58]

It was Jesus' immediate followers—the women and disciples—who,
refusing to accept his death, began to proclaim the supernatural Christ
and the dogmas that built the Christian church.

The discussion of Renan's continental impact may be left to
others.[59] Even before the English translation appeared, the British
press began printing reviews, extended serial assessments, and brief
appraisals. Virtually without exception, they were negative, ranging
from outrage and invective to serious, heavy-handed refutation and
amused sarcasm. As with Strauss, it seemed to be the denial of miracle
that offended most. "Like its German predecessor," wrote John
Tulloch, one of the more impartial critics,

> the "Vie de Jesus" marks the spring-tide of an advancing wave of
> thought inimical to Christianity. As the former was the result of
> Hegelian speculation, and of the crisis reached by rationalistic criticism,
> the natural consummation of the anti-Christian activity of the German
> intellect through many years; so the work of M. Renan is the result,

and, it may be hoped, the consummation, of the course of materialistic thought—known as Positivism—which since then has been active, not only in France, but in England, Germany, and elsewhere, and of an historical criticism divorced from all faith and true reverence.[60]

Wrote another, "It is his principles which are incompatible with belief, in the ordinary sense of the word. It is the premisses which are responsible for the conclusion . . . The *first* is a remarkable specimen of pure scientific dogmatism, viz. *that there neither is, nor can be, any such thing as a miracle.*"[61]

Though Renan was less sceptical than Strauss, he still did not hesitate to consign much in the gospels to the shadowy realm of legend, or to argue that the synoptics "long remained in a pliant condition" and grew up by a slow process of accumulation and revision of sayings and events.[62] To this the critic in *Blackwood's Magazine* retorted that "of all modes of producing a picture full of such divine unity, this is about the last which could be supposed successful."[63]

Renan also took a peculiar view of the gospel of John, contending that its sequence of events was accurate while its discourses placed in the mouth of Jesus were fictitious. This was a weak position, which succeeded in producing a rare instance of agreement between the Catholic *Dublin Review* and the rationalist *Westminster*, both of which attacked it as inconsistent and highly improbable.[64] Most repugnant of all, however, was Renan's suggestion that Jesus deceived men into believing he did miracles, then became victim of his own deceptions. The Methodist *London Quarterly,* a strident voice of orthodoxy, was incensed:

> The moral contradictions of this imaginary life are the most palpable and confounding . . . In the *Vie de Jesus* we find, however glozed over by fine words, duplicity, popular tact, self-seeking, higher than imperial ambition, moral weakness and cowardice in adopting opinions and conniving at practices which revolted him, falsehood, nefarious sorcery, rage in disappointment, ferocious invective at his enemies, the convulsions of insanity, and a wild clutch at death as the release from his desperate entanglements.[65]

Comments like this might be adduced from nearly the entire spectrum of religious opinion in Britain. "I trust that the sense of truth and reality . . . will reject the dream of one who pretended to establish a kingdom of God, who cheated men into the belief of it by exhibitions of imaginary power," wrote F. D. Maurice in *Macmillan's Magazine.*[66] "Infantile, ridiculous, ignorant, and off-hand" were the adjectives of the *Literary Churchman.*[67] R. W. Church, Richard Holt Hutton, and H. P. Liddon may be cited as only a few leaders of opinion who expressed similar, if less graphic, disapproval.[68]

There is, incidentally, a revealing side effect to be noted here. In its curious, negative way the menace of the new critical tradition as it first appeared on the British scene uncovered a certain underlying unity among religious factions which had been quarreling fiercely and publicly for decades. The infidelities of Strauss and Renan could be observed drawing various parties of British Christianity into a rather tight circle of defense around the dogmatic articles all regarded as the core of Christian belief. Protestant and Catholic, Church and dissent, High Church and Low, Ritualists and their opponents all seemed agreed that a traditional supernaturalist Christianity was crucial. Though there came to be some spokesmen for it, particularly in the mid-century Broad Church, a wholly naturalistic, liberal Christianity which stressed ethics and the moral teaching of Jesus never got the footing it acquired in Germany. Nor did it produce a Ritschl or Harnack. Instead, leaders from all the existing parties joined hands to attack the new criticism. Church and Liddon were High Churchmen, influenced by the Oxford movement; Tulloch was a Scottish Presbyterian; Maurice a mystical Broad Churchman; the *London Quarterly* spoke for conservative Methodism; the *Dublin Review* for literate Catholicism. Yet all came together in their opposition to the proposals of infidel critics. All held strongly to the inspiration of scripture, belief in miracles, the deity of Christ, the vicarious atonement, resurrection, and eternal life.[69]

Over against this conventional orthodoxy Britain had of course always had its intellectual rebels. There was the coterie of London rationalists whose roots went back to Deism and Tom Paine. As in the case of Hennell, the religious establishment did not feel greatly threatened by this group, particularly since the Evangelical and Oxford revivals of religion early in the century. Since the days of Joseph Butler, orthodoxy had produced apologists equal to the task. Even without such, the churches' entrenched position in the social order allowed them to argue from silence and ignore the gadflies. But the present circumstance was different; native rationalism was acquiring formidable foreign allies whose arguments drew their strength from the new historical science. Hence the urge to join arms against the foreign critics. It would be false to say that Strauss and Renan realigned the parties of British Christianity, but their threat did awaken a sense of shared tradition and disclosed a bond that, however temporarily, transcended disagreements over ritualism, legal disabilities, and even the age-old problem of popery.

The chief complaints against Renan focused upon his critical assumptions, which seemed arbitrary and unconvincing. While some of the attacks merely vented basic ideological differences, others disclosed the real problems with the book. There certainly was truth in G. K. Chesterton's verdict, uttered much later, that the *Vie* "discredits supernatural stories that have some foundation, simply by telling natural stories that have no foundation."[70] Serious New Testament scholars in France and Germany were unimpressed by the *Vie*, whatever its popular success.[71] Schweitzer's criticisms in the *Quest* bordered on ridicule.[72]

The narrative of the *Vie,* however, was more difficult to fault. There was something so striking, so vivid and imaginative in its execution that even the most embittered critics were forced into grudging compliments. There was in the first place Renan's elegant style, which even a fierce opponent like Liddon conceded to be the *Vie's* "one and only excellence."[73] Even in translation its fluid grace was apparent, as in this passage on Jesus' early ministry:

> Every one believed that at any moment the kingdom so much desired might appear. . . . No one, during the course of this magic apparition, measured time any more than we measure a dream. Duration was suspended; a week was as an age. But, whether it filled years or months, the dream was so beautiful that humanity has lived upon it ever since, and it is still our consolation to inhale its diluted fragrance. Never did so much joy expand the heart of man. For one moment, in the most vigorous effort she ever made to rise above the world, humanity forgot the leaden weight which fastens her to earth, and the sorrows of the life below. Happy he who could see with his own eyes this divine unfolding, and share, though but for a day, this unexampled vision.[74]

Imagery of this sort seldom wears well; to contemporary ears it seems slightly excessive and overdrawn. In its day, however, it had appeal, particularly when applied to a subject like the life of Christ, which had so often endured the dry prose of the harmonist.

More important, what Renan conveyed through this language was precisely that sense of romance and Oriental realism which writers like Lant Carpenter and Milman had been hinting at decades earlier. Most of the *Vie de Jesus* had been written in 1860-61, while Renan and his sisters traveled in Palestine with a party exploring ancient Phoenicia. In the Introduction he recorded the powerful effect of this landscape upon his thinking:

> I have traversed, in every sense of the term, the Gospel region; I have visited Jerusalem, Hebron, and Samaria; scarcely any important locality in the history of Jesus has escaped me. All this history, which seems at a distance to float in the clouds of an unreal world, took thus a form, a solidity, which astonished me. The striking agreement of the texts and the places, the marvellous harmony of the Gospel idea with the country which served it as a framework, were to me a revelation. Before my eyes I had a fifth Gospel, torn but still legible; and from that time, through the narratives of Matthew and Mark, I saw, instead of an abstract being who might be said never to have existed, an admirable human figure living and moving.[75]

As much as anything, it was this "fifth gospel," this aspect of ancient time and place, of Jewish customs and character and social life which added fresh color and a novel look to Renan's work. To be sure, he achieved some of this effect by artifice, as when he gave biblical characters Hebrew names rather than their customary Western Christian equivalents. As the *Dublin Review's* critic shrewdly observed,

> A good half of the effect of M. Renan's book would be destroyed if he were made to use the common established names for persons and things. We have heard before of the Children of Israel, with their Law and their Prophets; but we bow down with awe before the Beni-Israel, the Thora, and the Nabis. Annas and Caiaphas, Judas Iscariot, Bartholemew, Joseph of Arimathea—we have known them from our childhood: but they have quite a new look as Hanan and Kaiapha, Judas of Kerioth, Nathanael Bar-Tolmai, and Joseph of Haramathaim.[76]

Still, the peculiar texture of the *Vie* arose from more than clever verbalisms. Renan was suitably equipped for his task. He was a Hebraist, well-grounded in Talmudic learning, and intimately acquainted with the social and physical landscape of ancient Judaism. His success throughout Europe was no accident.

More precisely, what were the effects of the *Vie* in Britain? They were several—and significant. First, there was the impact of its style. Since the gospel story is as old as Christendom, it faces the perennial hazard of becoming stale through familiarity. Sermons, moral exhortations, pious meditations must return with numbing frequency to the same incidents, the same discourses, the same miracles, the same narrative of passion and death. With Renan the story passed to a hand with the novelist's touch, a writer whose sketches of character and scenes had a living quality. For all the controversy it aroused, Strauss's Life was obscure and unread; it made its mark, like many German books, by reputation. Renan's book was different. It could be read, and it was very interesting. If it was scandalous, so much the better; people seemed to read it both because of the outrageous views and in spite of them. After the *Vie,* it may be said, a fresh, attractive, novelistic style comes to be a virtual prerequisite for a successful Life of Christ.

Second, Renan had mastered the art of what we may call historical romance. His evocations of the ancient scenes drawn from visits to the Holy Land did indeed function as a fifth gospel, for readers as well as the author. Granted that some of this effect was achieved by such contrivances as the strange spelling of proper names. For readers it was nonetheless a pleasing experience to gain from the *Vie* the distinct "feeling" for ancient Galilee that one got from Walter Scott for medieval Rotherwood forest, or from Carlyle for Paris under the

Reign of Terror. Just how "religious" this romantic sentiment was is perhaps open to question. Yet there was little doubt that it seemed to further religious ends. Richard Holt Hutton of the *Spectator* confessed the paradox of the book: "I have never read a professedly sceptical book that tended more powerfully to strengthen the faith it struggles to supplant."[77] Renan's graphic style and historical romance had cleared a path for the kind of Life that transcended dry debates of the harmonists and the conventional style of the devotionists. Future writers could not ignore his work and still hope to succeed.

The *Vie* also taught a negative lesson, however. No matter how good the historical and stylistic innovations, no Life could be truly successful if it were wedded to such unequivocal anti-Christian scepticism. Success achieved on these terms could only be the success of scandal. The writer of Britain's definitive Life needed an orthodox voice.

6. *Ecce Homo*

As the interest in Renan subsided and the churches passed their final negative verdict on the *Vie,* none could have guessed that barely two years later the entire discussion over the life of Jesus would rekindle and spread with a new flame. Late in 1865 the presses at Macmillan produced an anonymous extended essay under the title *Ecce Homo: A Survey of the Life and Work of Christ.* Judging from the attention it was to draw, it was unquestionably the most important natively British contribution to life-of-Jesus study that had appeared so far; yet "definitive," or "final," or "forthright" are the very last words one would ever choose to describe it. The book began from, and ultimately ended with, ambivalence; its strategies were always oblique.

As the subtitle indicated, *Ecce Homo* purported to be a life of Christ in the newer, historical style. It was addressed to those "who feel dissatisfied with the current conceptions of Christ," and therefore sought "to trace his biography from point to point, and accept those conclusions about him, not which church doctors or even apostles have sealed with their authority, but which the facts themselves, critically weighed, appear to warrant."[78] This, clearly, was a promise of novelty, an approach that suggested the methods of the foreign critics. Like Strauss and Renan, the author announced a departure from the dogma of the churches and a determination to sift the biblical facts as a critic. The churchman or pastor who first looked into the preface of *Ecce Homo* might be forgiven if his first impulse was to brace for yet another infidel assault on the gospels. What he soon would have found, however, was something different. Instead of the confident scepticism so characteristic of rationalists both in Britain and on the continent, there was a curious modesty. "What is now published," wrote the author in preface,

> . . . is a fragment. No theological questions whatever are here discussed. Christ, as the creator of modern theology and religion, will make the subject of another volume which, however, the author does not hope to publish for some time to come.[79]

This author did not offer his work as a verdict or set of assured conclusions. He had come to the subject as a mere inquirer with the modest hope that "the inquiry which proved serviceable to himself may chance to be useful to others."[80] With this end in mind he chose not to deny the difficult theological dogmas of miracle, the deity of Christ, and inspiration of the gospels, but simply to postpone them. As he later wrote in a letter to the *Spectator,* the life of Christ is in part easy to understand and in part hard; that being so, the sensible course was to lay aside the vexing theological issues of the biblical story and begin with those human, historical phenomena which are easiest to grasp.[81]

This odd and intriguing strategy of postponement was to prove crucial for both the structure of the narrative in *Ecce Homo* and the way it was received by the Victorian public. It gave the book an elusive, mysterious flavor. It caused great difficulty for those who reviewed it. It helped tantalize readers with the question of the author's identity. (Not until late in 1866 was he discovered to be John Robert Seeley, Professor of Latin in University College, London.) It led, perhaps inevitably, to a Life of Christ quite unlike anything that had yet appeared in Britain. *Ecce Homo* was a work which edged its way quietly between the sceptical productions of continental criticism and the devotional, conservative works which prevailed in Britain. It produced its own unique, enticing image of Jesus.

In the narrative of *Ecce Homo* we are introduced to the figure of Christ on the day of his baptism and are invited to consider first his character and personality. Unlike John the Baptist, whose troubled soul and prophetic spirit drove him into the desert with a message of judgment and repentance, Jesus entered the public eye without declamations and with quiet composure. He moved about with a quality of inner peace which drew men to him as to a magnet. It was clear to John as it was soon after to others that Jesus was extraordinary; he seemed in all he did a man of unwavering purpose and vision.

> No other career ever had so much unity; no other biography is so simple, or can so well afford to dispense with details. Men in general take up scheme after scheme, . . . and therefore most biographies are compelled to pass from one subject to another . . . But Christ formed one plan and executed it; no important change took place in his mode of thinking, speaking or acting; at least the evidence does not enable us to trace any such change.[82]

The "plan" which Jesus formed could be best understood against the background of Jewish history and the ancient hopes of his people. From earliest days Israel had been a theocracy—a people ruled first by God directly and then through Saul, David, Solomon, and the monarchs of the divided kingdom. By the time of Jesus, however, the theocracy had come to ruin; its citizens had been deported and only a small remnant had returned to the homeland holding the pieces of Israel's shattered dreams.

Now in this broken world it flashed across the mind of Jesus that he might restore, in a new form, the faded monarchy of Israel. His plan was to adopt the old title of "king" and invest it with a wholly spiritual and universal meaning. He would be God's representative in a "divine society," a "Christian commonwealth" built on those two principles most essential to the old theocracy: belief in God and benevolence toward man. In Jesus the new society would find its founder, legislator, and judge.

Further, Jesus was remarkable not only for conceiving this Christian commonwealth but for the astonishing success with which he brought the vision into reality.

> It is not more certain that Christ presented himself to men as the founder, legislator, and judge of a divine society than it is certain that men have accepted him in these characters, that the divine society has been founded, that it has lasted nearly two thousand years, that it has extended over a large and the most highly civilized portion of the earth's surface, and that it continues full of vigor at the present day.[83]

In brief, the civilization of Christendom as it has existed for nearly two millenia is the proof of Jesus' success; it is his divine society. How was all of this accomplished? Chiefly, we are told, on the strength of Christ's unique and powerful personality as a teacher. Unlike Socrates and the Greek thinkers, who taught moral philosophy by precept and the logic of the head, Jesus provided an example, appealed to the heart, and asked men for their devotion to his person. "It was the personality of Christ exciting a veneration and worship which effaced in the minds of his followers their hereditary and habitual worships."[84] Jesus never asked for mere assent; he asked for devotion—for men who would commit their lives to him and to his program.

The name given to this intangible quality which Jesus both possessed in himself and imparted to his followers was the "enthusiasm of humanity." A positive, energetic pursuit of well-being, both physical and spiritual, for all mankind, it flowed from him "as from a fountain." With Jesus good will was contagious.

Having kindled in his disciples this fervor, this passion for the good, Jesus was careful also to give it form, to lay down definite moral prin-

ciples for his community. In fact, the latter part of *Ecce Homo*
departs almost entirely from a narrative Life of Jesus and becomes a
study of Christ as the founder of Christian morality. In this capacity,
says Seeley, Jesus instituted several laws which under all circumstances were to guide the conduct of his followers. The law of philan-
thropy required that they provide generously for the "physical needs
and distresses of their fellow-creatures."[85] The law of edification required that they both seek new members and guard the purity of one
another. It thus divided into the law of mercy, by which the faithful
offered help to "the neglected, outcast, and depraved part of
society,"[86] and into the law of resentment, which required criticism of
the proud and the willfully immoral. Finally, there was the law of forgiveness, which defined the way in which a Christian was to receive the
treatment of others. He must like his master be prepared always to
forgive no matter how serious the injury. Most important, these com-
mands were not external, but written on the heart, so that every
member of the commonwealth "is a lawgiver to himself." "Christ,"
said Seeley, "raised the feeling of humanity from being a feeble
restraining power to be an inspiring passion. The Christian moral
reformation may indeed be summed up in this—humanity changed
from a restraint to a motive."[87]

Such, in brief outline, were the Christ and Christianity of *Ecce
Homo.* It unquestionably provided a fresh, engaging approach to its
subject. But the instant readers compared it to Strauss or Renan, they
became puzzled. In some ways it too seemed a radical work. The very
nature of the inquiry as Seeley designed it dictated that there could be
no appeal to miracle, no clear assertion of Christ's divinity, no mention of resurrection or atonement, or the scriptures as divinely
inspired. Jesus had been depicted simply as an inspiring teacher of
morality and true religion, founder of a community marked by piety
and brotherhood. Though Seeley was no professional theologian, his
image of Jesus bore a strong resemblance to the non-miraculous,
humanitarian Christ found in Germany's "liberal Lives" of Jesus
written during this same period.[88]

Yet in spite of this the narrative of *Ecce Homo* hinted in another
direction. Throughout the text Seeley seemed careful to suggest that if
he *were* to take up theological matters, readers need not be alarmed;
they would find him on the side of orthodoxy. Thus, concerning
miracles, he writes,

> On the whole, miracles play so important a part in Christ's scheme that
> any theory which would represent them as due entirely to the imagina-
> tion of his followers or of a later age destroys the credibility of the docu-
> ments not partially but wholly, and leaves Christ a person as mythical as
> Hercules.[89]

The author of these lines could hardly be mistaken for another Strauss. He clearly believed in miracles, even if they played no part in his narrative. He offered similar reassurances about the sources. Whereas Strauss found the gospels riddled with myth and Renan freely dismissed what he saw as legend, Seeley declared the biblical evangelists "generally trustworthy." "If not," he claimed, "then of course this, but also every other account of Jesus falls to the ground"—a most unlikely conclusion.[90] There were even allusions to Christ's divinity. When Jesus uttered condemnations,

> he did so in a style which plainly showed . . . that he considered the ultimate and highest decision upon men's deeds, that decision to which all the unjustly condemned at human tribunals appeal, and which weighs not the deed only, but motives, and temptations, and ignorances, and all the complex conditions of the deed—that he considered, in short, heaven and hell to be in his hand.[91]

Phrases like these are perhaps open to several interpretations, but the most reasonable would be to suppose that the man Seeley described thus was divine. Here, as elsewhere, the author of *Ecce Homo* seemed to be planting reassurances. Proclaiming a moratorium on theology, the book seemed nonetheless to invite the judgment that it was orthodox.

Understandably, in view of all this, reviewers were perplexed about *Ecce Homo*. The *Spectator* was early to print an assessment, and its critic was ambivalent:

> The attempt to delineate from within the life and work of Christ, without making any fundamental theological assumptions as to his nature and the reality of his revelations, is almost like the attempt to paint a picture without making any assumption as to the quarter whence the light comes, and consequently whither the shadows fall. This strikes us as the only great fault of a very original and remarkable book, full of striking thought and delicate perception, a book that has realized . . . with far more power than Neander, and far more of both power and truth than Renan and Strauss—the historical magnitude of Christ's work . . . . The disadvantage which the author labors under as compared with Renan, for instance, is that he declines to assume any steady theological principle on which to interpret the true meaning and estimate the true worth, of the work he describes.[92]

Though it was not unkind to his book, Seeley disliked this review. He wrote immediately a (still anonymous) letter insisting that the critic had misconceived his plan and emphasizing that his book was merely a preliminary inquiry. "But pray do not suppose," he added, "that postponing questions is only another name for evading them. I think I have gained much by this postponement."[93] Brief as it was, this early exchange anticipated much of the very animated public debate that was to swirl about the book for fully a year. *Ecce Homo* managed to draw every kind of response from critics and church leaders who assessed it. They were inspired, bewildered, annoyed, or outraged. The reactions may be read as testimony to the importance of the book. For in a way more ingenious than Strauss or Renan, and more sensitive to the British conscience, it was raising again the crucial question of method—historical method—in approaching a sacred subject. Was it right, even in a provisional study, to look at a sacred subject only with the eye of the secular historian? Could one proceed without reference to the axioms of orthodox belief and still hope to secure approval from the churches? In Germany a significant number of scholars had already answered—with a strong affirmative, regardless of the opinion of the religious establishment. In Britain things were different; the claims of the historical method were only beginning to be pressed.

The *Spectator* review appeared late in 1865. As the new year opened, *Ecce Homo* began to attract notice from every quarter of religious Britain. The mood of the decade no doubt contributed to this, for the book appeared at a time of great theological ferment and at a moment when a flourishing press hurried to bring every controversial idea into public view. We have already noticed Renan. The *Origin of Species* had been published in 1859; the Broad Church manifesto *Essays and Reviews,* which among other things argued a more secular view of the scriptures, in 1860; Bishop J. W. Colenso's deeply disturbing *Pentateuch and Book of Joshua Critically Examined* in 1862; and Strauss's new *Life of Jesus* in 1864. Not surprisingly, the critic for the nonconformist *British Quarterly* immediately thought of Renan when he read *Ecce Homo.* "We shall be surprised if 'Ecce Homo' does not compete in fame with Renan's 'Vie de Jesus.' It is as novel in its treatments, as daring in its speculation, and as polished in its style, as its notorious rival."[94] This critic was also of two minds about the book. While it clearly was more religious than Renan's "sentimental romance," it still raised an "irritating distrust."[95]

The first really positive assessment came somewhat later, from R. W. Church, writing in the *Guardian.* To be sure, he felt the same puzzlement as others: "The first aspect of the book is perplexing; closer examination does not clear up all the questions which present themselves; and many people, after they have read it through, will not feel quite certain what it means."[96] But he went on in a more sympathetic vein to say that "there could be no question of the surpassing ability which the book displays" and called attention to "the deep tone of religious seriousness which pervades the work."[97] Though it was true that *Ecce Homo* ignored theological issues, Church preferred to see this as the design of a religious apology, a work addressed to a sceptical, agnostic age. Its point was evidently to concede all the advantages of Christian dogma and look at Jesus in purely human, historical terms, so that having seen his greatness as a man, readers would be led on to conclude he was also God. *Ecce Homo* was the work of a believer bold enough to step out from the protection of the church and meet unbelief on its own ground. Others agreed.[98]

Still others, however, were not so charitable. The comments which appeared in *John Bull* disclose not only a distaste for the book but also how deep ran suspicions of the Germans:

> The book is really an attempt to familiarize the English mind to the German sceptical habit of reasoning out a religion for itself from the historical facts of the four, or three synoptic, Gospels. The author professes to have put himself outside the supernatural atmosphere of these facts and to view them *ab extra* in their purely historic meaning. To our mind such is a false position from the beginning and even if its influences should accidentally turn out to be orthodox in the main, it is the one exception to a rule of faith which ninety-nine times out of a hundred would prove fallacious.[99]

The *Record* was just as severe:

> To postpone theology and religion to the future, and meanwhile to settle the object of Christ's life and work independently of them is to omit all of the important facts of the case . . . No scheme of orthodox belief could possibly co-exist with the view of Christ's life advocated in these pages.[100]

It would be difficult to find a wider range of views. Where Church saw the hand of the skilled apologist, these spokesmen could only find Germanism or ill-conceived logic. They contended that it was nonsense to deal with the divinity of Christ as a sort of belated footnote. One could either accept these claims as orthodoxy did, or deny them with Strauss and Renan; but one could not hope to succeed by pretending, like Seeley, that they did not even exist.

Soon the disagreements in the religious press spread to the literary journals, whose interest in *Ecce Homo* testifies further to the intense public interest it generated. Edinburgh's *North British Review* found in it one of the first vigorous counterattacks upon the scepticism that paralyzed modern civilization. Its "power and truthfulness" delivered a forcible Christian response to the doubts of science, mechanism, and aesthetic refinement.[101] The *Quarterly Review* saw things differently, however. Trading heavily in the elegant sneer, its critics did not spare the author of *Ecce Homo*: "As far as he is aware, the comments of learning, genius, and piety for upwards of eighteen hundred years have left the character of our Blessed Lord an enigma, and it has been reserved for the author of 'Ecce Homo' to solve the mystery."[102] The

Quarterly too focused upon Seeley's strategy of postponement, which it regarded as futile and absurd. As theology was the essence of Jesus' life, only a fool would seek to ignore it.[103] Edward Vaughan, writing in the *Contemporary Review,* followed the line of Church. "He whose argument is intended for minds in doubt or unbelieving must assume nothing which he intends to prove afterwards."[104] Persuaded that the reasoning of *Ecce Homo* was apologetic, he found it pointless to rail against its strategy of postponement. The only "postponement" in the book was that of any sensible author who allows his conclusions to wait upon his premises.

As it happened, Vaughan's comments were soon swept aside in the public clamor raised, almost accidentally, by Lord Shaftesbury. At the meeting of the Church Pastoral-Aid Society in May of 1866, he was reported to have made the comment that *Ecce Homo* was "the most pestilential book ever vomited from the jaws of hell." [105] It was a colorful piece of condemnation which immediately drew more readers to a book which in four months had already run to four editions and more than 8,000 copies sold.[106] Seeley later felt that the criticism won him a host of new readers, many of whom found his book not in the least scandalous; as for Shaftesbury, he later came to regret the remark he was never certain he had even uttered.[107]

Before long *Ecce Homo* went to a fifth edition, published with a new preface by the author. In it he elucidated further his approach to the sources, which accepted only those passages where all four evangelists agreed—a principle which, incidentally, revealed how innocent Seeley was of the progress of German criticism. What he sought from this was not a complete biography of Jesus, but "a rudimentary conception of his general character and objects."[108] Again he replied to those who criticized the "postponement" of theological issues: "To those who doubt whether it was justifiable to treat of one part of Christianity without treating at the same time of other parts, he [the author] replies that their scruple seems to be to him astonishing and unreasonable.[109]

The new preface was meant for clarification, but it did not end the disagreements. None less than John Henry Newman reviewed the book for the Catholic *Month,* and he too was perplexed. Its austere, profoundly moral Christ was impressive, but the concealments were annoying. It was impossible to decide whether the author "was an orthodox believer on his road to liberalism, or a liberal on his road to orthodoxy."[110] More enthusiastic endorsements came from Peter Bayne in the *Fortnightly,* who called it "the most important religious book that has appeared in England for a quarter of a century,"[111] and from Broad Churchman A. P. Stanley:

> If the view here taken of the essence of Christ's teaching be the truth, or anything like the truth, then, whatever theory we may form of His abstract nature will be wholly inadequate to shake His transcendent greatness in the scheme of history, human or divine, or His claim upon our moral allegiance.[112]

But conservatives like the critic in C. H. Spurgeon's Baptist *Sword and Trowel* remained unconvinced and looked to German infidelity for an explanation:

> one of our Broad-churchmen has been muddling his brains with the works of Renan and other blasphemers, and has in addition drank [sic] deep of German rationalism, and on the whole had been descending upon a sliding scale to the very depths of atheism, until, growing uneasy . . ., he desires to halt, and . . . pulls himself up by hanging upon a thornbush and pitching his foot against a crag; that process of pulling up he here describes.[113]

The High Church *Christian Remembrancer* was less colorful but just as suspicious.[114] To its side came also a pair of the *Remembrancer's* old foes, the Evangelical *Christian Observer* and the nonconformist *British and Foreign Evangelical Review.*[115]

It is interesting to note that *Ecce Homo's* elusive strategy worked its mysteries even upon the rationalist press. What alarmed the churches usually elated *Fraser's Magazine* or the *Westminster Review,* but free thought was troubled for the very opposite reasons. "We have here sufficient foundation for the whole of the Nicene and Athanasian dogmatism," ran the *Westminster* notice.[116] And *Fraser's* critic, James Fitzjames Stephen, insisted, "The skin is the skin of a rationalist wolf, but the voice is the voice of the tamer and more orthodox animal."[117]

In these curious reversals and realignments one may discern the first of *Ecce Homo's* several effects on religious opinion and interest in Lives of Jesus. Like Renan's, Seeley's venture into a purportedly historical study of the biblical gospels also played havoc with the traditional parties of British thought. As the assessments appeared, it became clear that allegiances based on liturgical or denominational interests gave no forecast of the responses to this intellectual question. In the Church of England it was odd to see Shaftesbury, the most celebrated Evangelical, on the side of Tractarians like Pusey and Liddon, who found themselves in the equally strange position of disagreeing strongly with fellow High Churchmen such as Church and Vaughan.[118] Free Church organs like the *British Quarterly* and the Methodist *London Quarterly* were allies in the struggle against the establishment, civil disabilities, and the "Romanism" of the High Church, but on the questionable tactic of *Ecce Homo* they broke ranks, the former finding in it much, the latter little, that was good. Among religious weeklies and higher literary journals, such odd bedfellows as the *Quarterly* and Evangelical *Record* were agreed in their contempt, while an equally peculiar pair, the Scottish *North British Review* and the High Church *Literary Churchman* freely praised it, though the latter did so with some reservations.[119] "There remains the fact," said A. P. Stanley, "that this same book has drawn to it the common sympathy of those who are agreed on hardly any religious topic besides, and the common antipathy of those who are disagreed on almost every other religious topic."[120]

Beneath the surface there turned out to be less diversity than these critics supposed. In fact, there was a substrate of considerable theological agreement among these parties which, as will be demonstrated in chapter three, made it possible for others to learn from Seeley and score literary successes with Lives of Christ. The attention given to *Ecce Homo*'s oblique approach concealed this at the time. What none could conceal, however, was that *Ecce Homo* had become an extraordinarily popular book. Nine months after publication it had sold more than 9,000 copies. By the end of its first year alone, it had nearly matched the entire sale of *Essays and Reviews*.[121] It passed into new editions almost every other year up to 1888 and beyond. It was reviewed extensively not only by the religious press but by nearly every one of the major literary magazines and in essays by several of religious Britain's most distinguished spokesmen. It called forth at least nine different essays and responses published in book form.[122]

Among its effects, then, *Ecce Homo* could list not only the bewilderment of scholars, but also the fascination of the public. The translation of the *Vie de Jesus* had made an impact on British public opinion, but it was still a foreign work. Seeley's book was by an English author and for English readers; that fact sparked much of the popular interest and widespread curiosity. In the Isles both the *Leben Jesu* and the *Vie* gained readers chiefly through scandal, and the refutations were left to the theologians. Their works had drawn predictable criticism, and the orthodox replies received equally perfunctory words of approval. *Ecce Homo,* because it baffled, was different. It would almost be accurate to say that what Renan did for the continent Seeley achieved for Great Britain. He lifted all of this discussion out of the university common room or cathedral chapter, brought it into the marketplace and vented it in the broad forums of public discussion. He awakened the minds of readers to the real attractions of the sacred story as told in the accent of the modern historian.

Finally, *Ecce Homo* convinced scholars and makers of opinion that a definitive historical Life of Jesus could indeed be written for Victorian believers. It had become apparent through the reception of this work that a Life which joined religious edification with modern historical inquiry could quickly sweep away the specters of Strauss and Renan; perhaps it could even rehabilitate faith in a time of doubt. The critic for the *Edinburgh Review* was persuaded that *Ecce Homo* had in fact done precisely that:

> At present we wish . . . to show sufficient cause for our judgment that it [*Ecce Homo*] is, without any exception, the most important contribution towards a restoration of belief that our generation has seen . . . we hold ourselves justified in saying that in this book—incomplete, undramatic, and not very critical, as it confessedly is—we have the English "Life of Jesus," thoroughly adapted to, and characteristic of, the country whence it sprang; and not only worthy of comparison with more scientific and more histrionic works which have proceeded from Germany and France, but distinctly taking the lead of them in point of successful handling of the question.[123]

This judgment was too enthusiastic. Whatever its merits, the reception just chronicled shows there were genuine obstacles to its assuming so prominent a place as *the* English Life of Jesus. There was in the first place its announced incompleteness. Lacking a clear affirmation of the old theological verities, *Ecce Homo* could not hope over the long term to be a work for the British churches. When the prominent Congregationalist Joseph Parker read the book, he was so gripped by this void and so impatient for it to be filled, that he wrote his own sequel, appropriately titled *Ecce Deus,* which was rushed into print to give theology its due.[124] Others, like the statesman Gladstone, who took keen interest in the controversy, felt the same.[125] Besides this, there were other gaps. Though Seeley aimed at a psychological portrait of the personality of Jesus, he made no use at all of Palestinian romance, despite the enormous success Renan had realized with this strategy. Nor had he really given a narrative life of Jesus in any detail. The number of incidents chosen from the gospels was quite small, and the latter, larger half of the book departed from narrative almost entirely in order to concentrate on an exposition of Christian moral principles. There was little on the passion or crucifixion.

Yet if in the end *Ecce Homo* failed to be a definitive success, it proved a most instructive failure. The reactions to the book from nearly every quarter of religious Britain—from Church to dissent, from Scottish Presbyterian to Irish Catholic—disclosed that there was a surprisingly broad-based consensus on what should be a proper approach to the life of Christ. Since on certain implicit assumptions most were agreed, the writer able to build on them was sure to gain an audience. Suppose, for example, there were someone able to combine the merits of

Ecce Homo with those of earlier efforts while avoiding their several faults. Suppose one were able to begin with Seeley's fresh literate style and focus upon the human qualities of Jesus, his earnest character and sublime teaching. Suppose too that along with the old devotional authors one were able to affirm forthrightly the supernaturalist theology of the churches while displaying, like Ellicott and the Germans, a thorough acquaintance with the newer historical scholarship. And suppose finally that, like Renan, one were to learn from the books of Jewish antiquity and fill the narrative with a traveler's glimpses of the color and landscape of Palestine. Such a writer surely would be furnishing a Christ for the times. The lessons of Seeley were not lost; new attempts were soon to follow.

NOTES

1. The significance of Osiander and other early harmonists has been pointed out by Theodore Zahn in *The New Schaff-Herzog Encyclopedia*, s. v. "Harmony of the Gospels"; see also McArthur, *Quest,* 90-93.

2. This and a long register of other harmonies which span several centuries may be found in *The British Museum General Catalogue of Printed Books* (hereafter, *Brit. Mus. Catalogue*) (London: Trustees of the British Museum, 1965), s.v. "Bible-Gospels-Harmonies [English]."

3. John Lightfoot, *The Harmony, Chronicle, and Order of the New Testament,* in *The Whole Works of the late John Lightfoot,* ed. John Rogers Pittman (London: G. Cowie and Co. Poultry, 1825), vol. 3.

4. In the *Quest,* 223, he notes that the first real advances upon Lightfoot's studies, particularly his *Horae Hebraicae et Talmudicae in quatuor Evangelistas,* did not take place until the work of August Dillmann and Adolph Hilgenfeld in the 1850s.

5. James Macknight, *Harmony of the Four Gospels in Which the Natural Order of Each is Preserved,* 2 vols. (London: Printed for the author, 1756).

6. Joseph Hall, *Contemplations upon the Principal Passages of the Holy Story,* in *The Works of Joseph Hall,* new ed. (Oxford: D. A. Talboys, 1837). For a closer study of the *Contemplations* see T. F. Kinloch, *The Life and Works of Joseph Hall 1574-1656* (London: Staples Press, 1951) 61-79.

7. In the Introduction to his *Place of Christ in Modern Theology,* Amer. ed. (New York: Charles Scribner's Sons, 1911), first published in 1894, A. M. Fairbairn sketched the theological library of the British clergyman as it might have looked in the 1830s and its very changed appearance some sixty years later. Although the earlier collection would have been notable for its "poverty in books dealing with Jesus as an historical person," he observed that it would have been rich in works of devotion, among them à Kempis, Jeremy Taylor, and Bishop Hall's *Contemplations* (p. 17).

8. C. J. Stranks, *The Life and Writings of Jeremy Taylor* (London: S.P.C.K., 1952) 95-96.

9. Jeremy Taylor, *The Great Exemplar of Sanctity and Holy Life . . . Described in the History of the Life and Death of the Ever-Blessed Jesus Christ, the Saviour of the World,* in *The Whole Works of the Right Rev. Jeremy Taylor, D. D.,* ed., Reginald Heber (London: Longman, Green, Longman, Roberts, & Green, 1864) 2:2.

10. Citations of these and other such works may be found in Ayres's bibliography, *Jesus Christ our Lord,* and in *Brit. Mus. Catalogue,* s.v. the respective authors.

11. John Fleetwood, *The Life of Our Lord and Saviour Jesus Christ,* Amer. ed. (New Haven: Nathan Whiting, 1832). The *Brit. Mus. Catalogue* lists new editions of Fleetwood as late as 1852, 1853, 1854, 1856, 1857, and the 1870s. Fairbairn included Fleetwood in his imaginary library of the 1830s, noting that his Life "was everywhere, especially in the homes of the people,

but seldom read, scarcely worth reading, certainly not worth a place amid the books of a serious theologian" (see n. 6 above).

12. Fleetwood, *Life,* 20.

13. Thomas Woolston, *Discourses on Miracles,* in *The Works of Thomas Woolston,* 5 vols. (London: J. Roberts, 1733) 1:40-57. A comprehensive survey of Deist authors and writings may be found in John Orr, *English Deism: Its Roots and Fruits* (Grand Rapids: Wm. B. Eerdmans, 1934); the classic intellectual history of English Deism remains Leslie Stephen, *History of English Thought in the Eighteenth Century,* 2 vols. (London: Smith, Elder, 1876).

14. Orr, *English Deism,* 131-32.

15. Ibid., 112.

16. Ibid., 146.

17. Ibid., 112.

18. Ibid., 132.

19. "Introduction," in Herman Samuel Reimarus, *The Goal of Jesus and His Disciples,* tr. with introduction by George Wesley Buchanan (Leiden: E. J. Brill, 1970) 5-6.

20. Orr, *English Deism,* 132-33.

21. On the causes of the Deist decline see Stephen, *English Thought,* 1:80-90 and Orr, *English Deism,* 171-76.

22. Orr, *English Deism,* 172.

23. The works of Willan and others are cited in *The New Schaff-Herzog Encyclopedia,* s.v. "Harmony of the Gospels." Fellowes's harmony was entitled *The Guide to Immortality; or, Memoirs of the Life and Doctrine of Christ,* 3 vols. (London: Printed for John White, 1804). Greswell's work was the *Harmonia evangelica sive quatuor evangelia Graeca* (Oxford: University Press, 1830); the four thick volumes of *Dissertations* which accompanied it reached a new edition in 1837.

24. For a recent discussion of the issues and participants see Horton Harris, *David Friedrich Strauss and His Theology* (New York: Cambridge University Press, 1974) 66-84.

25. Schweitzer offers a brief portrait of the man and his misfortunes in his chapter "David Friedrich Strauss—The Man and His Fate," *Quest,* 68-77, and closes with some poignant comments on his trials. See also Leander E. Keck, "Editor's Introduction," in D. F. Strauss, *The Christ of Faith and the Jesus of History,* Lives of Jesus Series (Philadelphia: Fortress Press, 1977) xv-cxii.

26. The *Foreign Quarterly Review* 22 (October 1838) 101-35, where the critic was generally hostile. Thomas Arnold, the early Broad Churchman, had also taken note of Strauss and remarked unfavorably on the *Leben Jesu,* though he had only read the German notices of the work. See A. P. Stanley, *The Life and Correspondence of Thomas Arnold,* 2d Amer. ed. (New York: D. Appleton & Co., 1956) 289, n.

27. Philip Harwood, *German Anti-supernaturalism: Six Lectures on Strauss's "Life of Jesus"* (London: Charles Fox, 1841).

28. See the comments by J. R. Beard in the preface to his *Voices of the Church in Reply to Dr. D. F. Strauss* (London: Simpkin, Marshall, and Co., 1845) xii-xiii. Beard provides no title of the work he describes, but he may have been referring to the same cheap translation mentioned by John Sterling in a letter to Carlyle. For a helpful recent discussion of these developments see Valerie A. Dodd, "Strauss's English Propagandists and the Politics of Unitarianism, 1841-1845," *Church History* 50 (December 1981) 425-29.

29. David Friedrich Strauss, *The Life of Jesus Critically Examined,* 2d ed., tr. (from the 4th German edition) George Eliot (London: Swan, Sonnenschein & Co., 1892). Both Amy Cruse and B. M. G. Reardon contend that the *Leben Jesu* was a popular success of sorts. Reardon, *Coleridge to Gore,* 18, cites W. G. Ward, who "remarked at the time [1846] that it was selling more than any other book that had appeared on the market." Cruse, *Victorians and Their Reading,* 91, states that the translation "was widely read and had great influence, especially among workingmen." In neither case, however, is any further documentation provided. If Strauss was read by workingmen, it is difficult to believe they were really convinced by his arguments, or even understood them. Chadwick, *Victorian Church,* 1:325-36, observes that workingmen of the 1830s and 1840s were not so much anti-Christian as anti-church; their real grievances were social and economic, not theological; if Strauss did appeal, therefore, it was likely to be in an indirect fashion, as a symbol of defiance to be held before the churches.

30. W. H. Mill, *Observations on the Attempted Application of Pantheistic Principles to the Theory and Historic Criticism of the Gospel,* 2d ed. (Cambridge: Deighton, Bell, and Co., 1861). The work was never finished.

31. See n. 28 above. The collection had an international flavor, revealing perhaps Britain's inability to produce a formidable opponent of Strauss. Among the essays were two from France, by Edgar Quinet and Athanase Coquerel, and three from Germany: a critique of the theory of myth by Julius Müller and extracts from F. A. C. Tholuck and J. A. W. Neander.

32. Mill, *Observations,* 83-84.

33. "Strauss's Life of Jesus," *British Quarterly Review* 5 (February 1847) 247. Other critical assessments included "The Straussian Controversy," *Eclectic Review* 83 (March 1846) 362-75; and "Strauss' *Leben Jesu,*" *Dublin University Magazine* 28 (July 1846) 268-84. At about the time of Miss Evans's translation, the replies to Strauss began to multiply rapidly. Among the earliest were J. R. Park, *An Answer to Anti-supernaturalism: Directed at Strauss & Harwood* (London: n.p., 1844), and Orlando T. Dobbin, *Tentamen Anti-Straussianum: The Antiquity of the Gospels asserted, on Philological Grounds, in Refutation of the Mythic Scheme of Dr. D. F. Strauss* (London: Ward, 1845). Others may be found in the *Brit. Mus. Catalogue,* s.v. "Strauss, David Friedrich."

34. "The Study of Christian Evidences," *Edinburgh Review* 86 (October 1847) 416.

35. A brief discussion of the *Inquiry* may be found in Reardon, *Coleridge to Gore,* 252-53 and n. 1, where Hennell's "originality" is overrated. Schweitzer, *Quest,* 161, had a low opinion of the *Inquiry* and doubted the wisdom of Strauss in translating it.

36. H. H. Milman, *The History of Christianity,* 3 vols. (London: John Murray, 1840) 1:121. Though Milman was more receptive to novelty than most clerics, he shared the difficulty of others in grasping the true nature of the revolution effected by Strauss. Charles Kingsley captured the new situation vividly in a passage from *Alton Locke,* Amer. ed. (New York: Harper & Brothers, 1854) 275, where Alton Locke declares of his prison chaplain: "The fact was, he was, like most of his class, 'attacking extinct Satans,' fighting manfully against Voltaire, Volney, and Tom Paine; while I was fighting for Strauss, Hennell, and Emerson. . . . He had never read Strauss—hardly ever heard of him; and, till clergymen make up their minds to do that, and to answer Strauss also, they will as he did, leave the heretic artisan just where they found him."

37. Crowther, *Church Embattled,* 40-81, provides two helpful chapters on the connections between British and German theology during these years. See especially pp. 46-58 on the translations of Clark and Bohn, as well as other channels by which German approaches became known in Britain.

38. William Palmer, "On Tendencies towards the Subversion of Faith," *English Review* 10 (December 1848) 399-444.

39. The word coined to describe German liberal views on biblical inspiration; see Chadwick, *Victorian Church,* 1:530.

40. "Harmonies of the Gospel," *British and Foreign Evangelical Review* 5 (October 1856) 722.

41. "Contemporary Literature: Theology and Philosophy," *Westminster Review* 83 (July 1862) 186.

42. Lant Carpenter, *An Apostolical Harmony of the Gospels,* 2d ed. (London: Longman, 1838) v.

43. On Robinson's researches see J. Benzinger, "Researches in Palestine," in *Explorations in Bible Lands During the 19th Century,* 2d Amer. ed., ed. H. V. Hilprecht (Philadelphia: A. J. Holman and Co., 1903) 579-622.

44. On the origins of the Fund see "The Exploration of Palestine," *London Quarterly Review* 45 (January 1876) 277-322.

45. Milman, *History of Christianity,* 1:53.

46. On the early Anglican historians see Duncan Forbes, *The Liberal Anglican Idea of History* (Cambridge: University Press, 1952) 42 et passim.

47. G. P. Gooch regarded Carlyle as the best in this circle; he was "the greatest of English historical portrait-painters"; for a full estimate of the literary historians, see Gooch's *History and Historians in the Nineteenth Century,* 2d ed. (New York: Peter Smith, 1949) 323-39.

48. H. H. Milman, *History of the Jews,* 3 vols. (London: John Murray, 1829) 1:35.

49. On the controversy over Milman's work see Reardon, *Coleridge to Gore,* 243-45.

50. The general suspicion of continental works clouded the judgment of critics and threw up obstacles to the reception of Lives by any of Germany's evangelical or mediating theologians. Though Neander's conservative Life was translated by two Americans and circulated in Britain in the 1850s, it moved in a hostile climate created in some measure by Palmer's misguided article. His comment on Neander ("Tendencies," 441) is worth reproducing: "We will not waste more time on this weak, heretical, and disgustingly pedantic book than to remark, that in denying, as it does, the literal correctness of the Holy Scripture, it throws doubt on all the facts, and all the doctrines of Christianity." But Palmer was not alone. The nonconformist *British and Foreign Evangelical Review* 2 (September 1853) 736, found Neander suffering from "the disease of subjectivity." Some years later, when T. & T. Clark undertook to publish an English version of a Life by the conservative J. P. Lange, General Editor Marcus Dods begged his readers to "judge considerately" a work which emerged "from the turmoil of German opinion"—this despite the manifestly orthodox character of Lange's views. The work does however illustrate another feature of German Lives which reduced their appeal in Britain—length. Lange's Life ran to six volumes. See J. P. Lange, *The Life of our Lord Jesus Christ,* ed. Marcus Dods, tr. Sophia Taylor, et al., 6 vols. (Edinburgh: T. & T. Clark, 1864-72). For Dods's comments see "Editor's Preface," 1:xx.

51. C. J. Ellicott, *Historical Lectures on the Life of our Lord Jesus Christ: Being the Hulsean Lectures for the Year 1859,* Amer. ed. (Boston: Gould and Lincoln, 1862) 32. Dissatisfaction with the older harmonies grew throughout the 1860s; see, for example, E. T. Vaughan, "The Life of Our Lord," *Contemporary Review* 2 (August 1866) 416: "When we come nearer to the present day, we meet usually either mere collections of dissertations, or else 'harmonies,' at least equally dry, constructed too often on the most arbitrary and untenable hypotheses, too often elaborate blunders from first to last, of which the great aim is to settle precisely what cannot be settled on the only available evidence, and would be quite unimportant if it could."

52. Ellicott, *Historical Lectures,* 34.

53. Ibid., 26.

54. Marcus Dods, "Editor's Preface," in Lange, *Life,* 1:xiii.

55. See the *Dictionary of National Biography* (hereafter *DNB*), s.v. "Ellicott, Charles John"; the *Historical Lectures* were first published in 1860; for later editions see *Brit. Mus. Catalogue,* s.v. "Ellicott, Charles John."

56. Neill, *Interpretation,* 193.

57. Schweitzer, *Quest,* 180.

58. Ernest Renan, *Life of Jesus,* tr. and rev. from the twenty-third ed. (Boston: Little, Brown, and Co., 1917) 402. The *Vie* was the first volume of a projected series on the "Origines du Christianisme"; it was in the second volume, "Les Apôtres," that Renan traced the rise of the dogmatic Christ of Paul and the apostles. For the sake of brevity, references to specific passages of the *Vie* have been omitted from the summary of its narrative.

59. A brief discussion of Renan's impact on the continent may be found in Maurice Goguel, *The Life of Jesus,* tr. Olive Wyon (1932; New York: Mac-

millan, 1944) 50-53; p. 53 n. 3 provides a list of some of the numerous responses to Renan in France and Germany.

60. John Tulloch, *The Christ of the Gospels and the Christ of Modern Criticism: Lectures on M. Renan's "Vie de Jesus"* (London: Macmillan and Co., 1864) 3-4.

61. "Renan's *Life of Jesus,*" *Edinburgh Review* 119 (April 1864) 578.

62. Renan, Introduction to the *Life of Jesus*, 44: "That the Gospels are in part legendary is quite evident, inasmuch as they are full of miracles and of the supernatural."

63. "The Life of Jesus," *Blackwood's Edinburgh Magazine* 96 (October 1864) 428.

64. "Renan's 'Vie de Jesus,' " *Dublin Review,* n.s. 2 (April 1864) 406-10; "Contemporary Literature: Theology and Philosophy," *Westminster Review,* n. s. 24 (October 1863) 540.

65. "Renan's Life of Jesus," *London Quarterly Review* 22 (April 1864) 296.

66. F. D. Maurice, "Christmas Thoughts on Renan's Vie de Jesus," *Macmillan's Magazine* 9 (January 1864) 196.

67. "Ernest Renan," *The Literary Churchman and Critical Record of Current Literature,* 1 October 1863. This was the second in a series of chapter by chapter reviews of the *Vie de Jesus* which ran into 1864. The *Literary Churchman* also gave extensive coverage to French replies to Renan.

68. Church reviewed the *Vie de Jesus* unfavorably in the *Guardian*, 9 September 1863; his essay is reprinted in R. W. Church, *Occasional Papers,* 2 vols. (London: Macmillan and Co., 1897) 190-204; Hutton's review, "M. Renan's 'Christ,' " appeared in the *Spectator* and is reprinted in Richard Holt Hutton, *Theological Essays,* 3d ed. rev. (London: Macmillan & Co., 1888). Liddon had severe words for Renan in a note on "Lives of our Lord" appended to the published version of his Bampton Lectures for 1866; see H. P. Liddon, *The Divinity of Our Lord and Savior Jesus Christ,* 7th ed. (London: Rivingtons, 1875) 506-7. A register of pamphlets and book-length replies may be found in the *Brit. Mus. Catalogue,* s.v. "Renan, Joseph Ernest."

69. Tulloch was somewhat of an exception since he did not hold as keenly to traditional doctrines, and he grew more open to new views as time passed. See chapter three (p. 113 below) on his support for the Theological Translation Fund.

70. G. K. Chesterton, *Orthodoxy* (1908; Garden City, New York: Image Books, 1959) 43.

71. Goguel, *Life of Jesus,* 50-53, records the disillusionment of Eduard Reuss and the Strasbourg scholars when they opened the *Vie.*

72. Pp. 180-92.

73. Liddon, *Divinity of Our Lord,* 506.

74. Renan, *Life of Jesus,* 218-19.

75. Ibid., 72.

76. "Renan's Vie de Jesus," 396. The author, according to the *Wellesley Index to Victorian Periodicals,* ed. Walter Houghton, 2 vols. (Toronto: University of Toronto Press, 1966, 1972), s.v. "Dublin Review," was Father Henry James Coleridge, S. J., who was later to contribute much to British Catholic literature on the life of Christ.

77. "M. Renan's 'Christ,' " 306-7.

78. [J. R. Seeley], *Ecce Homo: A Survey of the Life and Work of Jesus Christ,* Amer. ed. (Boston: Roberts Brothers, 1866) 3.

79. Ibid., 4.

80. Ibid.

81. See his letter to the *Spectator,* 30 December 1865.

82. *Ecce Homo,* 24.

83. Ibid., 50.

84. Ibid., 146.

85. Ibid., 208.

86. Ibid.

87. Ibid., 201.

88. On this see Schweitzer, *Quest,* 193-222.

89. *Ecce Homo,* 51.

90. Ibid., 49.

91. Ibid., 47-48.

92. "Ecce Homo," *Spectator,* 23 December 1865.

93. *Spectator,* 30 December 1865.

94. "Epilogue on Books," *British Quarterly Review* 43 (January 1866) 229.

95. Ibid., 230.

96. *Guardian,* 7 February 1866. In a curious way there may have been a circumstance other than the issues which led to this favorable review. Writing at the end of the century, the well-known Scottish journalist, William Robertson Nicoll, noted that at the time Church reviewed *Ecce Homo,* he believed the (still unknown) author to have been Newman! It is not hard to imagine that the man who so affectionately recorded the Oxford movement struggled to give his former mentor the benefit of every doubt. See W. R. Nicoll, *The Church's One Foundation: Christ and Recent Criticism* (New York: A. C. Armstrong, 1901) 85.

97. *Guardian,* 7 February 1866.

98. *The Literary Churchman,* 24 February 1866, insisted that it "bates not a jot of Christ's pretensions."

99. Quoted in the *Record,* 28 February 1868.

100. *Record,* 14 March 1866.

101. " 'Ecce Homo' and Modern Scepticism," *North British Review* 44 (March 1866) 126.

102. "Ecce Homo," *Quarterly Review* 119 (April 1866) 515.

103. Ibid., 516.

104. Edward T. Vaughan, "Ecce Homo," *Contemporary Review* (May 1866) 44.

105. Quoted in Edwin Hodder, *The Life and Work of the Seventh Earl of Shaftesbury, K. G.,* 3 vols. (London: Cassell, 1887) 3:164.

106. See Macmillan's advertisement in the *Spectator,* 19 May 1866.

107. Hodder, *Life,* 3:164; see also Chadwick, *Victorian Church,* 2:65.

108. "Preface Supplementary," to the fifth edition of *Ecce Homo,* iv.

109. Ibid., xiv.

110. [J. H. Newman], "Ecce Homo," *The Month* 4 (June 1866) 564.

111. Peter Bayne, "Ecce Homo," *Fortnightly Review* 26 (June 1, 1866) 129.

112. A. P. Stanley, "Ecce Homo," *Macmillan's Magazine* 14 (June 1866) 141.

113. "Ecce Homo," *Sword and Trowel,* July 1866.

114. "Ecce Homo," *Christian Remembrancer* 52 (July 1866) 131.

115. *"Ecce Homo,"* British and Foreign Evangelical Review* 15 (July 1866) 563; see also *Christian Observer* 66 (July 1866) 498-520.

116. "Contemporary Literature: Theology and Philosophy," *Westminster Review* 85 (April 1866) 521.

117. "Ecce Homo," *Fraser's Magazine* 73 (June 1866) 747. This extended two-part critique, which ran into the July number, was by far the most perceptive of the major reviews. Chadwick, *Victorian Church,* 2:65-66, supposes the author to have been J. A. Froude, the historian, but it actually was James Fitzjames Stephen; see *The Wellesley Index to Victorian Periodical Literature,* 2:468. The article pointed out in unsparing terms that though the book proposed to be historical, the author ignored the tangled critical problems associated with the New Testament gospels. Like Renan's *Vie,* wrote the critic, *Ecce Homo* belonged to the category of "historical novel," and it was a rather poor one. See part two of the review in *Fraser's Magazine* 74 (July 1866) 52.

118. See Liddon's reply to Gladstone, *Divinity of our Lord,* 509-11. On Pusey's reaction see Somervell, *English Thought,* 119-20.

119. *"Ecce Homo,"* London Quarterly Review* 53 (October 1866) 76-77; *Literary Churchman,* 24 February 1866.

120. Stanley, "Ecce Homo," 140.

121. Altick, *English Common Reader,* lists *Essays and Reviews* as one of the more popular nonfictional books of the age, with sales of over 20,000.

122. For a consideration of several of these and a list of the remainder, see my *"Reception of Ecce Homo,"* Historical Magazine of the Protestant Episcopal Church,* 16, 1 (March 1977) 80-81 and n. 72.

123. "Strauss, Renan, and 'Ecce Homo,' " *Edinburgh Review* 124 (October 1866) 467-68.

124. Edinburgh: T. & T. Clark, 1867.

125. W. E. Gladstone, *Ecce Homo* (London: Strahan, 1866) 200.

2) THE MID-VICTORIAN DECADE

FROM ECCE HOMO *TO FARRAR'S* LIFE OF CHRIST, *1865-1874*

No capon priest was the Goodly Fere
But a man o' men was he.
                                        Ezra Pound

The preceding survey, which centered upon Strauss, Renan, and Seeley, tends to give a slightly misleading impression of our subject. Besides these more creative and controversial figures, one may point to any number of lesser writers who in the second third of the century also produced serious studies of the life of Christ. If they were less talented, they were nonetheless moved to undertake the enterprise, though usually in a more conventional fashion. A glance at the 1850s will turn up perhaps a dozen such works. There were, for example, the English translation of Neander's Life (1851); Stephen Thomas's *Gospel History of our Lord and Saviour Jesus Christ* (1853); an anonymous *Scenes from the Life of Jesus* (1855); George Rogers's *Footprints of Jesus* (1856); John Hiffernan's *Sketches of Our Lord's History* (1856); A. L. R. Foote's *Incidents in the Life of our Saviour* (1856); and Hugh Martin's *Christ's Presence in Gospel History* (1860).[1] The *Leben Jesu,* the *Vie* and *Ecce Homo* thus were only the most prominent in an entire gallery of portraits, both British and foreign, which testified to a resurgent interest in gospel study.

From about 1860 onward, moreover, the number of writers to try their skills on the life of Christ multiplied rapidly. The historian who surveys this expanding literature must search for landmarks, for works that signal most clearly the course of the developing inquiry. Here we begin with a brief look at some of the lesser works and translations that appeared alongside Renan's and Seeley's in the early 1860s. We can find something interesting in at least two works which came out in the aftermath of the *Vie* and *Ecce Homo*—Lives by another French author, Edmund de Pressené and by the Scot William Hanna. Some space must also be given to social and cultural circumstances—the book trade, economics of the reading market, religious attitudes and social habits—which came to play a part in the fortunes and spread of the Lives. We shall further look at two rationalist Lives—by Richard Hanson and Thomas Scott—which kept alive the freethinkers' approach, despite very limited success. The excursion finally will take us to the book which in several ways was the most important of the century for the Victorians: F. W. Farrar's *Life of Christ*. This enormously successful work was to set a pattern followed by most Victorian Lives throughout the quarter-century after its publication.

1. Older and Foreign Lives

We have already taken note of the devotional tradition in Britain which, along with harmonies, reached back through Bishop Hall and Jeremy Taylor, through the Reformation and Middle Ages to the very earliest centuries of Christendom. Despite the first stirrings of the critical style and the vogue of historical romance, these Lives had a perennial appeal, and they continued to turn up in reprints, abridgments, and new editions. New editions of *The Great Exemplar* appeared in 1849 and 1850; reprints of Fleetwood reappeared until late in the century, as noted earlier.[2] Newer works in the purely devotional tradition, such as Désiré Pinarts's *Meditations on the Suffering Life on Earth of Our Lord* were also available. Nor were new attempts at harmonies an uncommon sight. The *British and Foreign Evangelical Review* was able in 1856 to review five recently published works by an international group that included Constantine Tischendorf, Johann Griesbach (in revised form), William Stroud, American James Strong, and Isaac Da Costa.[3] Still, after mid-century it was yearly becoming more evident that books of this sort were survivors of a bygone era. After 1860 even authors of middling ability who chose to work along the newer historical lines could be seen edging these classics out of the market. William Thomson, Archbishop of York, contributed a very good study under the heading "Jesus Christ" in the first volume of Smith's *Dictionary of the Bible* (1860). This piece might have had even wider influence had it not been couched in a reference book, and it was never separately published. There were also works by popular preachers like Joseph Parker, whose *Ecce Deus,* written in response to *Ecce Homo,* enjoyed some success, and the Scottish millennial preacher John Cumming. Cumming's *Life and Lessons of Our Lord* was offered in 1864 in a variety of bindings and prices as "the cheapest gift-book of the [Christmas] season."[4] There were anonymous Lives, Lives in verse, and Lives by noted popular Bible expositors like W. J. Irons.[5]

Taking its place beside these works was an ever-growing collection of foreign Lives. American works did not need translation of course, so they had easy access to the British market. Horace Bushnell's chapter on "The Character of Jesus" in *Nature and the Supernatural* was not really a Life of Christ, but it was close enough to merit separate publication by two British firms, and in fact it sold very well.[6]

Another work which won approval from critics was Samuel Andrews's *Life of Our Lord Upon Earth.*[7] This was an unpretentious study, which did not claim to be a definitive Life of Christ. As a kind of gospel handbook, halfway between a Life and a harmony, it supplied summaries of recent scholarship on the gospels and, revealingly, a good deal of ancient Jewish history and geography—the stuff of historical romance—which testifies to the growing interest in such things manifested by readers.

From Germany came scholarship, some of it rather laborious, much of it profound, and nearly all of it quite theologically conservative. We have noticed how a truly critical spirit was beginning to spread in Germany in the earlier nineteenth century. It was an academic revival whose import for biblical study was most apparent in linguistic and historical disciplines: textual analysis, philology, the study of Semitics, investigation of the biblical world unencumbered by the old framework of classical studies. In the case of Reimarus, Strauss, and others, these new skills and approaches were associated with a deep ideological scepticism of the inherited dogmas of Christianity, thus creating the Germanic image of learned infidelity. There remained, however, scholars in the German lands who employed the same skills but without rationalist, anti-dogmatic presuppositions. They were allied in one form or another with the German churches, and they put their scholarship to the cause of reassurance. Through the middle decades of the century, it was mainly these writers whom the British read in translation. With the exception of Strauss, British readers had the opportunity to meet Germany's new critical tradition only in derivative ways. They depended on R. W. Mackay's *The Tübingen School and its Antecedents* for their knowledge of the famous Ferdinand Christian Baur and his circle, or on J. R. Beard's translation of French critic Amand Saintes's *Critical History of Rationalism in Germany* for a discussion of larger thought-patterns.[8] The direct translations were of more conservative thinkers—Hengstenberg, Stier, Olshausen—whose ports of entry were publishers like Bohn and T. & T. Clark. Around 1860 there appeared several new translations dealing in various ways with the life of Christ. In 1859 appeared I. A. Dorner's five volumes on the *History of the Development of the Doctrine of the Person of Christ,* a chiefly theological work, but of obvious relevance to life of Jesus study. The same year Clark published Ebrard's *Gospel History;* in the next came Karl Hase's *Life of Jesus;* in 1864 J. P. Lange's *Life of Our Lord;* and in 1867 H. G. A. Ewald's Life, which formed the sixth volume of his *History of the People of Israel.*[9]

There were fewer translations from the French, chiefly because the French contribution in this area was much smaller. After 1863, moreover, French scholarship on both the Catholic and Protestant fronts was obsessed with the idea of refuting Renan. An enormous literature of controversy sprang up, most of it contributing little new or creative to the genre of Lives. The *Literary Churchman* ran a series of reviews which attempted to notice these "Answers to Renan," but only a few of the replies were ever translated.[10]

2. Edmund de Pressensé

Among Renan's opponents there was one whose theological assumptions formed a natural bridge to British nonconformist churches. Edmund de Pressensé was a French Reformed pastor at Strasbourg and a skilled controversialist. His reply to Renan earned a wide readership in France, appeared in English quickly, and made his name known among the theologically educated in Britain. In addition, he had been to Palestine and had written a sort of travelogue entitled *The Land of the Gospel*, which in 1865 also appeared in an English version. Then in 1866 came a more ambitious work: *Jesus Christ: His Times, Life, and Work.*[11] The book was translated from the French proofs and thus appeared almost simultaneously in English and French. It appeared in March, when the controversy over *Ecce Homo* was beginning to reach its peak.[12]

Pressensé's work, foreign and more conventional as a Life, could not hope to gather the same attention accorded the mysterious *Ecce Homo*, but it received in the main a most favorable reception from those critics who took note of it. The book exhibited a number of those qualities notably absent in the Lives which had gained so much attention earlier. It was in the first place unequivocally orthodox. Pressensé took great pains to make clear his belief in miracles, in the deity of Christ, the trustworthy character of the sources, and the classic Christian doctrines of sin and redemption through the blood of Christ.[13] In contrast to Strauss and others in the German critical tradition, he offered a militant defense of the gospel of John as a source for the life of Jesus, though he by no means rejected the methods of historical criticism. He also wrote in a vivid, if somewhat declamatory, style and displayed some acquaintance with the Near Eastern scene, which he himself had visited. There could be no doubt that he aimed at the historical mode, even while presenting the Christ of traditional orthodoxy—at once teacher, example, redeemer, and God.

There were certain limitations to the book. Though Pressensé referred to the Jewish Palestinian landscape, it was surprising in light of Renan's success and his own travel there that he made so little use of it. There was little in the *Jesus Christ* to remind one of the *Vie de*

Jesus. Nor did it possess the unexpected insights and turns of phrase that Seeley, a layman, scattered throughout *Ecce Homo.* The French work was patently from a clergyman who was more at home in the world of controversy than in the realm of popular literature or Near Eastern romance. Pressensé was an apologist, unable to speak with the same confidence and sensitivity as Renan when the subject turned to the nuances of source traditions, the Talmud, or the nature of rabbinic teaching.

The predilection for the role of advocate was evident in the very structure of Pressensé's Life, nearly half of which was devoted to "Preliminary Questions." These included all the traditional topics of dispute between rationalist and Christian: the possibility of miracles, the truth of the biblical sources, the claims of supernaturalism and theism over against naturalism, pantheism, and atheism. It was perhaps indicative of the author's talents and failings that while one British critic regarded this section as the finest part of the book, another felt it inappropriate to a Life of Christ.[14] Though Pressensé was a man of ability, his abilities seemed misplaced. Beyond this lay a final difficulty; the author was French. Though translated works were turning up frequently and Britain was fast acquiring a more international outlook, it was still difficult for readers to recognize as definitive and widely acceptable a Life which came from a foreign author. The critic in the *London Quarterly* suggested as much when he noted of the work that "its value *in France* can hardly be exaggerated."[15] Its merits in Britain were substantial, but limited.

Jesus Christ, then, was not natively British, not free of limitations, and unlike *Ecce Homo,* had little chance of being carried through the marketplace on the waves of controversy. Yet for just over a dozen years after publication, it stayed in print and managed to reach seven editions.[16] Hodder and Stoughton, the prominent nonconformist house, originally issued Pressensé's book in an octavo volume at 14s. In 1868 the price was reduced to 9s. for a second edition, and a third at the same price appeared the following year. In 1871 the cost dropped further to 5s. for a new duodecimo edition.[17] Hodder and Stoughton was, of course, following a typical practice of publishers: reissuing books that had some ongoing appeal in cheaper formats and at cheaper prices. In fact, this strategy points out how important the practices of the book trade were to the success of Lives of Jesus. Since Britain's Lives in this era always aimed beyond pure scholarship to a more general audience, the decisions, forces, and interests at work behind the scenes in the publishing industry were crucial to their success. A short excursion into the world of the Victorian publishers should demonstrate this more clearly.

3. The Book Trade

During the early years of the century, Britain's book trade, and not least the religious trade, was in the hands of a small circle of prestigious old publishers. Their names—Murray, Blackwood, Longman, Rivington, Macmillan—are in some cases as recognizable today as they were well over a century ago. Unfortunately in the early Victorian years certain of their commercial practices were almost as time-worn as their names, and they succeeded in keeping the price of most books well beyond the reach of working- and middle-class readers. As a rule, only the wealthy bought books, and even they bought few.[18] Since 1829, in fact, when the London firms banded together to eliminate competitive underselling, the publishing trade amounted to a rather thinly disguised cartel. There were, to be sure, a few early renegades: the London houses of Bentley and Colburn had since 1832 issued cheap 6s. reprints of popular fiction; the Chambers brothers in Edinburgh and Charles Knight made similar pioneering efforts in nonfiction and cheap periodicals. But the landscape of publishing prior to the 1850s also showed the wreckage of firms that had gone under in the attempt to supply cheap literature. What some forgot was that in the severe economic climate of the 1830s and 1840s, even 6s. was often too much for a middle-class reader to pay; as for workingmen, who were on the verge of starvation, the last thing they needed was, in Cobbett's bitter phrase, "ample *food for their minds.*"[19]

In this set of circumstances the older, dominant firms preferred to remain elitist. They sold aristocratic literature—elegantly bound, printed, and priced—to those who could afford it. The rest of the populace did without. In time the resulting gap between poor readers and expensive books came partly to be filled by an institution which held an important place in early Victorian society, the circulating library.[20] The most legendary and successful of these was the firm established by Charles Mudie, who set up his shop in the early 1840s and came to eminence a decade later when his headquarters were moved to New Oxford Street, London. Mudie won a peculiar sort of infamy for his activities as the unofficial censor of books and guardian of public morality, but the control he and other circulating librarians exercised over the economics of the book trade was in some ways even greater. The circulating library, though designed to meet popular needs, operated on a premise which, strange as it may seem, also suited the elitist publishers: that the people need not own books, only use them. The publishers preferred selling a few hundred or a few thousand copies of a new book at a rather high price to a reliable purchaser like Mudie to casting it freely upon the turbulent and unpredictable waters of an open market. Thus the conservatism of the publishers was fed by

the conservatism of the circulating libraries to create a powerful institutional opposition to the idea of a free, cheap market in books. It is
scarcely surprising that in time, when the popular mood began to turn
against the publishers, Mudie and others like him remained their
strongest supporters.

Whether promoted or resisted, however, change in the publishing
industry was on its way. In the very decade of Mudie's dominance, the
1850s, a growing number of firms were experimenting with popular
novels at 6*s.* and less. Unlike the previous decades, when economic
adversity worked against the innovators, the 1850s were relatively
prosperous. When a few firms cut prices to as little as 2*s.* for cheap
fiction, the popular demand was instant and astonishing.[21] The era of
the "yellow-back," the inexpensive novel so convenient to purchase
and carry, so suitable for empty hours of travel, had begun in earnest.
"Yellow-backs" were also known as railway novels; they were ideal
companions for a journey of an hour or two, when one wished to
occupy the mind, but not too intensely. Before long the booksellers
expanded to non-fiction, including adventure, travel, history, and religion. It was also with the railway in mind that the enterprising W. H.
Smith hit upon the notion of locating bookstores conveniently for the
traveling citizen; his "railway bookstalls" were to become as prominent a feature of the 1860s as Mudie and the circulating libraries had
been in the two decades before. Like Mudie, Smith was also careful to
guard public morality; only respectable fiction was offered at the
stalls, and along with other uplifting literature he supplied every rail
station with a Bible on a bookstand—spiritual food for the hungry
traveler.[22] Another innovator, who accumulated a fortune by minis-
tering at once to morality and the popular reader, was John Cassell.
Education was the peculiar bent of Cassell's enormously successful
literature. He published popular history, mechanics, literary classics,
and religion. *Cassell's Popular Educator,* launched at a penny a
number in 1852, was to become one of Britain's most successful
popular periodicals, perfectly suited to those who were struggling to
practice what Samuel Smiles and the gospel of self-help were beginning to preach.

In the same year that Smith established his bookstalls and Cassell
his *Popular Educator* (1852), there occurred an even more momentous
change in the trade. John Chapman, a maverick bookseller, decided
to challenge the pricing practices of the more established firms. He
made his case first in a *Westminster Review* article, and soon afterward a
campaign against the publishing cartel was on its way. It quickly
acquired the backing of Gladstone in Parliament and of the *Times* and
the *Athenaeum.* Driven to concessions, the publishers agreed to arbi-

tration by a government commission. The commission decided against them, and competitive underselling at last became a reality throughout the industry. Almost immediately it became possible to buy most of the books published by the major firms at a discount of 2*d*. or 3*d*. on a shilling. The publishers complained bitterly, but the populace benefited, not least because bookselling, now a less lucrative trade, emerged as a sideline in shops that sold other commodities. In place of the single bookstore appeared a variety of new, and often more accessible, book outlets for interested purchasers.

The changes that took place in the 1850s amounted, in short, to a kind of renaissance in the book trade. Once in motion, moreover, they took added momentum from the manufacturing and social changes of the succeeding decade. Of the period after 1860 Richard Altick has observed:

> The three great requisites of a mass reading public—literacy, leisure, and a little pocket-money—became the possession of more and more people. Though there were temporary setbacks, particularly during the serious depression of the mid-seventies, the period as a whole was one of remarkable economic progress. The number of families with an income of over £ 150 a year more than trebled in thirty years.[23]

He concedes that "it was still the middle class, far more than the workers, who benefitted from the prosperous times."[24] Nonetheless, in a climate of burgeoning prosperity, spreading education, and an expanding population, the demand for books of all kinds grew rapidly. Shorter days, shorter workweeks, better housing and lighting all contributed in small ways to the new leisure and comfort of would-be readers. It is worth noting that throughout the economic changes of the last quarter of the century, prices continued to fall, and up until 1896 the average reader's buying power steadily increased.[25]

At the same time, the cost of printing books was declining. Around 1860 North African esparto was introduced as a cheap raw material in papermaking. In 1861 the paper duty was repealed. The American Hoe press, so successful in high-speed printing of newspapers, made its appearance and was eventually used to turn out paperbound books in great numbers. There were also new methods of printing illustrations and a variety of related inventions which brought the cost of production steadily downward.[26]

But that was not all. The sudden changes in Victorian business practice and publishing economics opened new doors to an expanding middle class, which was in many ways favorably disposed to instructive literature. During the mid-Victorian years the common citizen, whether he liked it or not, faced a network of cultural forces which induced him to read, to read seriously, and often to read religion.

There is space here to touch only on a few of these underlying pressures and attitudes, but they should at least be sufficient to disclose something of their effect on middle-class habits in reading.

There was first the curious alliance of Benthamism and religious Evangelicalism, whose advocates differed profoundly in some respects, but agreed on the value of education and self-help, and on the paramount importance of serious "improving" literature.[27] Indeed, the mention of improvement and self-help immediately conjures the image of Samuel Smiles, whose popular works on those subjects sold in great quantities through the late sixties and early seventies. His individualist gospel of self-education, industry, and ambition conferred an almost sacred status on good, instructive books. Reading was a way to moral improvement and personal success.[28]

Among religious Evangelicals, seriousness of purpose was just as intense, though often it manifested itself, unpleasantly, in a general suspicion of fiction and frivolity. In such an atmosphere, anything whose purpose was strictly entertainment found itself under a cloud. It is possible, of course, to make too much of this. The practice of many Evangelical leaders who opposed the popular novel on religious grounds was often very different from their principle, and in any case, Altick has noted, the severe strictures against imaginative literature were weakening by mid-century.[29] Yet the Evangelical ethos certainly did no harm to the sales of serious nonfiction. Thomas Burt, the working-class boy who rose to leadership of the labor party, grew up in his Primitive Methodist home on a steady diet of serious religious literature, from Paley's *Natural Theology* and William Cook's *Theology* to Albert Barnes's *Notes,* the *Christian Witness,* and the *Primitive Methodist Magazine.* Nor was he alone; Burt mentions a circle of friends who with him made it a practice to discuss "the merits of their favorite preachers and books."[30]

Evangelicals were also responsible for the social institution which, through devious ways, fostered the habit of serious reading. Owen Chadwick has reproduced a Victorian proverb: "Ennui was born in London on a Sunday."[31] The testimony of mid-century travelers in Britain provides an interesting picture of the social and recreational restrictions this eminently Victorian institution placed upon the populace. Railroad travel was restricted, coffee houses were closed, museums shut, and a brief but intense campaign initiated by Evangelical leaders led even to the closing of the Crystal Palace.[32] In such circumstances of enforced leisure, many seem to have had no choice but to remain at home and read; when they did, the reading was frequently religious. Amy Cruse's comments on the mid-Victorian affection for sermons might be extended to commentaries, tracts, religious pamphlets, and, one may suspect, Lives of Christ:

Everybody read them; some with the drowsy attention that came with the consciousness of a Sunday afternoon duty carefully performed, many with keen enjoyment and spiritual satisfaction. There were many households like that of Squire Hamley of *Wives and Daughters,* where the unwritten laws for the regulation of conduct on Sundays included "cold meat, sermon reading, and no smoking until after evening prayers" . . . In houses where only half a dozen books were to be found one of them was almost sure to be a volume of sermons.[33]

A number of Lives of Jesus, it might be added, seem to have begun as sermons.

In a culture with such an abiding interest in religious literature, even the author or pastor whose skills as a writer bordered on mediocrity could still sell books. The truly talented or learned men, like H. P. Liddon, A. P. Stanley, C. H. Spurgeon, or more flamboyant ones, like John Cumming, who read the signs of the millennium, could reach sales well into the tens of thousands. They always had a sizeable audience, whether in the pulpit or in print. One may, of course, ask how widespread this interest really was; some have suggested that it was confined chiefly to the overt religiosity of the social orders above the working class. Much has been written, after all, about the superficiality and hypocrisy of Victorian Christianity. Much of it may be true, but it must be balanced against some revealing, recently discovered data. The results of one inquiry show that in 1859 nearly one-third of all books published, including fiction, were religious![34] A similar survey devoted to the circulation of periodicals in 1864 is cited by social historian Geoffrey Best:

> The total circulation of non-daily London-published periodicals in that year was reckoned by a trade expert to be: 2,203,000 weekly newspapers (more than half being of the *Reynold's* sort); 2,404,000 other weeklies (a third being predominantly religious and/or educational); and 2,490,000 monthlies *nearly two million of which were religious.*[35]

Religious publication on *this* scale is difficult to explain in terms of merely superficial or hypocritical interest. It tends rather to lead credence to R. C. K. Ensor's remark that "among highly civilized societies . . . Victorian England was one of the most religious the world has known."[36] Adding Scotland and Ireland would only reinforce the verdict.

Religious literature thus benefited from cultural changes—from the railway and increased leisure, which allowed men to read more; from social choices, like the "serious" Sabbath, which produced a weekly day of gravity and enforced leisure. It profited conveniently from inherited attitudes about self-education and personal improvement, which were applied as diligently to the spiritual life as they were to the secular. It reaped the fruits of economic prosperity and the renaissance of cheap literature in the publishing industry. The end toward which these forces converged was plain to see. By the 1860s the Victorian market was ripe for mass reading, and not least for the reading of informative, uplifting books on religion.

4. William Hanna

In view of this, it need hardly be said that the religious writer of ability had the chance to fare exceedingly well. Among those works that did sell widely after 1860, Lives of Christ were becoming more and more common. For a profile of such works we may draw upon the example of William Hanna, Scottish Free Church pastor, editor, and biographer of Thomas Chalmers. In 1862 Hanna published a semi-devotional history, *The Last Day of our Lord's Passion,* a work which turned out to be very popular.[37] The success was gratifying enough to make new efforts worth attempting, and in subsequent years, Hanna published new volumes to fill in the remaining periods of Christ's life. By 1869, when the project was finished, he had completed what was the most ambitious Life of the 1860s. *The Life of our Lord upon Earth* ran to six volumes. Unlike Pressensé, who seemed born a controversialist, Hanna designed his work along practical and devotional lines. It would have been almost indistinguishable from the old devotional works of Jeremy Taylor and Joseph Hall were it not the case that it provided a striking instance of the new historical sensitivity, the keen desire to recover a sense of ancient place and time.

In the Spring of 1863, Hanna journeyed to Palestine, hoping to satisfy a special curiosity about all of the locations—cities, plains, rivers, groves, mountain ridges—that figured in the life of Jesus. Of the advantages offered by such a fresh acquaintance with the actual setting of Jesus' life he had little doubt. "Besides its use . . . in removing pre-existing doubts," he wrote in preface to the second volume of the *Life,* "a journey through Palestine is of the greatest service in giving freshness and vividness to one's conceptions of the incidents described by the Evangelists, which nothing else can impart."[38] The words recall Renan of course. Hanna presumed that religious ends could be served by drawing upon historical romance. Somehow Jesus seemed more real when seen against the backdrop of Galilean meadows and rugged Judean hills. The strength of Hanna's antiquarian curiosity could be measured by the keen sense of loss he felt in his inability fully to satisfy it. In the same passage he went on, a bit ruefully:

But if any one goes to the Holy Land full of expectation of gazing on spots, or limited localities, once hallowed by the Redeemer's presence, and closely linked with some great event in his history . . ., he will be doomed, I apprehend, to disappointment. I had the strongest desire to plant my foot upon some portion of the soil of Palestine, on which I could be sure that Jesus once had stood. I searched diligently for such a place, but it was not to be found. . . . The nearest approach you can make to the identification of any such spot, is at the point where the lower road curves round the shoulder of Mount Olivet . . . It is here that Dr. Stanley supposes Jesus to have passed and beheld the city, and to have wept over it.[39]

Sadly, Hanna's confidence even on this last point was shaken when he met an expert topographer who disagreed with Stanley, author of the popular *Sinai and Palestine* noted earlier, and "destroyed the impression which absolute certainty would have produced."[40]

Elsewhere Hanna did try to find some comfort in the thought that perhaps Providence did not want believers attached too firmly to the accidental first-century circumstances of Christ's life and times, but that did not restrain him when the opportunity to recreate the ancient setting presented itself in the course of his narrative. His account of Nazareth was typical:

Near to the foot of the highest of these surrounding hills, nestled in a secluded upland hollow, lies the village of Nazareth. No village in Palestine is liker [sic] what it was in the days of Jesus Christ, and none more fitting to have been his residence during the greater part of his life on earth. The seclusion is perfect . . . Nazareth is closed on every side, offering to us an emblem of the seclusion of those thirty years which were passed there so quietly. Pure hill breezes play over the village, and temper the summer heat.[41]

Further quotation would be redundant. It is sufficient to observe that the narrative continues in this fashion for several pages, a vivid instance of the way, in such Lives, strands of history, geography, and a fair measure of free speculation were deftly interwoven.

The brilliant descriptive sketches of Renan, it must be remembered, clothed a radical denial of the orthodox Christ. Hanna, in contrast, wrote only to reassure. In their initial form the various chapters of his work were delivered as sermons to his Edinburgh congregation. It was thus understandable that he could write in preface to his work, "The author has abstained from all historical, critical, and doctrinal discussions, as alien from his object."[42] This abstention meant acceptance in general of the construction which orthodoxy put upon the gospels. The four evangelists were equally trustworthy, and fully inspired; miracles happened; Christ was divine. The best way to neutralize sceptics like Renan was "by a simple recital of the Life of Jesus, so as to show that the blending of the natural with the miraculous, the human with the Divine, is essential to the coherence and consistency of the record; . . . that the fabric of the Gospel history is so constructed that if you take out of it the Divinity of Jesus, the whole edifice falls to ruins."[43]

By now it should be apparent, incidentally, that the historical romance of Palestine which British writers saw in Renan and imitated themselves is a rather different thing from the historical work which was emerging from the new critical tradition of Reimarus, Strauss, and their successors in Germany. Most German scholars had little use for journeys to the Holy Land or charming literary portraits of antiquity. Their work could be done almost entirely with the help of a library and a lexicon. They engaged in comparative, critical analysis to dissect differences and discern dependencies among the gospels, as one might with any group of related ancient texts. Till well into the 1860s British writers were for a variety of reasons—theological and otherwise—very uncomfortable with such techniques.[44] After this time, however, they came gradually to embrace the critical approach, at least in principle. In the dynamics of this transition, which will be explored in a later chapter, the earlier romantic style played a most intriguing part.

At this juncture the mingling of antiquarian romance and solid theological orthodoxy made Hanna's Life and others like it quite acceptable to a wide spectrum of readers. Unfortunately, its gains in these respects were somewhat diminished by what it sacrificed in others. A set of sermons, no matter how skillfully reworked, was not likely to escape the obvious limitations of the original format. The flights of rhetoric, appeals to the audience, and attempts at dramatic effect which sometimes suit the pulpit do not wear well over the course of a long, involved narrative. In the *Life of our Lord* there were repetitions and interpolations which the author failed to excise before publication, as, for example, when the passage on Jesus weeping over Jerusalem was interwoven with a grave meditation on the death of the Prince Consort.[45] What might have been fitting and proper in a sermon from 1861 seemed slightly inappropriate in a book of 1869. The sermonic origin of the work may in fact have contributed to its most glaring weakness—at least for the popular audience. It was exceedingly long: a series of devout reflections that required seven years to complete and in final form extended to six forbidding volumes. Such a work was likely to have far greater circulation in its separate issues than as a single, unitary Life of Christ. The evidence on publication and sales seems to bear this out. Whereas the first and most successful volume reached seventeen editions and 50,000 copies over a period of years, and another achieved five editions, the circulation of the completed work seems to have been not nearly so large.[46] Although the Religious Tract Society republished it in 1883, and in 1869 it was noticed by a number of religious quarterlies, the higher literary journals passed over it almost entirely.[47]

5. Rationalists

In the hands of translated writers like Neander, Lange, Pressensé and native authors like Hanna, then, the tradition of orthodox Lives held its own. Even a man of modest ability and mediocre learning could manage to win a measure of success by writing an orthodox narrative. There existed both the need and the means to fill it in the form of a growing, religiously conservative middle class eager to read instructive books on Christian faith and for the first time acquiring the means to purchase them. But the orthodox were not the only ones to address this market. Freethought maintained a tradition devoted to vigorous criticism of both the religious and social orthodoxy of the land. In the years after *Ecce Homo* several rationalists entered the debate on the life of Christ, two of whom deserve some notice.

Richard Davies Hanson's *Jesus of History* appeared in 1869. Hanson was a jurist of some distinction. Long active in colonial affairs, he had been a member of the Durham Commission, Advocate-General in South Australia, and later chief justice of its supreme court. His *Jesus of History* was the first important rationalist account to appear since Hennell's *Inquiry*.

"My object in the present work," he wrote, "has been to place myself, as far as practicable, in the position of an inquirer living before the fall of Jerusalem."[48] Such a strategy was certainly defensible as a way for the historian to get behind the clouds of dogma and speculation which tend to obscure the real Jesus of Nazareth. In a sense it was what writers like Hanna also sought. To it, however, Hanson added his determination to be a critic of the sources in the manner of the Germans. Like Strauss, Renan, and his fellow rationalists, he was not convinced by traditional arguments for the deity of Christ. Though he was not dogmatic in rejecting miracles, he repeated the argument of Hume that such events could only be accepted if the testimony in their favor overwhelmed the natural tendency to disbelief. In the gospel writers he found no such overwhelming testimony and, for that matter, not very much even in the way of agreement. He engaged in the free criticism of sources, rejecting whatever to him seemed inconsistent, legendary, or the result of later accretions.

In Book I Hanson made an extensive study of the sources. The gospel of John, he concluded, was a later document, the product chiefly of speculative Hellenism and utterly unacceptable as history.[49] Luke and Mark were not quite so suspect, but they were less reliable than Matthew, which represented a tradition reasonably historical and traceable ultimately to Judea, where the events of Christ's life actually took place. Even here, of course, miracles and legends had to be pared away; but what remained was reasonably historical. Jesus was a Jewish prophet who regretted the enslavement of his nation to Rome and looked forward to a coming Messiah who would establish the kingdom of God. The nature of this kingdom was unclear. Some saw it as moral and spiritual, others as a revolution in arms and blood. Jesus was uncertain too, but he did believe himself to be the herald, or precursor, of the kingdom. His teaching stressed its spiritual side, and he urged men to obedience and love.

For a time this teaching brought success. Jesus won a following; he gathered disciples whom he sent out as evangelists and predicted the appearance of the Messiah before their return. But the prophecy failed, and his popularity began to fade. Searching his soul he slowly reached the conviction that he himself was the Messiah. His mind grew ever more otherworldly, ever more hostile to the ruling orders. He determined to go to Jerusalem and lay before Jewish and Roman leaders his extravagant claims. Although this road was filled with danger, he seemed with each step to become more certain that at the crucial moment God would supernaturally intervene and open all eyes to his Messianic role.

But this did not happen. Jesus was seized and executed by the alarmed magistrates. Through a misunderstanding for which neither party was really to blame, the innocent but misguided teacher of love and obedience was martyred by anxious men who imagined him more dangerous than he ever hoped to be.

That was Jesus as his contemporaries knew him. Jesus as the churches came to paint him was a very different figure, and the master artist was the man known today as St. Paul. "There appears to be a measure of truth in the claim sometimes made in behalf of Paul, that he was the founder of Christianity," Hanson concluded.[50] It was Paul who under the influence of Gnostic ideas fashioned a sect of Judaism into a religion applicable to all humanity.

> And he did this by raising Jesus from the position of the King of the Jews to that of a pre-existent being who had been invested with divine attributes in order to their manifestation [sic] to mankind, and who embodied, to the spiritual apprehension of his followers, the wisdom, power and love of God, the universal Father.[51]

To this process of spiritualization and universal application begun by Paul, the Fourth Gospel added a capstone in the thoroughly Greek doctrine of the *logos*.[52]

Although a brief summary like this might give the impression that Hanson very nearly anticipated the revolutionary eschatological theories of Johannes Weiss and Albert Schweitzer late in the century, such was not in fact the case. Most of these similarities are accidental; they reflect no all-embracing theory, nor do they arise, as did the later views, from an intimate knowledge of the language and history of intertestamentary Judaism. His approximations of the theory of myth and use of psychological interpretation show that he had borrowed rather heavily from both Strauss and Renan. He knew of both and in fact admitted his debt to a review of Renan for "many valuable suggestions."[53]

Hanson was complimented, predictably enough, by the rationalist *Westminster Review,* but most of the literary journals and church organs passed over his book.[54] One verdict of the *Westminster,* as it happens, gives us a clue to the ambitions and fate of such rationalist writers in the Victorian years. The critic insisted that *The Jesus of History* was "well worthy to take its place by the side of Strauss, Renan, and *Ecce Homo.*"[55] It was hardly so; but such a plaudit would have been taken as high flattery by British freethinkers. They wanted from the religious establishment the compliment of being taken seriously; but they never, or very rarely, got it. The *Jesus of History* certainly left no visible mark on British biblical scholarship. Among the populace, it could scarcely be expected to fare better, partly because of its sceptical thrust, but equally, it would seem, because it read like one of the justice's legal briefs and demonstrated that even the most startling thesis could result, in the words of Owen Chadwick, in "a sober dry book."[56]

Were it possible to bring the New Testament evangelists into Justice Hanson's courtroom, Thomas Scott, a Catholic turned militant free-thinker, would have taken the prosecution with delight. Scott brought to freethought all the enthusiasm of the newly converted. An associate of Colenso, he had guided the controversial prelate's studies of the Pentateuch to publication. Between 1862 and 1877 he had issued a variety of rationalist pamphlets attacking Christianity. Contributors to this series included the leading lights of English freethought: F. W. Newman, W. R. Greg, Charles Voysey, Charles Bray, and others. In 1872 Scott published *The English Life of Jesus*, a work self-consciously designed to make the author into Britain's David Strauss. Though the book seems to have been partly written by Colenso's biographer, G. W. Cox, Scott took sole responsibility for it, and Cox's name appeared nowhere in the text. (Scott's name will be used here for the author, whoever he was.) There were the usual complaints of inattention. The *English Life* had first appeared in serial form, its various parts distributed as pamphlets, but, admitted Scott, "the form thus given to the book furnished to editors of journals a reason for putting it aside as a series of pamphlets."[57] In another effort to gain notice from the "public press," he then decided to publish the parts in a single bound volume. The results were less than spectacular. They could be measured in the notice of the *British Quarterly Review* which consumed *in toto* twenty-one lines of print.[58] Others did not trouble to give it even this.

In a sense that was unfortunate. Although he wrote with belligerence, venom, and occasional distortion, Scott had several important things to say. Hardly the British *Leben Jesu* it pretended to be, the *English Life* was nonetheless a book worth noticing.[59] In fact, partly because it was written in imitation of Strauss, whom the popular audience had not read, it offered such readers a quick introduction to the arguments and strategy of the *Leben Jesu.* Like its prototype the *English Life* was negative in design, virtually an essay on the impossibility of writing a Life of Jesus. Scott noted that Christians frequently take comfort in the fourfold character of the gospel accounts. If four men, each with his own point of view, observe the life of Jesus and nevertheless tell substantially the same story, believers may take it as confirmed. But is this really so? A few moments of cold analysis will do away with the illusions:

> The discourses in the fourth Gospel present a marvellous contrast to the simple and single-minded addresses in the Synoptics. There is little in the Sermon on the Mount which the least instructed Galilean could find serious difficulty in understanding; there is scarcely a step in the Johannine arguments which is not calculated to irritate or baffle even a well-skilled dialectician. There is no trace in the Synoptics of any attempt to confound his hearers, or to involve them in mist: there is not one discourse in the fourth Gospel which is not designed to glorify Jesus by exhibiting those who converse with him as wholly unable to apprehend his high spiritual meaning. . . . Is it possible that two modes of teaching so utterly antagonistic should characterize the same teacher? Is it possible also that one who had put forth in the Sermon on the Mount a seemingly complete summary of his faith and a complete code of moral practice, should in that sermon make not the slightest reference to any of those great topics which form the burden of the Johannine discourses?[60]

For Scott this was only the beginning. Elsewhere contrasts become contradictions. In John Jesus ministers at Jerusalem and occasionally in Galilee; in the synoptics these circumstances are reversed. In the synoptics Jesus is tempted in the desert; in John he is not only not tempted, the sequence allows no room for it. In John the temple is cleansed at the outset of the ministry; in the synoptics at the close. In the former Jesus' ministry apparently is two years; in the latter, barely two months. In the one, he is crucified on the Passover; in the other, the day after. The candid reader, concluded Scott, cannot harmonize these antinomies and must not choose blind faith. He must admit that one gospel—John—is quite simply unhistorical.

Scott went further. It will not work, he said, to retreat to the synoptics alone, at least if we want history. Both internally and by comparison with each other, it can be shown that they are "utterly heedless of historical order, and that no trust can be placed in their sequence of events, unless they are strengthened by collateral testimony."[61] In sum, the gospels are so riddled with legend and credulity, with manifold variations inherent in documents arising from oral traditions and a primitive age, that the modern reader trusts in them only what can be established in the face of insistent, unrelenting scepticism.

As anyone might guess, the profile of Christ left by Scott's scepticism was slender in the extreme. Jesus was born to Mary and Joseph, poor Galileans from Nazareth. He became a teacher and claimed to be Judaism's Messiah, though whether in a spiritual or in a political sense is unclear.[62] He looked forward to a future moral regeneration of man and perhaps to a universalism which placed Jew and Gentile alike under the Mosaic law. His message was practical, at times ascetic. He neither did nor claimed to do miracles. In the end he was a good, compassionate, self-giving man, no more. Scott concluded that his work had

> drawn out the image of one, of the facts of whose life we know indeed but a little, but who stands out in himself, pure, loving, gentle, and merciful to all men. We see before us one who embraced all the suffering and heavy-laden in the wide circle of his love, and who spoke of his mission specially as a charge to seek out and save that which was lost. It is no wish of ours to tarnish a picture so fair and true; that unworthy office is performed by theologians who proclaim him as the head of a hard and ecclesiastical system.[63]

This humane, rationalist Christ is by now a pedestrian figure, still very much alive in the mass mind. Like Hanson's, Scott's liberal Jesus is an arbitrary construction. But in spite of this the role of these rationalist works among the British Lives is significant, and in a measure paradoxical. They remind one of a potent medicine, wrongly mixed and slightly misapplied. Their strength is a remorseless, commonsense questioning of texts and truths the religious establishment too easily accepted. Rationalists constantly return to what is uncomfortable in the texts: the marks of legend in the birth narratives, the residue of myth and folktale in numerous miracles. They hammer away at the inconsistencies between the Fourth Gospel and the first three. They single out the reversals and missed connections in the narratives. They raise, in fact, urgent, real questions about the record of Christ's life that spokesmen for the more traditional portrait ought to have been answering.[64] Instead, they were ignored.

Why did this happen? In part, because of circumstances internal to the intellectual growth of the churches which chapter four will explore further. In part as well, it was because of rationalist disabilities largely self-inflicted. Much of the rationalist case against the gospels, however cogent, was derivative and perceived to be so by scholars within the churches. Scott virtually admitted this by announcing his intent to be the English counterpart of Strauss. The substance of the books bore it out. A major argument of both writers, that John differed from the synoptics, came directly from Strauss. When Hanson followed the psychic development of Jesus from dreamy youth to dark prophet of apocalypse, it was not hard to see that the plot came from Renan. In light of this, the religious establishment could be forgiven if it looked beyond the local scepticism to its foreign source.

In the second place, it was clear to many that rationalists were not really interested in a truly historical inquiry, as were the spokesmen of the German critical tradition. They were not serious students of Near Eastern antiquity. They were not skilled in the relevant languages, Hebrew, Aramaic, or Hellenistic Greek. Nor were they in any sense scholars of intertestamental Judaism, the Talmud, or pseudepigraphal literature. They were in fact present-day controversialists, carrying on a contemporary argument in historical guise. Their real quarrel was with the ascendant, supernaturalist, socially conservative Christianity of the Victorian years. Their "historical" Jesus thus turned out to be a first-century, socially progressive freethinker. The works in which rationalists presented this Christ were in the final judgment identical in form with religious Lives, since their aim was popular persuasion. It may well have been true, as these rationalists charged, that the Christ of the churches was a product of dogmatic presuppositions, but so, it appeared, was the Christ of freethought. Between two parties thus aligned there was, understandably, little ground for real debate.

6. Farrar's *Life of Christ*

The fate of the rationalists among most ordinary Victorians was something of a foregone conclusion. Were one to mention Scott or Hanson, the common reader would concede to having never heard of them. Disliking Christian orthodoxy, rationalists continued to write for a narrow but loyal audience which shared their distaste. Among those who read rationalist literature on a regular basis were some very interesting minds—independent souls from the upper and middle classes and a minority of disgruntled working people. The great majority of readers had little patience with dissection of the gospel sources or strident denunciations of miracle. What they preferred, if they could get it, was a basically orthodox Life of Christ. The profile of the author likely to please them thus required someone able to present the familiar gospel story, but in a fresh way: with true faith, but with evidence also of real scholarship (to answer the Germans); with a touch of the novelist's psychological insight and literary style; and with Renan's sensitivity to Oriental scene and circumstance. For many Victorians, the author and the book which managed perfectly to fit the profile finally turned up in 1874. In that year F. W. Farrar published his *Life of Christ.*

Frederic William Farrar was a churchman of some celebrity, a Cambridge Apostle, Headmaster of Marlborough College, and Chaplain to the Queen and the House of Commons. Versatile and prolific, his diverse writings in fiction, philology, and theology had by the 1870s made him a recognizable name. He had written two successful public school novels in the vein of *Tom Brown's Schooldays.*[65] His philological studies won him election to the Royal Society. In theology he had delivered the Hulsean lectures, published as *The Witness of History to Christ.* He had also demonstrated in a book on three Roman Stoics called *Seekers After God* considerable skill as a popular expositor of religious and historical topics. Alongside the literary endeavors, he kept active his church career, becoming a canon of Westminster in 1875. Though he soon became embroiled in controversy over *Eternal Hope,* a series of published sermons questioning eternal punishment, he held his ground and weathered the storm, eventually becoming Dean of Canterbury in 1895.[66] Farrar was a man of vast energies and various initiatives, but his greatest literary success, *The Life of Christ,* was not originally his idea.

The thought of producing a popular biography of Jesus, the work of a scholar but addressed to the populace, occurred first to the editors of that firm most skillful in capitalizing on the tastes of the popular market—Cassell & Company, now the combined house of Cassell, Petter & Galpin. Petter first broached the idea in a conversation with his chief editor, Teignmouth Shore. "In 1870," reports Cassell's historian, "Petter asked Shore to suggest the name of 'a real scholar' capable of writing, in a popular style, a Life of Christ."[67] The slot was not an easy one to fill, and Farrar was not the first candidate to come to mind.[68] At the firm he was known chiefly for articles he had contributed to Cassell's *Popular Illustrator* and to the *Quiver,* one of its more popular religious magazines. His schoolboy fictions, *Eric* and *Julian Home,* proved he could write for the large audience. His scholarly credentials were somewhat less impressive, consisting chiefly of his philological essays and the Hulsean lectures. Nonetheless, it was to Farrar that Shore turned when he was unable to get his first choice. Had he been alive to witness it, John Cassell would doubtless have seen the hand of providence at work in the decision. For as it happened, few men could have been more perfectly fitted for such a task than F. W. Farrar. He was a cleric deeply attached to the creedal center of Christianity, despite *Eternal Hope* (which then lay in the future). Although his family attachments and early training were rooted in the Evangelical tradition, he reached out in mature years ecclesiastically toward High Churchmen and intellectually toward the Broad Church party.[69] As a scholar his abilities were considerably greater than his published work at the time might have indicated. He stood in fact only a rank below B. F. Westcott, J. B. Lightfoot, and the leading British minds in biblical study. There was, of course, no question about his ability to write in a rich, colorful, eminently readable and engaging style. When in 1870 Shore offered him the commission for the *Life* at £500 and £100 for expenses of a trip to Palestine, Farrar accepted and left for the Holy Land the same year.

During the next four years he worked on the Life at intervals, using up vacations and carving spare hours out of his busy schedule as a school administrator. *The Life of Christ* was published, with a frontispiece by Holman Hunt, in the Spring of 1874. It was an immediate success.

Looking back, Cassell's historian Simon Nowell-Smith conceded that the success of Farrar's book "was far greater than either he or his publishers had dreamed of."[70] Before the year was out the *Life* had run to twelve impressions of 1,000 copies each, and this was to be only a small fraction of its sales over the next two decades. In the next quarter-century it continued to reach new editions, many of which required multiple printings; it was reissued, reprinted, published in illustrated versions, sold in ornately bound octavo gift editions and convenient duodecimos, issued in numbers, pirated in America, translated into most European languages; it even appeared in Russian and Japanese.[71] It was in a rather short time to exceed thirty editions and 100,000 in sales; and like other Lives that were to follow, it showed a remarkable staying power through the 1880s and 1890s. In the process the *Life* established permanently Farrar's reputation as a popular writer on historical and religious subjects. The success even served at one point as the occasion of a breach between author and publisher and led to a rather undignified public quarrel in which Farrar hinted that he had never been properly compensated by Cassell for the enormous profits the book had brought in.[72]

In the *Life* it immediately became apparent that there was much to

recommend Farrar's abilities as both author and scholar. He worked
quickly and with confidence through a wide range of materials. His
son had noted that his ponderous "book box," filled mostly with
heavy tomes of German scholarship, seemed to be a constant companion during the family's summer holiday at the sea.[73] His classical
training served him well in Greek, though as German critics were sensing, the Greek of the New Testament required a different grasp of the
language. His knowledge of Hebrew was adequate. He was at home
naturally among classical historians like Tacitus, who provided the
context of the Roman world, and Greek-writing authors like Josephus,
who opened one of the doors to Judaism of the first century. He also
made a real effort to acquaint himself with the work of Jewish antiquity—the Targums, Talmud, and Rabbinic literature, so far as they
were then known—as well as the German scholars who in the past two
decades had done so much to recover the world of ancient Judaism.[74]
His son later wrote that Farrar's scholarship belonged to the "extensive" rather than the "intensive" school.[75] It is true that he was less at
home when he attempted original research in the fashion of a Lightfoot or F. J. A. Hort than when he sought "to interpret and make
available the labours of the former class, whose work would otherwise
remain buried under its own weight."[76] There were thus limitations to
Farrar's scholarship which were to show up more clearly later on, as
learning turned more and more toward specialization; but what he did
he did well. *The Life of Christ* gave evidence of an author at ease with
his materials.

Farrar's actual procedure in applying the methods of biblical higher
criticism was conservative to say the least, but he defended his position with intelligence and, at times, surprising flexibility. He regarded
the gospel of John, for example, as an authentic and historical source
of data on Jesus' life. This was a backward position compared with
the views of the leading critics in Germany, but Farrar was not insular
in adopting it. As will become apparent in chapter four, he drew support in his views from the Cambridge scholars, Westcott, Hort, and
Lightfoot, and from conservatives in Germany who resisted the critical contention that the Fourth Gospel was late and unreliable.[77] At the
same time, he made concessions on the orthodox doctrine of inspired
scripture which, though small from today's perspective, were not at all
insignificant. He saw no need to contend for an accuracy or wooden
literalism which made both the Bible and its defenders look ridiculous
in the eyes of educated men. The evangelists were as reliable as any
four eyewitnesses with variant viewpoints and fallible memories could
be expected to be. Their writings were in the main trustworthy:

> The phenomena presented by the narratives are exactly such as we should expect, derived as they are from different witnesses, preserved at first in oral tradition only, and written 1800 years ago, at a period when *minute circumstantial accuracy,* as distinguished from perfect truthfulness, was little regarded.[78]

The "perfect truthfulness" of the evangelists could be vouched for; their perfect accuracy could not—at least not in all cases. On the other hand, not all inaccuracies cited by modern critics turned out to be such. Farrar found it possible to account for a number of difficulties by appealing to manuscript errors and what apparently was the faulty transmission of texts. The discovery of an erroneous gloss, or a variant reading, offered a way past apparent inconsistencies and occasionally helped to dissolve anachronisms.[79] In their original form the four gospels were not only trustworthy, but given the circumstances of their composition, strikingly accurate. If they seemed to differ, this was chiefly because of their supplementary character. What one gospel omitted the next intended to supply. Whereas the synoptics dealt chiefly with Galilee and Jesus' ministry in the countryside, the Fourth Gospel focused upon Jerusalem and Judea.

This cautious approach to criticism linked itself naturally with an orthodox position on theological issues. "This Life of Christ," wrote Farrar in preface,

> is avowedly and unconditionally the work of a believer. Those who expect to find in it new theories about the divine personality of Jesus, or brilliant combinations of mythic cloud tinged by the sunset imagination of some decadent belief will look in vain.[80]

"Believer" to Farrar meant several things, not the least of which was a resolute assent to miracles and an acceptance of Jesus not only as portrayed in the gospel narratives, but as interpreted in the theology of Paul, and definitively presented in the historic creeds of the church. Jesus spoke to his contemporaries not merely as a teacher or itinerant wonder-worker, but as nothing less than the savior of mankind. He was the unique God-man, revealer of the Father's love, redeemer of men from sin and evil, the founder of an everlasting kingdom whose present form is the Christian church and whose final glory will be evident to all at the end of time, when the risen, ascended Christ returns to judge the earth. Thus, Jesus claimed to be the Messiah, but in a sense which passed far beyond the limited interests of Judaism in his day. In the opinion of the Jews he was a blasphemer and insurrectionist; in truth, he was carrying out a far higher purpose—the redemption of men through his blood. While his preaching drew multitudes, it angered the Jewish leaders, who were jealous of his popularity, fearful of his free views on the Law, and consequently determined to bring about his end. During Passover week in the third year of his ministry he was seized, brought before the Roman governor, and executed. But death only accomplished his divine plan, and he arose on Easter morn, to the wonder of his now-awakened disciples and the baffled rage of his enemies.

Merely to summarize these convictions is to see why Farrar's narrative could be commended as warmly in the Catholic *Month* as in any of the journals of Protestant Britain.[81] The author spoke the thoughts of historic Christendom, of a creed which after many centuries, the trauma of the Reformation, and the rise of secularism, great sectors of the Christian world still managed to hold in common. Readers who feared a rationalist or another Renan were jubilant. The *Life of Christ* vigorously reassured.

Yet there was something about Renan that Farrar did not forget. The substance of the *Vie de Jesus,* he would readily have agreed, was unacceptable, but not its form. There was something in its manner— its vivid, fresh, picturesque presentation of the gospel story—that an orthodox writer would be foolish not to recapture. Renan steeped himself in the scenic romance of Palestine; so did Farrar. His own trip to the Holy Land had been a part of the original commission, financed by Cassell in the hope that the *Life* would give off just this sort of reflection from the primitive Jewish setting. Farrar needed no incentives, actually; his own testimony speaks for itself:

> I seized, in the year 1870, the earliest possible opportunity to visit Palestine, and especially those parts of it which will be for ever identified with the work of Christ on earth. Amid those immemorial customs which recalled at every turn the manner of life he lived—at Jerusalem, on the Mount of Olives, at Bethlehem, by Jacob's Well, in the valley of Nazareth, along the bright stand of the Sea of Galilee, and in the coasts of Tyre and Sidon—many things came home to me, for the first time, with a reality and vividness unknown before. I returned more than ever confirmed in the wish to tell the full story of the gospels in such a manner and with such illustrations as—with the aid of all that was within my reach of that knowledge which has been accumulating for centuries—might serve to enable at least the simple and unlearned to understand and enter into the human surroundings of the life of the Son of God.[82]

Except for the concluding doxology, Renan himself could not have said it better. The life and landscape of the Near East, the historian's "fifth gospel," offered an almost inexhaustible fund of romantic scenes and picturesque customs from which to draw. In the Victorian religious community, there was perhaps no writer more sensitive than Farrar to their magical power, or more able than he to recreate them with such a wealth of colorful and descriptive imagery. We have already observed instances where the arts of the travelogue, so popular with Victorian readers, had been applied to biblical subjects. Stanley had done it successfully with *Sinai and Palestine;* William Hanna, haltingly in his *Life of our Lord.*[83] Farrar became the first native English author to do it extensively with the story of Christ, and it contributed measurably to his success.

The *Life of Christ* thus indulged in embellished descriptions of the Palestinian locale whenever the occasion presented itself. Consider, for example, the brushstrokes with which Farrar fills in the scene of Christ's anguish in Gethsemane:

> It was . . . probably one of the secluded hollows . . . which witnessed that scene of awful and pathetic mystery. . . . although the exact spot cannot be determined with certainty, the general position of Gethsemane is clear, and then as now the chequering moonlight, the grey leaves, the dark brown trunks, the soft greensward, the ravine with Olivet towering over it to the eastward and Jerusalem to the west, must have been the main features of a place which must be regarded with undying interest while Time shall be, as the place where the Saviour of mankind entered alone into the Valley of the Shadow.[84]

This was Farrar's handling of a scenic backdrop; the same style came into employ when the subject turned to Roman or Jewish customs, to the life of the cities, and the folkways of the Jewish people. Sabbath practices, imperial coinage, the complexities of the Talmud and Torah, the disputes of the rabbis, the tensions between Sadducee and Pharisee, Essene and establishment, Zealots and Hellenizers—all were woven at appropriate places into the multicolored fabric of the story. Such subjects had of themselves a certain antiquarian charm, as Renan had shown. When gilded with Farrar's luxuriant, rolling prose, they seemed almost overdrawn. His sentences bent beneath the weight of adjectives which gathered in clusters. Where the sources lacked detail, historical fancy sometimes came to the rescue. The passage above, where the moonlight is "chequering" about the Saviour, the leaves are a moonlit "grey" up against the dark brown tree trunks, is typical of Farrar's attempt at the novelist's sense of vivid realism. Where there was human conflict, as between Jesus and the Pharisees, or among the disciples, Farrar readily supplied motives, occasions, reasons, and reactions for the interested parties. He had too a flair for the dramatic, which came to his aid especially in passages like the passion narrative. In the upper room, for example, readers are told of a "dark omen" which overshadowed the disciples at Jesus' announcement of the betrayer, and the scene quickly evolves into a tumult of whispered fears and horrified suspicions. Where the gospel sources so much as hinted at intrigue or conspiracy, it was enough. Farrar's fertile imagination took liberties to fill in the lights and shadows and colors.

This sort of bold intimacy with the biblical personages, conveyed in Farrar's rather florid prose, did not escape some censure from critics. In fact, the only feature of the book which came in for some rather severe criticism was its style, which in the view of many reviewers was so colored and rhetorical as to seem excessive. Although there was a complaint from an extreme orthodox voice about vagueness on the atonement, the substance of the *Life* met with almost uniform approval. Critics saw it as scholarly, theologically orthodox, critically sound; it portrayed Christ as the Son of God, yet as a flesh-and-blood human personality. But to sensitive ears, the author's ornate, effusive prose was another matter. It would be inaccurate to say that Farrar wanted to make the gospel story a sort of prose epic, and unfair to accuse him of stooping to mere sensationalism. But in places the *Life of Christ* suggested both, and this was what annoyed a number of critics. The *Spectator* was among the more severe: "here the words are too big for the thoughts, and the poverty of the fancies is not concealed by the tinsel epithets with which they are tricked out . . . epithets must not be introduced for ornament, but only to add real and pregnant meaning to the sentence."[85] Though others were more charitable, most agreed with the verdict of the *London Quarterly's* critic, who conceded that "the style glitters a little too much."[86] In general, magazines like the *Athenaeum,* which were concerned with upholding the standards of sophisticated taste, took most offense at the literary excesses; the religious reviews regarded them as a minor defect in an otherwise most valuable book.[87]

Whatever the judgment passed by literary critics and the guardians of good taste, there could be no quarrel with Farrar's tremendous popular success. Indeed the very thing about its style that most offended the elite—its tendency toward the sentimental or sensational, its inclination to vulgarize sacred things—was perhaps the secret of its success with the ordinary reader. Here was an author who made the story of Christ as captivating as a tale of adventure, as dramatic as a novel of crime. In truth the life of Christ was a tale of crime, also of intrigue and hatred, of the conflict between good and evil, of the insidious effects of human corruption which brought a man of divine goodness to a cruel and hideous death. If that was so, why should an author not be allowed to say it? Such was the argument that Farrar himself brought against his critics the following year in an able defense of his book written for *Macmillan's Magazine.*[88]

To the vast majority of British readers, however, the book needed no such defense. Farrar alone deserves the credit for striking at last upon the correct formula for a successful, historical approach to the life of Jesus, a blend of just those elements which satisfied the needs of conventional, middle-class Victorian piety. For such readers he was Britain's definitive answer to the petty carping of rationalists and the threat of the great foreign infidels, Strauss and Renan. All of those key features which earlier British Lives had exhibited in part—orthodoxy, scholarship, appealing style, a venerable human Christ, the glow of antiquarianism and Oriental romance—were fused into one in Farrar's book. He had managed to tell the story as many, both educated and unlearned, wished to hear it. The Victorian populace purchased the *Life* steadily and in sizable quantities over the next several decades, but sales were only one index of appeal. An even better sign was to emerge in the decades that followed. From 1874 to the end of the century almost every successful British Life was to draw heavily upon the model shaped by Farrar.

NOTES

1. Many of these Lives are cited in Ayres' bibliography, *Jesus Christ our Lord,* 49-88. More extensive information is available in the *Brit. Mus. Catalogue.* Most of these works are accessible in research and seminary libraries across the United States, but no one institution has a comprehensive collection.

2. See chap. 2, n. 11; for the successive editions of both Fleetwood and Taylor's *Great Exemplar* see the *Brit. Mus. Catalogue,* s.v. the respective authors. The *Catalogue* of course lists only those works and new editions which were submitted to the Museum library and thus cannot be regarded as an exhaustive record of works that were published in these years. From about mid-century, however, when librarian Antonio Panizzi began to enforce the copyright provision that copies of all new publications be deposited in the Museum, it gives an accurate record at least of first printings. On the work of Panizzi see Altick, *English Common Reader,* 215.

3. "Harmonies of the Gospel," 721-42.

4. *Publisher's Circular,* 31 December 1864. See also Patrick Scott, "The Business of Belief," 220 n. 29.

5. Irons's work was *The Sacred Life of Jesus Christ . . Taken from the Gospels* (London: J. Masters, 1867).

6. *Brit. Mus. Catalogue,* s.v. "Bushnell, Horace," lists this under the title *The Character of Jesus* (London: T. Nelson & Sons, 1861) and mentions another edition, by A. Strahan & Co., Edinburgh, as in its ninth thousand.

7. Samuel Andrews, *The Life of Our Lord upon Earth Considered in its Historical, Chronological, and Geographical Relations* (London: A. Strahan & Co., 1863).

8. On these and other sources through which British readers learned of developments in Germany see Crowther, *Church Embattled,* chap. 2, "The Threat From Germany," 40-65; the number of translations grew in the 1840s, yet nearly all were from conservative German works. In 1856 and 1865 Clark published translations of two German histories of religious ideas written from the conservative viewpoint: Kahnis's *Internal History of German Protestantism* and Hagenbach's *German Rationalism in its Rise, Progress and Decline.*

9. Probably because of their liberal tendencies, Ewald and Hase were not published by Clark; see *Brit. Mus. Catalogue,* s.v. the respective authors. Appreciative comments on the publications of Clark may be found, among other places, in the Anglican *Literary Churchman,* 16 January 1863: "At a time like this, it is a matter of thankfulness that the Bible reader is provided with all the means within reach, for a critical as well as practical understanding of every part of the word of God. And perhaps none of our publishers have done more than Messrs. Clark for the great cause of biblical investigation."

10. See the articles entitled "Answers to Renan" in the November and December issues of the *Literary Churchman* 9 (1863); another survey, which included some British works, appeared in the issue for 24 August 1864, 351-52.

11. Citations of this work will be taken from the American edition: Edmund de Pressensé, tr. Annie Harwood, *Jesus Christ: His Times, Life, and Work,* 2d ed. rev. (New York: Scribner, Welford, & Co., 1868).

12. See my "Reception of *Ecce Homo,*" 76-77.

13. On the theological issues see "Preliminary Questions" (book 1), *Jesus Christ,* 1-20 especially; the sources were treated in the same section, 110-85.

14. "The most valuable part of it is the long and elaborate Preliminary Dissertation," wrote the critic in the *London Quarterly* in his piece on "Pressensé's Jesus Christ," 27 (October 1866) 163; E. T. Vaughan, writing on "The Life of Our Lord" in the *Contemporary Review* 2 (August 1866) 417, agreed, but "would gladly have had M. de Pressensé's preliminary investigation separated from the remainder of the volume." For a comparative survey of the major Lives from H. E. G. Paulus through Pressensé, written from the viewpoint of a contemporary orthodox observer, see Appendix B in E. H. Plumptre, *Christ and Christendom* (London: Alexander Strahan, Publisher, 1867) 328-29.

15. "Pressensé's Jesus Christ," 163; italics added.

16. Ayres, *Jesus Christ,* 59, lists a seventh edition in 1879. One must be careful not to rest judgments about popularity solely on the register of new editions. In Victorian publishing the size of editions varied considerably; so the real popularity of a book must be measured in terms of copies sold. Where these records are not available, one must fall back, with appropriate cautions, upon the number of editions as the best guide. At the very least they testify to the durability of a book, its capacity to serve a certain part of the reading populace over an extended period of time. I have been careful to limit inferences about popularity in the case of those works whose new editions are the only clue to their success.

17. On the new editions and price changes see the entries under "De Pressensé, Edmund," in the listings of newly published works in the *Publisher's Circular,* 15 July 1868; 15 May 1869; and 2 October 1871.

18. Gladstone himself testified to this in a speech before Parliament; it is quoted in Altick, *English Common Reader,* 294.

19. Altick, *English Common Reader,* 275; for some of the material in this section I am indebted to Altick's comprehensive survey; to Henry Curwen, *A History of Booksellers, The Old and the New* (London: Chatto & Windus, 1873); to Patrick Scott, "The Business of Belief"; and to Geoffrey Best's illuminating social history, *Mid-Victorian Britain: 1851-1875.*

20. On the circulating library see Curwen, *History of Booksellers,* 421-32, which deals with Charles Mudie especially, and Altick, *English Common Reader,* 124-25, 217-18, 254-55, et passim.

21. Altick, *English Common Reader,* 299.

22. Best, *Mid-Victorian Britain,* 176; see Curwen, *History of Booksellers,* 433-40 on W. H. Smith.

23. Altick, *English Common Reader,* 306; see also Best, *Mid-Victorian Britain,* 224: "The fact is, that by the fifties a large and still enlarging middle-cum-working class public was ready to read all the cheap literature it could get."

24. Ibid.

25. Ibid.

26. Ibid., 307-9.

27. R. C. K. Ensor, *England 1870-1914,* is helpful on Evangelicalism, improvement and the doctrine of self-help. As for Benthamism, improvement was a central article in the utilitarian creed; see Altick's chapter on "The Utilitarian Spirit," *English Common Reader,* 129-40, and his treatment of one of the early monuments to utilitarian ideals, The Society for the Diffusion of Useful Knowledge, 269-73. Other pioneers in the "improving" literature movement were William and Robert Chambers, Charles Knight, H. G. Bohn, noted earlier for early contributions to religious literature, and the shrewd, shady Thomas Tegg; on these see ibid., 280-86.

28. On this aspect of Victorianism much has been misunderstood and misrepresented. Many would do well to begin with the engaging and sympathetic portrait of Smiles in Asa Briggs, *Victorian People: A Reassessment of Persons and Themes 1851-1867,* rev. ed. (1955; Chicago: University of Chicago Press, 1973).

29. Altick, *English Common Reader,* 115-23, surveys a number of families from the ranks of dissent as well as the Church who even before mid-century read fiction with no sense of guilt or fear of suspicion. Toward mid-century religious publishers themselves entered the fiction market with novels designed for moral instruction, particularly in the realm of juvenile literature. The sales of these works were often staggering; see Patrick Scott, "The Business of Belief," 215.

30. Quoted in Cruse, *Victorians and Their Reading,* 128.

31. *The Victorian Church,* 1:462; Chadwick's entire section, pp. 455-68, is very good on the problem of Sunday, the campaigns to keep it sacred, and the resulting social stress. A more recent, comprehensive study is John Wigley, *The Rise and Fall of the Victorian Sunday* (Manchester: Manchester University Press, 1980).

32. Chadwick, *Victorian Church,* 1:462-63; for the comments of foreign travelers on the Victorian Sabbath, see Best, *Mid-Victorian Britain,* 175.

33. Cruse, *Victorians and Their Reading,* 216.

34. Scott, "Business of Belief," 224.

35. Best, *Mid-Victorian Britain,* 226.

36. Ensor, *England 1870-1914,* 137.

37. See *DNB,* s.v. "Hanna, William," where this volume is said to have reached "a circulation of fifty thousand."

38. William Hanna, *The Forty Days After Our Lord's Resurrection,* vol. 6 of *The Life of our Lord upon Earth,* Amer. ed., 6 vols. in 3 (New York:

Robert Carter and Brothers, 1876) ix. These comments are taken from the preface to vol. 6, dated Edinburgh, 11 November 1863. Vol. 6, last in the sequence of Christ's life, was the second written and the first after Hanna's return from the Holy Land.

39. Ibid., ix-x.

40. Ibid., xi.

41. William Hanna, *The Earlier Years of our Lord's Life on Earth,* vol. 2 of *The Life of our Lord,* 362.

42. Hanna, General Preface to *The Life of our Lord,* vi.

43. Hanna, *The Forty Days,* xix.

44. On this contrast see the instructive discussion by Hans Frei, *The Eclipse of Biblical Narrative: A Study in Eighteenth and Nineteenth Century Hermeneutics* (New Haven: Yale University Press, 1974) 55-60.

45. This was noted among the otherwise favorable comments of the critic in the *North British Review.* See "The Life of our Lord," *North British Review* 50 (July 1869) 185.

46. The first volume published was volume five of the completed work. On reprints and new editions see *The English Catalogue of Books* (London: Sampson, Low, Marston & Co., 1801—), s.v. "Hanna, W." in the years from publication of the *Life* to the end of the century. Though new editions of selected volumes appeared in 1876 and 1878, the only new printing of the entire work was in 1882 by the Religious Tract Society; it was reissued once after the close of the century.

47. The exception was the *North British Review,* which however had somewhat of a vested interest in the work of Rev. Hanna. He was for a time its chief editor; see *DNB,* s.v. "Hanna, William."

48. Richard Davies Hanson, *The Jesus of History* (Edinburgh: Williams and Norgate, 1869) x.

49. Ibid., 70 on John as a later document; see pp. 199-217 on his rejection of John's historicity.

50. Ibid., 365.

51. Ibid., 365-66.

52. Ibid., 374-75.

53. Ibid., viii; how fully he was aware of Strauss's contribution none can say for certain, but Strauss is mentioned on p. ix.

54. A favorable notice appeared under "Contemporary Literature: Theology and Philosophy," *Westminster Review* 92 (July 1869) 235-39.

55. Ibid., 235.

56. *The Victorian Church,* 2:66.

57. Thomas Scott, *The English Life of Jesus* (London: Trübner & Co., 1872) xi.

58. See the notice of this and two other, anonymous works in "Contemporary Literature and Philosophy," *British Quarterly Review* 56 (July 1872) 269-71.

59. It did not escape the view of F. W. Farrar, who cited both Hanson and Scott in the preface to his *Life of Christ,* Amer. ed., 2 vols. (New York: E. P. Dutton & Co., n.d.) ix. On Farrar and his celebrated Life, first published in 1874, see below, pp. 77-85.

60. Scott, *English Life,* 152-53.

61. Ibid., 173.

62. Ibid., 130.

63. Ibid., 348-49.

64. Mention should here be made of two lesser-known rationalist Lives which proceeded in a manner very similar to that adopted by Hanson and Scott. P. W. Perfitt's apparently incomplete study (only one volume published), *The Life and Teaching of Jesus of Nazareth, The Friend of Freethought* (London: George Manwaring, 1861), betrays its conclusions in its title. The anonymous *Jesus the Messiah* (London: Trübner & Co., 1872) was also an attack on the Christ of orthodoxy. Like Hanson and Scott, both challenged the authenticity and historic value of the Fourth Gospel.

65. See the account by his son and biographer Reginald Farrar, *The Life of Frederic William Farrar* (London: James Nisbet & Co., 1904) 71-75.

66. See *DNB,* s.v. "Farrar, F. W."

67. Simon Nowell-Smith, *The House of Cassell 1848-1958* (London: Cassell & Company Ltd., 1958) 96.

68. Ibid.; Shore had first suggested, but was unable to secure, the Bishop of Derry.

69. Farrar's roots were Evangelical. His father was chaplain of the Church Missionary Society, and his early schooling was of a strictly Evangelical cast while he was at King William's College. In maturity he developed Broad Church sympathies evident in *Eternal Hope* and in the generous act by which he secured permission in 1882 for the burial of Charles Darwin in Westminster Abbey, where he preached the funeral sermon. See R. Farrar, *Life of Farrar,* 109. On Farrar's early life see R. Farrar, *Life,* 1-37 and *DNB,* s.v. "Farrar, F. W.," which notes that theologically he held a position "between the evangelical and broad church schools of thought."

70. Nowell-Smith, *House of Cassell,* 96.

71. On the sales and circulation of the Life see ibid.; on the translations see R. Farrar, *Life of Farrar,* 196; some of the many editions and reprints are listed in the *Brit. Mus. Catalogue,* s.v. "Farrar, Frederic William," and in *DNB,* s.v. "Farrar, F. W."

72. Nowell-Smith, *House of Cassell,* 95-100, gives an interesting account of this falling-out from the publisher's point of view.

73. R. Farrar, *Life of Farrar,* 195.

74. There is some merit in his son's claim, *Life of Farrar,* 194, that "he was the first great literary churchman of his day to appreciate and make effective use of the body of Talmudic learning made available by German scholars."

75. Ibid., 193-94.

76. Ibid., 193.

77. The consensus of British scholarship on the Fourth Gospel before 1900 is recounted in my "Victorian Religion and the British Lives of Jesus: 1860-1910" (Ph.D. diss., University of Chicago, 1975) 185-95; for the German disputes and factions see Schweitzer, *Quest,* 121-28.

78. Farrar, *Life of Christ,* 2:432 n. 1.

79. See for example the *Life of Christ,* 1:140; 2:108; 246 n. 2; 396. A particularly good illustration is Farrar's handling of Jesus' reference to "Zechariah the son of Berechiah" being slain at the altar of the temple. Since it was known that this event took place some thirty-four years later, liberal critics sometimes argued that the passage was a later interpolation of the sort that one could find frequently in the evangelists. Farrar contended that Jesus had actually referred to "Zechariah the son of Jehoida," who according to Jewish books had long before been murdered by Joash "in the courts of the house of the Lord." He then concluded that the phrase "Zechariah the son of Berechiah" found in New Testament MS D "is a very early and erroneous gloss which has crept into the text."

80. Farrar, *Life of Christ,* 1:vii-ix.

81. "Reviews and Notices," *The Month* 22 (September 1874) 98-101; the critic did not hesitate to express as well his disenchantment with some features of the *Life,* particularly what he saw as its Protestant tendency toward anti-dogmatism and a too free criticism of the sources.

82. Farrar, *Life of Christ,* 1:vii.

83. On this see above, pp. 29-30. As the Victorian appetite for travel literature from the lands of the empire grew larger, surveys of the Near East and biblical lands were among the most popular. Stanley's *Sinai and Palestine* (1856) was a staple of this diet; works that supplemented it in succeeding years included W. M. Thompson, *The Land and the Book* (1866); H. B. Tristram, *The Land of Moab* (1873); Richard Newton, *Rambles in Bible Lands* (1879); J. Cunningham Geikie, *Hours with the Bible* (1881-1896); idem., *The Holy Land and the Bible* (1887); and Thomas Nicol, *Recent Explorations in Bible Lands* (1892).

84. Farrar, *Life of Christ,* 2:307-08.

85. "Farrar's Life of Christ," *Spectator,* 11 July 1874.

86. "Literary Notices," *London Quarterly Review* 43 (October 1874) 243.

87. The *Athenaeum* review, which dealt almost exclusively with matters of style, appeared in the issue for 27 June 1874. Among the more favorable notices in the religious journals and newspapers were the following: *British Quarterly Review* 60 (July 1874) 281-83; *Literary Churchman,* 8 May 1875;

Guardian, 12 August 1874; and the *London Quarterly Review* 43 (October 1874) 241-44. The *Westminster* was predictably critical; see "Contemporary Literature: Theology and Philosophy," 102 (October 1874) 516-18. The *Quarterly Review* gave a mixed opinion, 138 (January 1875) 177-206; despite some reservations it congratulated the author on his great popular success.

88. F. W. Farrar, "A Few Words on the Life of Christ," *Macmillan's Magazine* 31 (March 1875) 463-71.

3 AFTER FARRAR
THE TYPICAL VICTORIAN LIVES OF JESUS, 1874-1900

If we will, we may now discern the true features of Jesus of Nazareth, as no generation but our own has been able to discern them, since those who had seen and handled passed away.

Robert Elsmere

Farrar's *Life of Christ* was an unprecedented success. Even the *Quarterly Review,* never generous or unstinting in praise, was moved to congratulate the author upon an achievement "to which the annals of English theology present no parallel."[1] His formula of orthodox theology, serious, if conservative, scholarship, Oriental romance, and graphic popular style secured an audience of a size rarely attracted by nonfictional literature. To be sure, Cassell had provided the *Life* with a strong advertising campaign and a publisher's imprint without equal in the field of popular literature. Yet even so, the success surpassed anyone's expectations. Nothing quite like it had been seen before; a great deal that resembled it was soon to come after.

This latter development is noteworthy, for even more important than the immediate success of the *Life* itself was its long-term effect. Over the next quarter-century and to the very end of the Victorian era, Farrar's book set the pattern for subsequent writers on the life of Jesus. Inadvertently or intentionally, writers of every type and talent who wanted a hearing found themselves working from the model of Farrar. The sheer number of such Lives by mediocre or unknown authors which found their way into print testifies to a certain confidence on the part of publishers: it was as if the subject alone seemed to reduce the risk. Almost any Life could find a readership, provided it made some effort to approximate the virtues of Farrar. In what follows several of the more noteworthy Lives in this lineage will be examined. Though they vary considerably in length and size and format, in depth of scholarship and psychological insight, they are strongly imprinted with those features first clearly visible in the *Life of Christ*. Some writers lay greater claim to learning; others are more subjective and impressionistic; still others are more concerned to reaffirm orthodoxy's old verities. Almost all recognize in some measure the importance of orthodox theological premises, serious scholarship, a popular, colorful style, an appeal to Oriental romance, and a Jesus of truly human character or personality. First to claim our attention will be J. Cunningham Geikie, a prolific expositor of biblical subjects whose Life was written in conscious imitation of Farrar's and enjoyed almost equal success. Works by James Stalker, A. M. Fairbairn, W. Robertson Nicoll, and others illustrate how theological and instructional concerns took precedence in several of the most successful Lives. In E. A. Abbott, Edward Clodd, and others we make a brief return to the rationalist tradition. In Alfred Edersheim and others one may observe the importance of historical romance. And some attention must be paid to foreign contributions, particularly to Catholic Lives translated from the French and to certain more critical works coming from Germany. The survey will take us up to 1900, which for reasons that will later become clear serves as a kind of end point of the Victorian Lives.

1. Cunningham Geikie; Scottish works

In the years immediately after the *Life of Christ* was published, several other works of note also made their appearance. Father Henry James Coleridge's *Public Life of Our Lord* (1874) was a devotional work conceived on the grand scale. One of the earliest significant Catholic attempts, the *Public Life* was actually the first installment of a long devotional work in the old style of Catholic spirituality. The author continued working for seventeen years and sixteen volumes.[2]

G. S. Drew's *The Son of Man* (1875) was a competent but far less ambitious work than Farrar's. Besides these, there were others.[3] From the standpoint of public notice, however, the most important was clearly Cunningham Geikie's *Life and Words of Christ,* published in two volumes by Henry S. King & Company in 1877.

John Cunningham Geikie, son of a Scottish Presbyterian pastor, received his education in Edinburgh and in Canada, where he entered the ministry and served his first pastorate. After returning to Britain he was ordained a deacon in the Church of England in 1876. The following year he published the *Life and Words,* dedicated "to my honored friend, F. W. Farrar," who was responsible for Geikie's first preferment in the Church.[4] One is tempted, however, to find something more symbolic than the obvious clerical gratitude in these words. Having seen the *Life of Christ,* Geikie seemed in a way to be writing the very same book. That his book and Farrar's were similar was evident even on a superficial comparison. Both were two-volume works whose prefatory lists of sources disclosed virtually identical research: earlier Lives and New Testament commentaries (both English and foreign), with special stress on conservative scholarship, travelogues from the Orient, and some of the newer German studies of late-Jewish literature, such as those of August Dillman and Adolph Hilgenfeld.

At other levels Farrar and Geikie were in similar agreement.

Geikie's theological axioms were wholly traditional and orthodox. If that were possible, he was even less in doubt about miracles than Farrar. The wonder of the coin in the fish's mouth—for liberal critics a sure instance of myth or folklore in the gospels—Geikie believed as firmly as he did the virgin birth, the multiplication of the loaves, or Christ's resurrection on Easter morn. Jesus was precisely what the churches had always described him to be: son of God and son of man, founder of a universal kingdom made up of people who trusted in him and acquired through him a new life of faith and love. The purpose of his deeds and words was to bring the Jewish people (and all mankind) to understand that they could be spiritually renewed by him. That the Jews misunderstood and executed him was tragic on a purely human appraisal, but not in God's plan, for by his resurrection he overcame death and inaugurated the Christian era—the age of forgiveness available to all through his sacrificial death.

This was traditional enough. What gave the work its element of novelty was the painstaking care with which Geikie filled in the historical scene and context. With the attention to fine detail manifest in so many aspects of Victorian culture—from lace handiwork and imitative rococo furniture to neo-Gothic cathedrals and the Crystal Palace, he sketched the history, economy, religion, society, and thought of Judea in the time of Christ. Like Farrar, he was a scholar of the "extensive" sort, a specialist in no single subject, but a skillful expositor with a capacity to understand his authorities, absorb their researches, and convey the results to his readers in lucid prose. For political background Geikie drew on Tacitus, Suetonius, and Josephus, as well as the books of the Maccabees, to fill in both the imperial and local scene. Along with Farrar he was one of the first in Britain to appreciate the significance of Jewish intertestamentary literature, not merely the Apocrypha, but also the more recently explored apocalyptic and pseudepigraphal literature. "No better key to the religious spirit of an age," he wrote,

can be had than its religious literature. That of Israel, as the age of Christ drew near, was more and more concentrated on the expected Messiah, and the preparation needed for his coming. The Book of Enoch, the Psalms of Solomon, and the Fourth Book of Esdras, successively reveal the white heat of the national hopes of which they were the expression.[5]

In 1877 few British writers were well enough versed in the world and writings of late Judaism to have written even this much; nor would they have been able to follow it, as Geikie did, with a close and careful description of the message of each book. In the same way the Talmud, mediated through the works of the German scholar Emil Schürer and through John Lightfoot's *Horae Hebraicae,* provided background for discussions of Jewish law, the rabbinical schools, and the intricacies of first-century Jewish ritual and belief.[6] Geikie was a lover of small out-of-the-way facts, which were gathered into the story whenever the biblical events offered him the slightest opportunity. The imprisonment of John led to facts and figures on Herod's fortress at Machaerus; the wedding in Cana to a discourse on Jewish marriage customs; the cure of the woman with an issue of blood to a survey of health practices and ancient medications. His eye for detail, for the small illuminative circumstance, was unfailing.

Nor was he less assiduous in matters geographical. The elevation, slopes, and shapes of the Palestinian hills he searched out and described with the same energy he devoted to temple ritual or sabbath practice. Unable to get to the Holy Land before writing his Life, he afterwards made several visits, following with great interest the researches of Claude Ranier Conder and the Palestine Exploration Fund. In fact, his keen interest in biblical lands was later to inspire his longest work, a vast compilation, eventually reaching twelve volumes and entitled *Hours with the Bible, or, the Scriptures in the Light of Modern Discovery and Knowledge* (1881-1896), as well as *The Holy Land and the Bible: A Book of Scripture Illustrations Gathered in Palestine* (1887). For the present work he depended heavily on travelogues like Canon H. B. Tristram's *Land of Moab,* Curtis's *Wanderer in Syria,* W. M. Thompson's *The Land and the Book,* and Stanley's widely read *Sinai and Palestine.* Guided by these sources, he described cities and sites as though he were the guide on a Near Eastern tour. Each town or village was depicted in its environs: Cana, in the plain of El Battauf, where grasses and grains flourished below fortified hills; Capernaum, on the Western shore of the Galilean Sea, a bustling, busy town through which ran the great trade route known as the "highway to the sea"; Jericho, in the luxuriant valley of the Jordan, scene of historic battles and thriving commerce; above all, Jerusalem,

> the vast white walls and buildings of the Temple, its courts, glittering with gold, rising one above the other; the steep sides of the Hill of David crowned with lofty walls; the mighty castles towering above them; the sumptuous palace of Herod in its green parks, and the picturesque outlines of the streets.[7]

Geikie relished such portrait painting and warmed to the task wherever it presented itself.

Although the passage quoted above suggests otherwise, Geikie as a stylist was rather more restrained than Farrar. He was less given to the unnecessary epithet and the ornate cadences which sensitive critics thought had been carried to excess in the *Life of Christ.* His prose was more direct, more suited to strictly historical narrative and more resistant of the temptation to indulge in heavy moralizing or devotional reflections. Like most others who followed Farrar, he occasionally fell to supplying motives and seemed at times to know his characters too well. That Jesus selected Peter as a disciple because of "the rare unbending firmness of purpose, the tenacious fidelity, the swift decisiveness, the Galilean fire and manliness, and the tender religiousness of spirit, which marked him to the end of his life" is considerably more than one can discern from the bare essentials of the gospel texts.[8] But indulgence of this sort was rare. Spurgeon described the author as "one of the best religious writers of the age."[9]

From a critical standpoint, the weakness of the *Life and Words* lay not in what it did but, like Farrar's work, in what it did not do. The tendency to psychologize characters might be overlooked on occasion if elsewhere Geikie could be found asking serious critical questions about his sources. Even a popular work could pay some attention to the troublesome conflicts between the Fourth Gospel and the first three, to puzzling matters of chronology and consistency within the synoptics, and to the debates over duplicate and triplicate narratives of seemingly the same events. Geikie said almost nothing on these topics. He seemed merely to assume that the four gospels were compatible, that there were two cleansings of the temple, two feedings of the multitudes, and that such matters could be dispensed with in a note that cited B. F. Westcott, Franz Delitzsch, or some other conservative authority. Such appeals hint at an important circumstance in British scholarship, to be explored further in chapter four. In fact, they illustrate a tendency that persisted in Britain's Lives down to the end of the century. Unlike many German works, where critical questions were regarded as central to any reconstruction of the narrative, British works kept to a less profound scholarship. They consulted a group of recognized conservative critics; they found in them the reassurances needed about the gospel sources, then built upon what they found. The Lives themselves, therefore, were often long on industry, short on analysis; they were derivative, not primary investigations.

The critical disabilities, of course, made no difference whatsoever to the popularity of the *Life and Words.* An extremely successful book, it enjoyed new editions and impressive sales well into the first decade of the twentieth century, achieving a circulation second only, it would seem, to Farrar's *Life.*[10] Critics generally were appreciative of the enormous industry and erudition that had gone into such a book. Of course opinions varied. The *British Quarterly* thought that "as a perfect cyclopedia of biographical circumstance" it was indispensable; the *Athenaeum* seized upon the critical deficiencies and pronounced it "unscholarly and slovenly."[11] This last judgment was unduly harsh, and in any case the reading public gave little notice to critical slurs. By the end of the century the *Life and Words* had been through several publishers, including Cassell and Longman.[12] It had reached thirty editions by 1885, when Cassell proposed to offer it in serial parts.[13] In 1896 Longman announced it in three forms: a presentation edition at 24s., a cabinet edition at half that price, and a cheap edition at 7s. 6d. In addition Longman even offered an independent *Short Life of Christ* by Geikie at a price of 3s. 6d .[14] It seems hardly surprising that, as with Farrar, the total sales of the *Life and Words* had by the author's death exceeded 100,000.[15]

Although proper allowance must be made for copies that graced furniture or were bought as gifts, success on this scale was impressive. Clearly a great many late Victorian readers found in Geikie, as in Farrar, an author whose Christ had magnetic appeal.

Both Farrar and Geikie wrote large books. In the years afterward came a number of works on a smaller scale which were almost as popular. Typical of these was a brief *Life of Jesus Christ* by James Stalker, a Scottish Free Church pastor from Aberdeen. Published in 1879 as a part of Clark's Handbooks for Bible Classes, it was only 154 pages long. It was designed chiefly for instructional purposes in Sunday school classes, yet it attracted an audience well beyond the church classroom. "Looking at the smallness of the book and its more immediate object," wrote the *British and Foreign Evangelical Review,*

> it might be thought fitted only for Bible classes, not for grown students of the Gospel History; but this would be a great mistake. Though we ourselves have . . . read and studied most of the works of any real value on the endless theme, . . . we are not ashamed to say that we have read this little book of Mr. Stalker's with real profit, as well as, in some places, with admiration.[16]

Stalker's purpose was not to present a piece of definitive scholarship, but to offer a sort of introductory sketch—a clear historical outline of Jesus' life and character as well as of the course of his ministry. Under this limitation he naturally was forced to dispense with the luxuriant descriptive passages and historical digressions that found a place in long works. Where these expatiated on the meadows of Galilee and Christ's feeling for nature, Stalker was content to offer the brief observation that "the preaching of Jesus shows how deeply he had drunk into the essence of natural beauty and revelled in the changing aspects of the seasons."[17] Beyond this, and a few scattered paragraphs on the Jewish sects and the Roman occupation, he did not choose to go. For Stalker such things were important but for reasons of space had to be subordinated to the simple recitation of the events of Christ's life.

Like others successful in writing for a wide audience, Stalker kept close to the traditional beliefs of orthodoxy and biblical authority. Assuming John to be as reliable as the synoptics, he engaged in no criticism of the sources. Miracles were essential to Jesus' work, although with others who perhaps felt discomfort in the uncompromising supernaturalism of earlier ages, Stalker insisted that Christ's teaching was "by far the more important."[18] Jesus' plan was "to establish the kingdom of God in the hearts of individuals, and to rely not on the weapons of political and material strength, but only on the power of love and the force of truth."[19] Jesus, in brief, was Israel's Messiah, but not as Israel knew the term. He had come to invest the old idea of the Messiah with a new meaning, emptying it of its political content and refashioning it into a symbol of divine redemption and love. In the process he demonstrated that he was no mere human teacher; he was fully God. "God was in Him, and His human nature was endowed with the Holy Ghost without measure. . . . He was himself the great miracle, of which his particular miracles were merely sparks or emanations."[20] Stalker went on to explain how his miraculous divine nature enabled him to perform the momentous final act of his life, atonement for the sins of man by his death on the cross.

This simple retelling of the life of Christ with an accent on the basic beliefs of orthodox theology won and held a large readership. In 1891, twelve years after it was first published, Stalker wrote of the book, "That, alongside of so many voluminous works, there is room for this little one has been amply proved by a large and steady demand for it up to the present time."[21] His remark was born out amply by the title page of the 1891 edition, which recorded the *Life* in its "Forty-fifth thousand."[22] Nor was this the end; the sales of his book also eventually reached 100,000.[23]

Stalker's work—brief, popular, and theologically reassuring—was one of several by Scottish divines, who in the last quarter of the century began to play an increasing role in British religious thought. Among these A. M. Fairbairn carved a place as important as any. Having moved to England to become principal of Airedale Theological College, he had become by the 1880s perhaps the most distinguished of British Congregational theologians. By temperament inclined to philosophical theology, he had studied at Berlin under Dorner, Tholuck, and Hengstenberg, who, though conservatives in Germany, pushed him to somewhat broader religious views than those prevalent in Scotland at mid-century.[24] At ease with German, he had read not only liberal critics like Strauss, F. C. Baur, Theodore Keim, and Gustav Volkmar, but also the newer investigations of ancient Jewish life and literature by German semitic scholars like Emil Schürer and Karl Hausrath. The wealth and accuracy of historical detail provided in works such as these were of great interest to Fairbairn; the sudden growth of such knowledge had opened a gateway to the first century. It was this kind of interest that at least partly inspired his *Studies in the Life of Christ,* published in 1880.

Although originally written as a set of Sunday evening discourses, the *Studies* gave scholarship and biblical science more than their due. "True faith," wrote Fairbairn at the outset,

> proves its truth by its willingness to use all the lights of modern science and all the eyes of modern criticism, that it may get the nearer to the historical Christ, convinced that it can look in His face without fear and without dismay. The men that best knew Him most loved Him, and to stand in His immediate presence is to be touched with a deeper reverence than can be awakened by the broken image reflected in the traditions or phantasies of men.[25]

The essays which followed were arranged chronologically through the life of Christ, so as to yield the effect of a connected biography; but they made no attempt to be comprehensive in the manner of Geikie or Farrar. Fairbairn viewed his book as to some extent preliminary and expressed the hope later "to return to this greatest of all Histories, and deal with it in a more critical and comprehensive spirit; especially in its relations to contemporary history."[26] In the meantime, he was content to borrow from other authorities and embellish as he saw fit. Like others, he sought to convey the charm of things Oriental, as when he wrote of Galilee "guarded by the snowy crown of Hermon and wooded slopes of Lebanon";[27] of Judaea, "so suggestive of heroic names and Messianic hopes, and the graves where grew 'the palm trees by the water, the rose plants which are in Jericho' ";[28] and of Jerusalem, "embalmed in the most glorious sacred poetry of the world, so humanly universal, so divinely immortal, that once man has learned to use it he can never cease to sing."[29] On Jewish social life the tone was somewhat less elevated, but the salient points received their due. The schools of the rabbis, Hillel and Shammai, the doctrines of the sects, the role of the temple rites, the priests, scribes, Sanhedrin—all these came into the narrative, with appropriate notes from the Talmud, Josephus, and Apocrypha.

Despite the importance Fairbairn accorded such topics, however, they did not figure at all as large in his shortened narrative as they did in Farrar or Geikie. For the chief purpose of the book was to reaffirm orthodoxy and, in the context of relating Christ's life, contend for the basic reliability of the gospel texts. Fairbairn thus returned frequently to the miraculous, and to the divinity of Christ:

The power to work miracles would never prove its possessor to be a person so extraordinary as we conceive Christ to be; but Christ once conceived to be the extraordinary person we believe Him to be, miracles become to Him both natural and necessary. They are symbols of the reality He is, the appropriate expressions of the force he embodies.[30]

It is perhaps possible to discern in Fairbairn, as in Stalker, some sensitivity to the doubts of rationalists and German critics about miracles, for he does not stress them inordinately. He fully believed that Jesus' miracles were of less religious value than his teaching—a position common among critics who wrote what Schweitzer called "liberal" Lives. He disapproved strongly of the theologians of the eighteenth century, who made miracle the chief testimony of biblical truth and thereby placed the faith in an untenable position. Yet he was equally clear on the point that a purely naturalistic Christianity, wholly without miracle, was inconceivable. "The objections that annihilate miracles annihilate Christ."[31] It was as simple as that. Even the most controversial of the biblical miracles—the resurrections of Lazarus and of Christ himself—he defended against the alternative theories of rationalists and sceptics including Strauss, Ferdinand Christian Baur, Eduard Zeller, and Renan. The raising of Lazarus he described as "the greatest of Christ's miracles,"[32] and the resurrection on Easter morn was of singular importance:

The Resurrection of Christ is in the Christian system a cardinal fact, one of the great hinges on which it turns. Certain miracles have only an accidental, while others possess an essential value. The first are but incidents in the gospel history; the second belong to its essence, constitute, as it were, its substance.[33]

Like other orthodox writers, Fairbairn held that all four gospel narratives were trustworthy; that the ministry of Jesus lasted for a period of about three years, during which he preached a spiritual message of repentance, forgiveness, and the love of God for man. This was Jesus' idea of the kingdom, which brought him into conflict with the Jewish officials who then contrived his death. The stunning event of the resurrection, however, vindicated his message, utterly changed his despairing disciples into messengers of the risen savior, and gave rise to the Christian church.

Obviously, a Life that reflected so fully the official theology of the churches could expect favorable opinions in the religious press, and the *Studies* received a warm welcome. The Baptist *Sword and Trowel*, not usually indulgent of men with Fairbairn's broad views, commended his book: "In this volume there is a broad philosophy, a wide grasp of historical forces and influences, together with a keen eye for every dramatic detail and touch of beauty."[34] As for the book's popularity with the general reader, the best measure lies in the record of new editions, three of which were needed in the first year. Between 1880 and 1907 the *Studies* passed through fourteen editions in all; it was translated into Dutch, and was regarded by Fairbairn's biographer as "perhaps the most popular of all his writings."[35]

Fairbairn's effort was followed by that of another Scot, William Robertson Nicoll, a man well known in religious circles as a journalist, editor, theologian, and man of letters. From the 1880s on through the early decades of the next century Nicoll spent extended intervals editing the monthly *Expositor* and the widely circulated *British Weekly*. From these platforms his opinions issued regularly, and they had considerable effect on those who thought seriously about religion. The *Expositor,* which he edited from 1885 till his death in 1923, became synonymous with intelligent, if conservative, theology and biblical criticism. Serving from the 1880s on as one of the few professional forums for critical discussion, it drew some of Britain's best biblical scholars to its pages, especially as the century came to a close.[36]

Even before these ventures, Nicoll contributed to the Lives of Jesus with *The Incarnate Saviour,* first published in 1881. The book was, in several ways, a virtual duplicate of Fairbairn's. He avoided the extensive compilation of travel notes, the lore of the East, and the accumulated findings of modern scholarship. Assuming the value of all these things, Nicoll proceeded instead to a restatement of those perennial truths which in his view neither archaeology, travel, textual criticism, nor historical inquiry, however important, may be allowed to obscure.

> The scenery of Palestine, the customs of the changeless East, the idioms of Oriental speech, the literary phenomena of the gospel history, and the modes of contemporary thought,—these have been set forth with the highest skill and learning. There is a place, doubtless, for all these things, for Jesus Christ belongs to human history. But He is living still, and the events of His life are not separated from us by eighteen hundred years of the sorrowful experiences of humanity. While they have their place in time, they yet transcend it, and are of extraordinary significance. To that inward significance we turn our thoughts in the following pages.[37]

The "inward significance" that readers were invited to examine was chiefly theological. The narrative, Nicoll asserted, was designed to illustrate three basic Christian beliefs: that "Jesus Christ was God and man in two distinct natures and one person"; that he "came to suffer in order that he might save"; and that there was during his life a "sweet and perfect accord of . . . words, works, and thoughts."[38] None need question the author's orthodoxy; it was written clearly in the opening pages and never faded in what followed.

Yet even in such a "theological" Life as this, there were signs of the sensitivity to historical romance set in motion by Renan. Though he had not travelled there, Nicoll worked the landscape of Palestine occasionally into his text:

> There is no place in Palestine even yet that is so haunted by flowers as Nazareth is. It lies in a dell surrounded by hills, and one hill, of some five hundred feet high above the village, gives one of the most magnificent spectacles in the world,—a spectacle on which the eyes of Jesus must often have rested with rapture. We may suppose also that Joseph taught his reputed son the rudiments of his trade, and thus the quiet years wore on.[39]

The Incarnate Saviour was a comparatively short work, however, and reflections of this sort were brief and rare. Like Stalker, Nicoll kept closely to the biblical events, accepted the conventional view that the four evangelists wrote complementary and equally valid historical accounts; he made only modest attempts at anything like historical criticism.[40] This was to be expected in Nicoll's case; the strengths of his mind lay on the strictly expository side, not in a knowledge of texts or source criticism. On these matters, like most others, he accepted the word of authorities.

Although exact sales records are unavailable, *The Incarnate Saviour* seems to have generated some measure of interest. It was noticed, albeit briefly, in a healthy cross-section of religious periodicals. Though it did not enjoy the success of Stalker's Life or reach as many editions as Fairbairn, it did run through a large number of impressions and reached a new, cheaper edition in 1897.[41] It was thought valuable enough to be translated, for mission purposes, into both Japanese and Chinese.[42] As a theologically reassuring book, it stood clearly in the tradition most acceptable to British readers and most in keeping with the official theology of the churches.

Nicoll's work, a modest book as we have seen, may serve as a reminder and representative of other small-scale Lives which appeared in the same years. Though in their ways they employed the techniques of Farrar and Geikie, they aimed beneath the exhaustive study, the comprehensive survey. There were in fact enough of these shorter, single-volume studies in the early 1880s to prompt journalists to begin their reviews with references to the "voluminous" literature which the subject had already produced. Voluminous or not, Lives of Christ in a variety of shapes, sizes, and prices kept appearing in numbers sufficient to show they were still meeting a widely felt need. In 1881, the year of Nicoll's book, for example, there also appeared F. A. Malleson's *Jesus Christ: His Life and Work* and Eustace Conder's *Outlines of the Life of Christ*. Though the latter was not strictly speaking a Life, its close attention to chronology and topographical detail of Palestine showed that the concern for historical authenticity was still very much alive. By 1883 one could point to William Scrymgeur's *Lessons on the Life of Christ*; W. G. Blaikie's *Public Ministry and Pastoral Methods of our Lord*; and Henry Wace's *The Gospel and its Witnesses*. Even in selecting these there is perhaps a certain arbitrariness. They enjoyed a slightly larger circulation, if we are to judge by notices in the press and registers of new impressions or editions; but in design they differed only slightly from others in a genre that allowed each author to mix the elements of serious biblical science and popular devotion to his personal taste. Those cited here are not unique, but typical.[43]

2. Alfred Edersheim

The single work of the 1880s which stood apart from this class because it was unmistakably unique was written by a converted Jewish emigré, Alfred Edersheim. With the publication of his *Life and Times of Jesus the Messiah* British Lives reached a level of Oriental scholarship which suddenly superseded even the detailed funds of information gathered by Geikie and Farrar. The two-volume *Life and Times* was a monument to Edersheim's industry, patience, intimate knowledge of the ancient Jewish world, and deep preoccupation with the life of Christ. The book was (with certain reservations) British scholarship on a German scale. Nor is it surprising, when one considers that Edersheim was born in Vienna to wealthy German Jewish parents and had studied under Hengstenberg and Neander in Berlin. In Pest, where he had traveled to be a language instructor, Edersheim came under the tutelage of Dr. John Duncan, a Scottish Presbyterian pastor, and there converted to Christianity. After study in Edinburgh, he became a Presbyterian pastor until 1875, when he took an Anglican living in Dorsetshire.[44] His complete command of English, German, and Hebrew served him well in the composition of two earlier books, *The Temple: Its Ministry and Services at the Time of Christ* (1874) and *Jewish Social Life in the Time of Christ* (1876). He then began the *Life and Times,* originally a two-year project, which eventually required "seven years of continual and earnest labour" before its completion, fittingly enough, on Easter morn, 1883.

To the reader presented with this work's two large volumes, 1,300 pages of text and 150 pages of closely printed notes, even seven years seem short for the task. By the time it was completed, Edersheim's work had expanded his already formidable grasp of the Jewish world, its life, literature, and social landscape, to a place where no other English-speaking scholar was a match for him. He was thoroughly steeped in both Babylonian and Palestinian Talmuds, in Philo, Josephus, the Apocryphal and pseudepigraphal literature, and of course the Old

Testament. He knew the recent literature of archaeology, the works of travel by Tristram, Karl Baedeker, and C. R. Conder, the Oriental studies of Renan, the cultural surveys of such Germans as Hausrath and Schürer, and not least the newer work in the intertestamentary period done by Hilgenfeld, Dillmann, and H. L. Strack.

This extensive erudition was poured into the large octavo pages of the *Life and Times*. Although Edersheim insisted that his notes had been pared to a minimum, his book was crowded at every turn with quotations from the Talmud and explanations of minute features of Jewish life. There were passages on eating habits and crops, on exports and commerce, on clothing and domestic life, on the Jewish religious sects and their history, teaching, and practice, on the Essenes and the apocalyptic writers, on Jewish magic, medicaments, and angelology, on Hillel and Shammai and their schools, on Philo and the Hellenistic Jews, Persia and the Babylonian Jews, Herod and the Roman occupation, the Midrash, Haggadah, and Halakah, on temple rites and legal practice, the synagogue, the Sanhedrin, and all the previous and subsequent misfortunes of ancient Judaism. The reader who worked at the book could pass many a Victorian Sunday exploring the labyrinthe. Such details had, of course, been touched on briefly by other writers, but Edersheim treated them in depth, often devoting pages of explication to a matter as minute as the rabbis' clothing or the precise character of Jewish writing materials.

Near the end of the century few British students of biblical literature excelled William Sanday, yet he fully appreciated the scope of Edersheim's achievement. When Longman decided to offer the *Life and Times* in abridged form, it was Sanday who assisted in the editing and furnished a preface. There he was quick to point out the depth of Edersheim's penetration into both the mind and circumstances of ancient Judaism.[45] Elsewhere he already had written that in this respect the book was superior even to the best of the German works:

> One quality it possesses. . . . Neither Schürer nor Hausrath were so steeped in the knowledge of Jewish life and thought at the time of Christ. Schürer himself recognized his master here. In sureness and precision of statement on all subjects connected with the Jewish background of the Gospel history, Dr. Edersheim has no equal.[46]

The curious thing about this vast storehouse of information, however, was that it apparently coexisted in the same mind with a critical innocence difficult to fathom. Even though Edersheim did accept the priority of Mark as established by German scholars and conceded that Matthew, for example, was not always strictly chronological,[47] he seemed virtually incapable of feeling the force in the more rigorous doubts of higher critics. The appendices, for instance, contained discussions of every subject from proselyte baptism to the Talmudic sabbath law, but nowhere was there a thorough analysis of the gospel sources.[48] For these matters, as will become clear shortly, he tended to lean on other scholars. This policy of dependence was typical of the British Lives; it was of great import for the shape which the quest of the historical Jesus assumed in Britain. The evangelical records were taken as authentic and accurate, the products of the apostles themselves, or, in the case of Luke and Mark, those who had direct access to apostolic testimony as a supplement to their own reminiscence. Like others who held his conservative view of the sources, Edersheim did not hesitate to argue for duplicate events behind duplicate traditions. There were two cleansings of the temple, two feedings of the multitudes, numerous journeys made by Jesus to Jerusalem and back; there was no conflict between John, whose eyewitness account seemed to date Jesus' death on the day of Passover, and the synoptics, who placed it a day later. The authenticity of John could be intuited from the description of Jesus and the woman at Jacob's well:

> Indeed, there is such minuteness of detail about the narrative, and with it such charm of simplicity, affectionateness, reverence, and depth of spiritual insight, as to carry not only the conviction of its truthfulness, but almost as instinctively to suggest to us "the beloved disciple" as its witness.[49]

This sort of subjective reasoning prompted the *Athenaeum* to describe the *Life and Times* as a work "where manifold learning parts company with sound criticism."[50] Yet it was not untypical of those who wrote Lives in Britain. If it was more noticeable here, that was perhaps because it seemed out of place in a work otherwise so learned and mature.

Edersheim's critical conservatism found its natural complement in his strict theological orthodoxy. Miracles not only happened; they were crucial to the gospel record. Of the widow's son, raised by Christ at Nain, he wrote,

> The only real ground for rejecting this narrative is disbelief in the Miraculous, including, of course, rejection of the Christ as the Miracle of Miracles. But is it not vicious reasoning in a circle, as well as begging the question, to reject the Miraculous because we discredit the Miraculous? And does not such a rejection involve much more of the incredible than faith itself?[51]

The miracle at Bethesda brought from the author one of many affirmations of Jesus' deity:

> In this also the Gospel-narrative proves itself true, by telling that He did, what alone would be true in a Messiah, the Son of God. It is, indeed, impossible to think of Incarnate Deity—and this, be it remembered, is the fundamental postulate of the Gospels—as brought into contact with misery, disease, and death without their being removed.[52]

So it went through the narrative. Edersheim defended inspiration, atonement, resurrection, and supernaturalism. He carried on a running battle with Strauss, whose theory of myth was often attacked, and with Renan, whose *Vie* he regarded as "frivolous and fantastic," as well as "superficial and often inaccurate."[53]

To these other earmarks of the classic Victorian Life of Christ we should also add in Edersheim's case an explicitly popular intent, most evident in his narrative style. This may seem surprising in view of the heavy learning that went into the *Life and Times,* but Edersheim was set upon it. "Here," he commented in his preface, "I may be allowed to state that throughout I have had the general reader in view, reserving for the foot-notes and Appendices what may be of special interest to students."[54] Anyone who has ever tried to popularize scholarship intelligently will know how difficult a task this is; yet Edersheim was at least partly successful. The mass of archaeological, literary, linguistic, and historical detail at his disposal was frequently in danger of crumbling into amorphous fragments, particularly when there were digressions on trivia. Yet with the help of a fluid, clear, colorful, occasionally ornate style, he managed the task. To his credit Edersheim was not as prodigal with florid rhetoric as Farrar, but he could at times draw upon a high style with great effect. His sketch of Jerusalem at worship captured the crowded vitality and expectant devotion of Jewish culture in the first century:

> When the silver trumpets of the Priest woke the city to prayer, or the strain of Levite music swept over it, or the smoke of the sacrifices hung like another Shekhinah over the Temple, against the green background of Olivet, or when in every street, court, and housetop rose the booths at the Feast of Tabernacles, and at night the sheen of the Temple illumination threw long fantastic shadows over the city; or when, at the Passover, tens of thousands crowded up the Mount with their Paschal lambs, and hundreds of thousands sat down to the Paschal supper—it would be almost difficult to believe, that heathenism was so near, that the Roman was virtually, and would soon be really, master of the land, or that Herod occupied the Jewish throne.[55]

To the ordinary reader this sort of vivid portraiture made the *Life and Times* often appealing despite its length. To observe Jesus amid these surroundings was to view him as he had really lived; it was to gain, in the words of the *Edinburgh Review,* an authentic "reflection of the figure the Messiah must have presented to His contemporaries."[56]

More important, to see him as a Jew among Jews was to see how much more he was than another rabbi or itinerant teacher; his teachings, acts, life and death were evidence that someone utterly unique had appeared in Israel.[57]

Critics were quick to perceive the special qualities of the *Life and Times:* its erudition, its wealth of insight derived from Jewish lore and the author's lifelong intimacy with Hebrew life and literature. The religious press was understandably pleased with such a unique contribution to the subject, especially since Edersheim's theological and critical assumptions were, again, congenial to the interests of the churches. Periodicals without religious connections also recognized the book's merits, at least if we judge by organs like the *Edinburgh* and *Saturday Reviews.* Criticism was restricted chiefly to the author's neglect of any real attempt to analyze the sources, and on this, only the *Athenaeum* was actually severe.[58]

With the reading public Edersheim could scarcely hope for success on the scale achieved by a Geikie or Farrar, or perhaps even by some of the smaller efforts which had appeared in the interval. The *Life and Times* was too massive, too thick with obscure learning for that. At the same time, it is one work whose sales records remain extant, and the records tell a revealing tale. For a full twenty-five years it never really went out of print. The book appeared late in 1883; a second edition was required by June of 1884; and new printings were made at regular intervals till 1908.[59] These were supplemented after 1890 by the abridged edition, which enjoyed small, but similarly consistent, sales over most of the same period. The *Life and Times* was not a best seller, but it was a durable book—able in the words of the *Saturday Review,* to "meet the wants of some who are not quite 'learned' but have had education enough to take an interest in other men's learning."[60]

3. Other Rationalists

Writers of orthodox Lives seemed able to score a modest success without much of an effort. The subject alone and the reaffirmation of old verities seemed sufficient to draw some interest toward their books. Rationalists, as noted, did not enjoy this luxury. They complained that their books received scarcely any attention, no matter how impor ant the issues they raised. Despite this, freethinkers persisted, and in the years after Farrar several produced new works on the Life of Christ. A look at two of them will disclose how rationalism fared with the topic.

Philochristus: Memoirs of a Disciple of the Lord (1878) was written by E. A. Abbott, headmaster of the City of London School. Edwin

Abbott Abbott was one of those intriguing minor Victorians whose multiple talents placed him at the intersection of several professions. A classicist, educator, Shakespeare and Bacon scholar, and author of handbooks like *How to Write Clearly,* he was nonetheless able to produce learned works on biblical literature, including a historical, critical commentary on the Fourth Gospel and several imaginative, semi-historical works on early Christianity.[61] *Philochristus* was one of these. It purported to be the recollections of a certain Joseph, son of Simeon, who in his youth had become a follower of the prophet Jesus and now, a decade after the fall of Jerusalem, had chosen to record something of what he remembered. A devout Jew, loyal to the temple and Torah, expectant of Israel's restoration, Joseph was nevertheless a restless soul. Philo, Shammai, Hillel, the Essenes, the Pharisees were but a few of the teachers he had followed; but he came away from all dissatisfied. Only when he fell under the captivating influence of Jesus did he begin to find a measure of peace. Joseph was drawn irresistibly to the new prophet, to the strange mixture of tenderness and authority with which he spoke, to the surpassing beauty of his utterances about the love of God for men, and the love each man must show toward his human brother. Jesus had unusual powers that made even the raving demoniacs grow silent or fearful. He often spoke of a kingdom, but few understood the meaning of this metaphor. In fact, its meaning became clear only after Jesus himself had been cruelly executed through the conspiracy of Jewish leaders.

After Jesus' death, Joseph, who had taken the new name Philochristus, despaired of the future. But then, beginning on Easter morn, he discovered with the others through a series of incredible visions that Jesus was with them again. He had—somehow—risen, in spirit perhaps, or idea, or memory; however it was, Jesus after death returned to fill his little band with the hope that his kingdom—now perceived to be wholly spiritual—could indeed become an ongoing historical reality.

On a balanced view, much of this is not quite so unorthodox or shocking as Abbott evidently supposed it to be when he wrote his publisher insisting that it be brought out anonymously.[62] His letter to Macmillan, dated 23 January 1877, indicates that he actually feared removal from his position as headmaster and was "quite sure the Oxford people will want to strike me off the list of select preachers to which I have just been appointed."[63] It was true that the book had a heterodox ring to it. The author passed by the gospel of John in developing his material and, except for his rather ambiguous account of the resurrection, recounted only those miracles of healing—such as the cures of demoniacs—most susceptible of modern explanations. But considering early freethinkers like Hanson or Scott, one could hardly regard the book as a scandalous assault on orthodoxy. When it was let out that Abbott was the author, it cost him neither his headmastership nor his office as select preacher. Abbott might have learned from the fate of his predecessors that the most typical reaction of the churches to rationalists was to pass them by briefly in the fashion of A. B. Bruce, who classified *Philochristus* as "sentimental naturalism"—the work of writers who endeavored "in their whole delineation of Christ's life and character to embrace in the picture as much as possible of the extraordinary, while recognizing in no sphere the strictly miraculous."[64]

In defense of Edward Clodd it could at least be said that his naturalism was certainly not sentimental. His *Jesus of Nazareth* appeared in 1880. The son of simple Suffolk parents, Edward Clodd had by his twenties discarded his Baptist beliefs for a more flexible Congregationalism, and he had taken a keen interest in science. He was drawn steadily into rationalist circles, and after gaining notice through the success of *The Childhood of the World* (1873) he joined the Century Club, where he met Samuel Butler, W. K. Clifford, E. B. Tylor, John Tyndall, and others of their sort.[65]

Jesus of Nazareth bore the marks of its rationalist origin. Drawing upon the evolutionary hypothesis of Kuenen, Clodd sketched first the history of Israel: its beginnings amongst Semitic nomads, the pilgrimage and stay in Egypt, the coming of Moses, the escape, wanderings, conquest, monarchy, exile, and return. Parallel with this ran the growth of Hebrew religion: from an unfocused primitive faith in clan gods and mythology to the belief in Jehovah, God of righteousness introduced by Moses; thence into syncretism under the judges and kings, purification under the monotheist prophets, and final ossification at the hands of the priests of the post-exilic age. By its conclusion, the sketch of Israelite history occupied nearly half the volume.

Clodd's analysis of the gospel history worked along the same lines, aptly summarized in his dictum that "as knowledge advances, the number of events which are looked upon as miracles or the wilful acts of superhuman beings lessens."[66] Though many primitive superstitions had disappeared by the time of Christ, the inability to distinguish legend and miracle from true history survived. The New Testament gospels betrayed this sort of confusion. The gospel of John therefore had to be rejected as "so clearly the work of a man full of the views of a certain school about Jesus . . . that, although it is of exceeding beauty it is of small value for our [historical] purpose."[67] The synoptics too came under suspicion, though in them a modicum of history was discernible. This fact made it clear that there was little value in the work of those orthodox writers who were very busy "constructing lives of Jesus as minute and wordy as if every detail about him, with undisputed vouchers of its truth, were in their hands."[68]

Clodd's own conclusion was different. It would "suffice to show," he wrote,

> that a *life* of *Jesus,* in the usual sense of that word, is *impossible*; that all we can hope for, as we read the obscure phrases and varying statements of these ancient gospels, is to gather some idea of the secret of the enduring power of a man whose influence for good in this world cannot be overrated.[69]

We have seen this stance before in rationalists. While they preferred scepticism, their scepticism was never total. For Clodd at least, the essential features of Christ could be easily discovered. Jesus was a teacher born in Nazareth and raised in the lovely rural province of Galilee. He was a precocious youth, and though without the libraries and scrolls available to Jerusalem scholars, he nonetheless taught with great wisdom, originality, and power. Denouncing the formalism of the Jerusalem cult, he preached inner religion, the fatherhood of God, and the brotherhood of men. He was not divine and did no miracles, though both these notions were later affixed to him, at great detriment to his real purpose.

Jesus' teaching—"a change of the inner self; the heart as the source of good or evil, made pure, that the stream of thoughts and acts might flow clear"[70]—naturally was not well received by the Pharisees, who formed the religious establishment of Israel under the Romans. Conflicts arose; Jesus became gloomier, more visionary, and more determined to face martyrdom for his faith. In the end he achieved his aim, but he went to death willingly, "exalting the cross into the sublimest symbol of self-surrender, at whatever cost, to the will of God, and abiding in larger form than he himself had dreamed, as the holiest and tenderest influence of all time."[71]

Like *Philochristus,* and even more like the earlier works of Hanson and Scott, as well as Germany's "liberal Lives" of the 1860s and 70s, *Jesus of Nazareth* repeated a familiar formula: the moralist-teacher-humanitarian Jesus, opponent of the fossilized religious establishment of his day. To this liberal, rationalist framework Clodd added several of the favorite touches of orthodox writers: a considerable literary talent, some applications of Palestinian romance, and his own gleanings from the study of comparative religion. It was understandable that *Jesus of Nazareth* earned its author compliments from men like T. H. Huxley and Leslie Stephen. It was equally understandable that except for a few brief notices, it was dismissed by the religious press and disregarded by the reading public.[72] In Britain such rationalist portraits did not persuade.

Nonetheless, they kept coming. In 1879 the heterodox cleric Charles Voysey, who had been removed from Church office, published a translation of Reimarus's infamous exposé of the gospel under the title *Fragments from Reimarus.* In 1888 H. R. Haweis provided an engaging *Picture of Jesus* which suggested departures from orthodoxy. In 1890 the Unitarian C. J. Street's *Jesus, Prophet of God* returned to the liberal theme: that Christ was a noble, human teacher, not a miracle-working divine Savior. This view, which was soon to come under withering attack from Johannes Weiss and Schweitzer in Germany, had also come to find favor with certain American scholars; and some of their works circulated in Britain. A. K. Rogers of Yale University had adopted this stance in his *Life and Teachings of Jesus* (1894), which received a measure of attention in the British press. The work that occasioned perhaps the most heated argument in conservative circles during the nineties was Alexander Robinson's *Study of the Saviour in the Newer Light,* which appeared in 1894. In it the gospel sources, miracles, and the unique deity of Christ all came under attack. Robinson was a pastor in the Church of Scotland at the time his work was published, and the book brought immediate ecclesiastical action. Within six months the General Assembly had condemned it, and a year later Robinson himself, after refusing to repudiate its teaching, was deposed from his ministerial position.[73] With the turn of the century came the translation of Adolph Harnack's *Wesen des Christentums,* whose English version *What is Christianity?* gave a new statement, but no new justification, of the liberal view. It was followed in 1903 by Goldwin Smith's *Founder of Christendom,* which enunciated the same liberal position.

In following this lineage it matters little which author or decade is selected. The strategies and responses discernible in the 1860s still appear at the close of the century. Like the orthodox, Britain's rationalists are popular writers, bringing their case to a wider circle of readers than the cloistered academy affords. They profess an unprejudiced and hence more intellectually defensible approach to the gospels than that adopted by scholars speaking for the religious establishment. The claim to scholarly superiority is, however, something of a charade, since all of the rationalists' most serious criticisms of the scriptures are derived from continental scholarship and their Jesus, as Schweitzer would insist, is as arbitrary as the Christ of the churches. For these and other reasons to be explored in chapter four, their fate was to issue proclamations to a void. Slighted by scholars and unread by the public, they died, or very nearly died, a death of benign neglect.

4. More Foreign Lives

While rationalists struggled, traditionalists flourished. In the decades after Farrar Britain felt the impact of an ever-widening stream of foreign works which supplemented native efforts and flowed in, not only from America, but from France and Germany via translation. Henry Ward Beecher's fragmentary Life of 1872 was one of the better known American works of the 1870s, and it was warmly received in a few periodicals.[74] German translations as well continued to appear after 1870 and in significant numbers. By 1880 Clark's Foreign Theological Library, still the chief source of translated German works, numbered more than one hundred volumes.[75] Although many of these dealt with other disciplines and topics, such as systematic theology and Old Testament criticism, Lives of Christ and related works were well represented. By 1893 the series included, in addition to the earlier Lives by Lange and Ebrard, the commentaries of Ernst Luthardt and the French critic Godet on the gospel of John, Ewald's *New Testament Theology,* and the complete three-volume *Life of Christ* by the mediating scholar Bernhard Weiss.[76] Early in the 1870s, moreover, a new channel for translations opened up. Dissatisfied with the uniformly conservative character of the Clark translations, a small group of liberal divines which included Benjamin Jowett, A. P. Stanley, James Martineau, and Scotland's John Tulloch established the Theological Translation Fund. Its purpose was to create by subscription a fund large enough to pay translators to put into English those works which were representative of the more critical wing of German scholarship.[77] The translations were to come out at a rate of several volumes yearly, and the first, Theodore Keim's learned *Jesus of Nazara,* appeared in 1873.[78]

With regard to French works, the situation was somewhat different. Renan's *Vie* had of course been translated several times and was well on its way to becoming a classic.[79] The French Protestant contribution consisted chiefly of works already mentioned: Godet's commentaries, Pressensé's popular *Jesus Christ,* and a few less ambitious works, like Ernest Naville's apologetic piece, *The Christ,* translated and published by T. & T. Clark in 1888. Beyond these, it was the Catholic writers of France who were most frequently translated, particularly toward the end of the century. This is understandable considering that for various reasons, the life of Christ was a subject on which British Catholics chose to write little.[80]

In 1863 Father Henry James Coleridge wrote in the *Dublin Review* a sharp criticism of Renan's *Vie de Jesus* which nevertheless concluded with a sort of confession:

But if we ask ourselves for a written Life of Christ—one that may be a household book with Christians of all classes—a simple and short narrative, at once popular and scientific, that would give men of this generation the true results of genuine and orthodox criticism, and allow them to enjoy what light can be gained from the boasted progress of knowledge on collateral matters, without shrinking their faith or scarring their devotion—we are obliged to answer, that the Catholics of our time have not yet such a work to show.[81]

A "household book" that was "at once popular and scientific" is precisely what British Protestant writers like Farrar and Geikie so successfully produced. Catholics in Britain did not. Coleridge himself is an illustration. As indicated earlier, in the same year as Farrar he published *The Public Life of Our Lord* (1874), two volumes which over time grew into a long, homiletic and meditative treatise that meandered through many digressions till it reached a massive sixteen volumes.[82] This sort of work had little chance of exciting public interest, though along the way there were some favorable reviews even from non-Catholic journalists.[83] Catholic harmonies and other works, in some of which Father Coleridge had a hand, did not fare much better.[84]

It must be remembered that Catholics never formed more than a small part of the British populace. The most generous estimate would allow hardly more than 5,000,000—chiefly in Ireland—at the close of the century, the vast majority of whom were too poor and ill-educated to make up a substantial middle-class market where Lives might be sold and read. On the side of the writers, it must be remembered too that the Catholic clergy were proportionately many fewer; priests were neither as educated as their Protestant counterparts nor as familiar with sermons, which more talented Protestant pastors often found convenient to turn into Lives or related works.

The vacuum left by British Catholic writers thus came in part to be filled by translations of works from fellow Catholics in France. Père Lacordaire's conferences delivered at Notre Dame and published under the title *Jesus Christ* comprised one of the earlier works translated for this purpose (in 1869). Lacordaire's fervent devotion and brilliant style were warmly appreciated by critics in the Protestant religious press, but strictly speaking, the work was not a Life of Christ.[85] Through the 1870s and 1880s no works of importance were translated, partly because Catholics with an interest in the topic found themselves drawn to Farrar, Geikie, and Edersheim—works that could be read, but not with equal enthusiasm, by Catholics. It was in fact not until the 1890s that two of the best, and most popular, French Lives were able to leave their mark on British readers. Abbé Constant Fouard,

Professor of Theology in Rouen, had in 1880 published a two-volume study, *La Vie de N. S. Jesus Christ.* It had enjoyed considerable success throughout France, reaching five editions before 1890, when it was translated and brought before British Catholics with what was, outside of the signature of Newman himself, the best of passports—an introduction by Cardinal Manning. Fouard's book is an interesting illustration of both the limits and opportunities facing the Catholic writer of the late nineteenth century. Committed by the authority of the church to the infallibility of the evangelists, he could not really enter discussion with even the more moderate Protestant higher critics. Although a set of notes appended to the preface contained summaries of the views held by negative critics (which were omitted from the English version), the notes in the text itself were drawn solely from the scriptures. Fouard was free to harmonize, not to select from or assess, his sources.

Palestinian romance, on the other hand, was an open field to the Catholic, and here Fouard, like Farrar, made the best of his opportunities. He journeyed to the Holy Land where the scenes of Jesus' life came before his eyes too with the vividness that once again elicited memories of Renan's phrase about the "fifth gospel."

> An inestimable advantage has been accorded to us . . . which has enabled us to make the places in which the Saviour lived better known and realised. . . . we traversed the Holy Land, "from Dan to Beer-Sheba," from Gaza to Libanus, following the Master step by step, over those hilltops which were the witnesses of His birth, into the valley of the shadow of death, wherein He faced temptation; and along the borders of the Lake which He loved. On every hand we have seen the same world which met the eyes of Jesus. . . . In the Gospels all these pictures are indicated in a line, by a single stroke; it is only when viewed under the Eastern sky that they regain their fresh colours, in their clear native atmosphere.[86]

Fouard also recognized the value of recent Oriental studies, of Aramaic literature, the Talmud, and other investigations of Egyptian, Assyrian, and Hebrew antiquities; these were all used where helpful. But he reserved special affection for the Oriental landscape, the ageless beauty of its sunsets and dawns, its cities, streams, and vineyards, all of which were bathed in a mist of hallowed biblical associations. At the center of this colorful antiquarian scene Fouard placed the traditional Jesus; though slightly more humanized, he was still the divine, saving Christ of the church.

Fouard's Life enjoyed success; it reached fourteen issues by 1908.[87] Another French Catholic work that went into multiple editions was Father J. H. Didon's *Jesus Christ: Our Saviour's Person, Mission, and Spirit,* which was translated in 1891. This was a large two-volume account in which the author divided his time almost equally between devout homilies and serious scholarship. The theories of Baur, J. G. Eichhorn, Friedrich Schleiermacher, and Eduard Reuss were taken up briefly and dispensed with just as briefly in the introduction, where Father Didon preferred to give greater space to the testimony of the early fathers.[88] In the text itself, however, he made good use of Josephus and the Talmud on occasion, and manifested an intimate acquaintance with geographical and archaeological data. This last was chiefly because he, like Fouard, followed the by now accepted convention of making a journey to Palestine. In fact, Didon had made the pilgrimage twice, in the conviction that the facts of Christ's life were inseparable from the land. The fruits of the journey did turn up in the narrative. Consider:

> We always resemble our native land; our imagination takes the tints of the heaven in which our sight loses sight of itself; the highest are those in which echo profoundest harmonies with the nature in which they develop. . . . Whoever has not gazed long on the heaven of the East, Palestine, the mountains of Nazareth, the Lake of Tiberias, will never understand the outward frame of Jesus, the tone of his thoughts, the images in which he loved to clothe them, and the originality of his parables.[89]

It is perhaps unfair to expect from these Catholic writers any real appreciation of the doubts raised by historical science concerning the gospels; Didon in any case certainly showed little of it. He took up the tools of the new historians, but knowing that among Catholics their use was not wholly permitted, he found them uncomfortable in his hands.

Within its limits, however, Didon's work was a satisfactory achievement—well-researched, graphic, and instructive. "We are impressed everywhere," wrote a Protestant critic, "with the evidence of such complete and careful preparation as the sacredness of the subject demands. The work can only have been the fruit of years of study, travel, and thought."[90] The same critic went on to commend the "serene atmosphere of untroubled faith" pervading the book.[91] A fair number of readers must have agreed, for there was sufficient demand to produce a new and cheaper edition of Didon's Life in 1893.[92]

There is one further Catholic Life which deserves more than a mere mention, even though it stands slightly outside the form of the works under discussion here. James Tissot's *Life of our Saviour,* published in English in 1897, was a three-volume collection of watercolor sketches designed to illustrate Christ's life from the scenes and personages of Palestine and accompanied by passages from the Vulgate and the author's notes. Tissot was not a biblical scholar, but a painter who had studied under Ingres and found in the gospel story a set of appealing subjects and scenes. Yet his work demonstrates from another perspective just how intensely those who approached Christ's life in these years concentrated upon historical realism. "Is it not time in this exact century," he wrote,

> when such words as nearly or almost have no longer any value, to restore to reality . . . the rights which have been filched from it? This is why, attracted as I was by the divine figure of Jesus and the touching scenes recorded in the Gospels, I determined to go to Palestine on a pilgrimage of exploration, hoping to restore to those scenes as far as possible the actual aspect assumed by them when they occurred. For this, was it not indeed absolutely necessary to study on the spot, the configuration of the landscape, and the character of the inhabitants, endeavouring to trace back from their modern representatives through successive generations the original types of the races of Palestine, and the various constituents which go to make up what is called antiquity?[93]

Obviously, the intense visual realization of scene and character was important to Tissot because he was an artist. But in this age his words are just as good a clue to the mind of the historians and writers of Lives. Their works sprang from a distinct new sensibility: the desire to know the past in those peculiar shapes and scenes, things and places, habits and customs which made it quite different from the present. At the outset of the age, as we have seen, this impulse could be found in historians like Carlyle and novelists like Scott. In biblical studies it emerged early on as a diffuse sentiment, found brilliant application in the hands of Renan, blossomed in the works of Farrar and Geikie and Edersheim, and in varying measures became an essential feature of British Lives to the end of the century.

Toward the last decade of the century, writers of all types as well can be found exploring in their own ways this same historical sentiment, usually in the interests of the same, reassuring picture of Jesus. There was S. D. F. Salmond's very traditional *Life of Christ* (1888). There was Henry Latham's *Pastor Pastorum* (1890), strictly speaking, not a Life, but written with the same sensitivity to the historical. There were also David Milne's *Years and Eras of the Life of Christ* (1892); G. F. Pentecost's *Life of Christ* (1893); A. J. Mason's *Conditions of Our Lord's Life on Earth* (1896); and A. F. Winnington-Ingram's *Christ and His Friends* (1897). As Protestants, most of these writers enjoyed a measure of freedom in moving beyond historical sentiment to some appreciation of historical science. Unlike Catholic scholars, they were able to treat sceptics with a certain objectivity, accepting various minor points made by the newer criticism against the scriptures so long as the dogmatic supernaturalism they valued remained intact. They did not hesitate to question the evangelists on certain minor points, to admit certain errors of fact, place, or number in the narratives, or to rearrange selected fragments of the gospel chronology. But as was the case from early in the century, the concessions only went so far. Even as they welcomed much that the new scholarship of Germany insisted on, the writers of the standard British Life drew back quickly from conclusions likely to undermine the conventional Christ of orthodoxy. Their readiness to take in hand the tools of criticism found its match in a reluctance to use them whenever it appeared they might cut too deeply. In particular, two pillars of traditional faith were very carefully defended. Higher criticism was rejected whenever it linked itself, as it did so often among British freethinkers, with a direct challenge to supernaturalism; and whenever it produced, as it did with Strauss, a frontal assault on the historical value of all four biblical gospels. This resolute refusal to practice criticism beyond certain severe limits had the profoundest impact on Victorian inquiry about Jesus from the days of Strauss to the end of the century. It accounts for many things already observed: the failure of rationalists, the conventionality of the orthodox Lives, their popularity with readers, their fixed character during more than a half century of study and discussion.

In fact, the hesitance to practice criticism may be taken as a clue to something still larger. Beneath the Lives lay an entire network of popular needs, scholarly axioms, cultural images, religious beliefs, and institutional ties which were linked closely to their fortunes. These forces converged to produce the literature on the life of Christ, then found themselves subtly altered by it. The relation was complex and reciprocal; the next chapter will explore it.

NOTES

1. "Farrar's Life of Christ," 183 (January 1875) 177.

2. See below, p. 114.

3. A number of these ephemera, which survive in the British Library and are recorded in Ayres's bibliography, *Jesus Christ our Lord*, seem to have left little imprint on the contemporary culture. I have not been able to check more than a few of the more important among Victorian Britain's countless dailies and religious weeklies, where these works might have received some attention. The brief book notices in religious quarterlies have been carefully checked. In these there is no mention of minor Lives by writers like George Stretton, Henry Southgate, C. B. Johnson, and Alfred Hood, all of whom appear in Ayres's bibliography. Since such works would have found some brief recognition in these reviews if they were of any significance, I have seen fit to exclude them from the present survey.

4. John Cunningham Geikie, *The Life and Words of Christ*, rev. Amer. ed., 2 vols. in one (New York: D. Appleton and Co., 1894), dedication page.

5. Ibid., 1:317.

6. On Lightfoot see above, p. 20. Schürer was regarded as Germany's foremost scholar of Judaism in this era; his works included *The History of the Jewish People in the Time of Jesus Christ*, tr. John McPherson, Sophia Taylor, and Rev. Peter Christie, 5 vols. (Edinburgh: T. & T. Clark, 1885-1890).

7. Geikie, *Life and Words*, 2:374.

8. Ibid., 1:441.

9. *DNB*, s.v. "Geikie, John Cunningham."

10. Geikie's work is one of those whose sales records have in part survived the ravages and salvage needs of two World Wars. Copies of the Longman sales sheets were kindly supplied by Mr. J. A. E. Higham, Divisional Managing Director, and the archivist of Longman Group Limited, Burnt Mill, Harlow, Essex. The records indicate that with at least one of its publishers, Geikie's *Life* and a shorter version each sold at almost 500 a year to the end of the century. In itself this modest figure is not impressive, but by this time the *Life and Words* had been made available by no less than seven different publishers, several of whom were offering their editions simultaneously! Henry S. King published the *Life and Words* first; Hodder and Stoughton offered it in three forms, 1882-1883; Alexander Strahan, James Nisbet, Cassell, and Hatchards all made it available at one time or another before the end of the century. On this see also *The English Catalogue of Books*, s.v. "Geike, C.," in the volumes covering the relevant years.

11. "Contemporary Literature: Theology and Philosophy," *British Quarterly Review* 66 (October 1877) 553; *Athenaeum*, 8 September 1877.

12. Cassell's acquisition of the *Life and Words* is noticed in "New Editions," *British Quarterly Review* 81 (January 1885) 251. Longman acquired the corpus in 1896.

13. Ibid., 251.

14. Copy of "Longman's Monthly List," 1896, appended to sales records of Dr. Geikie's works supplied by Longman Group Ltd.

15. *DNB,* s.v. "Geike, John Cunningham."

16. "Current Literature," *British and Foreign Evangelical Review* 30 (April 1881) 373.

17. James Stalker, *The Life of Jesus Christ,* 2d ed. (Edinburgh: T. & T. Clark, 1891) 22.

18. Ibid., 64.

19. Ibid., 45.

20. Ibid., 63.

21. Ibid., 8: "Extract from the preface to the second edition."

22. Ibid., title page.

23. For this figure I am indebted to the firm of T. & T. Clark Publishers, Edinburgh, Scotland. Their letter of 25 October 1974 states that Stalker's Life "has run through many editions and impressions, some 133,330 copies." There is no terminal date for this figure. If we extrapolate from the first twelve years, 1879-1891, during which 45,000 copies were sold, we reach a figure of 90,000 by 1903, the remainder being sold by about 1915—all on the premise that sales remained reasonably steady over these years.

24. See *DNB,* s.v. "Fairbairn, Andrew Martin"; also W. B. Selbie, *The Life of Andrew Martin Fairbairn* (London: Hodder & Stoughton, 1914) 37-42.

25. A. M. Fairbairn, *Studies in the Life of Christ,* 11th ed. (London: Hodder & Stoughton, 1899) 3.

26. Ibid., preface. The essays of the *Studies* had been separately published earlier in the *Expositor* between 1876 and 1880. See Selbie, *Life,* 115 and the bibliography of Fairbairn's works in C. Silvester Horne, et al., *Mansfield College Essays: Presented to the Reverend Andrew Martin Fairbairn* (London: Hodder and Stoughton, 1909) 368-69.

27. Ibid., 10.

28. Ibid., 13.

29. Ibid., 16.

30. Ibid., 151.

31. Ibid., 152.

32. Ibid., 201.

33. Ibid., 331.

34. *Sword and Trowel,* August 1881, 441.

35. Selbie, *Life,* 115.

36. On these and other aspects of Nicoll's multifaceted career see T. H. Darlow, *William Robertson Nicoll,* Amer. ed. (New York: George H. Doran Company, 1925).

37. William Robertson Nicoll, *The Incarnate Saviour: A Life of Jesus Christ,* new and cheaper ed. (Edinburgh: T. & T. Clark, 1897) 1.

38. Ibid., 2, 4, 5.

39. Ibid., 26.

40. He did concede, for example, that there were certain inconsistencies in the various narratives of the passion; see ibid., 241.

41. Darlow, *Nicoll,* 454, Appendix III. Without providing figures T. & T. Clark, Edinburgh, have indicated by letter, 25 October 1974, that *The Incarnate Saviour* "has run through many impressions but the total is less than Stalker's."

42. Darlow, *Nicoll,* 454.

43. The best single collection of these lesser titles is Ayres, *Jesus Christ our Lord.*

44. On Edersheim's life see *DNB,* s.v. "Edersheim, Alfred."

45. William N. Sanday, Preface to Alfred Edersheim, *Jesus the Messiah* (London: Longmans, Green, & Co., 1890) vii.

46. William N. Sanday, "The Future of English Theology," *Contemporary Review* 56 (July 1889) 46. Others who recognized this as Edersheim's special contribution were the *British and Foreign Evangelical Review* 33 (January 1884) 185; *British Quarterly Review* 79 (January 1884) 224-27; and the *Edinburgh Review* 159 (January 1884) 121-44. It was noticed also in the reviews presented by two of the leading literary magazines, *The Athenaeum,* 9 February 1884, and the *Saturday Review,* 24 November 1883.

47. This was hardly a modern position, however; Calvin had taken it as early as the sixteenth century. See McArthur, *Quest,* 12, and John Calvin, *Harmony of the Gospels,* 3 vols. (Edinburgh: T. & T. Clark, 1845-46) 1:258.

48. Sanday also recognized this in his Preface to *Jesus the Messiah,* ix, and offered a modest defense of the procedure.

49. Alfred Edersheim, *The Life and Times of Jesus the Messiah,* 2d ed., 2 vols. (London: Longmans, Green, and Co., 1884), 1:406.

50. *The Athenaeum,* 9 February 1884.

51. Edersheim, *Life and Times,* 1:559.

52. Ibid., 1:467.

53. Ibid., 1:279 n. 4.

54. Ibid., 1:xviii-xix.

55. Ibid., 1:119.

56. "Edersheim's Life and Times of Jesus the Messiah," *Edinburgh Review* 159 (January 1884) 139.

57. See Edersheim, *Life and Times,* 1:508 especially; also 1: 525 and 2:192.

58. See *The Athenaeum,* 9 February 1884.

122 *Victorian "Lives" of Jesus*

59. This information was also supplied by Mr. J. A. E. Higham and the Longman archivist. It should be noted that 1908 is not the end of the Edersheim printings. The archivist has indicated that after this point the impression books record new printings of the *Life and Times* (1,000 copies, abridged edition, in 1910, 1,000 of the one-volume edition in 1912, 500 of the abridged edition in 1916, and so forth) to as late as 1926.

60. *The Saturday Review,* 24 November 1883.

61. For biographical information see *DNB,* s.v. "Abbott, Edwin Abbott," which also contains a list of his works.

62. Abbott to Macmillan & Co., 6 January 1874, Simon Nowell-Smith, *Letters to Macmillan* (New York: Macmillan & Co., 1967) 145-46.

63. Abbott to Macmillan & Co., 23 January 1877, ibid., 146-47. Abbott, who certainly was not overly afflicted with humility, dedicated the book to the author of *Ecce Homo* and seems to have been convinced that the controversy aroused by *Philochristus* would rival the 1866 debate over *Ecce Homo* in public interest. Nothing of the sort ever happened.

64. A. B. Bruce, "Current Naturalistic Opinions Concerning the Person of Christ," *British and Foreign Evangelical Review* 28 (January 1879) 16-17.

65. See *DNB,* s.v. "Clodd, Edward."

66. Edward Clodd, *Jesus of Nazareth: Embracing a Sketch of Jewish History to the Time of His Birth* (London: C. Kegan Paul, 1880) 57.

67. Ibid., 225.

68. Ibid., 230.

69. Ibid., 230-31.

70. Ibid., 256.

71. Ibid., 357.

72. Some religious periodicals did carry brief notices, as for example the *British Quarterly Review's* "Contemporary Literature: Theology, Philosophy, and Philology," 71:533-34. Beyond this there was little.

73. See Robinson's preface to the second edition of *A Study of the Saviour in the Newer Light* (London: Williams & Norgate, 1898) v.

74. See, for example, "Contemporary Literature: Theology, Philosophy, and Philology," *British Quarterly Review* 55 (July 1872) 583-84.

75. See Crowther, *Church Embattled,* 52.

76. For these facts I am indebted to T. & T. Clark of Edinburgh, which loaned me the firm's copy of the 1893 *Classified Catalogue of Books Published by T. & T. Clark,* Edinburgh.

77. On the Theological Translation Fund's purpose and initial membership see the preface to Theodore Keim, *Jesus of Nazara,* tr. Arthur Ransom, et al., 3 vols. (London: Williams and Norgate, 1873-83).

78. Edersheim, who by no means shared Keim's assumptions, had high

praise for this work. See, for example, *Life and Times,* 1:337 n. 1, where he speaks of Keim's portrait of John the Baptist, then adds: "Would that he [Keim] had known the Master in the glory of His Divinity, as he has understood the Forerunner in the beauty of his humanity!"

79. After the *Vie,* Renan's other works on early Christian history received considerable attention in both the religious and secular press of Britain. He was not always liked, but was never ignored.

80. This is a phenomenon that can perhaps only be explained by looking into the whole ethos of Catholicism in Britain, including the official attitude of Catholic leaders toward the growth of biblical criticism. By the last quarter of the century, there was certainly no dearth of educated clergy capable of writing a scholarly, yet popular, Life. But as Chadwick notes, leaders like Cardinal Manning were not eager to have their flocks know *too* much about the scriptures during an era of such enormous critical change. "The atmosphere of simplicity was not of the credulous," adds Chadwick, "but of the childlike. And a sophisticated leader like Manning preferred to have it so." He also recalls that a "Catholic publisher complained, as late as 1890, that Roman Catholics did not read books," *Victorian Church* 2:408, 409. This set of factors certainly did not encourage the diffusion of religious knowledge to the same degree that the individualist Protestant culture of self-improvement through reading did.

81. "Renan's 'Vie de Jesus,' " *Dublin Review,* n.s. 2 (April 1864) 418.

82. See "Two Lives of our Lord: Father Coleridge's and Dr. Joseph Grimm's," *Dublin Review* 19 (April 1888) 354-80. Father Coleridge's work was finished with three volumes on *Passiontide* in 1891 and one on *The Passage of our Lord to the Father,* bringing the completed work to a total of sixteen volumes. For a full listing see the *Brit. Mus. Catalogue.*

83. For a favorable non-Catholic review of *The Life of our Life* see the *Guardian,* 20 June 1877.

84. Ayres, *Jesus Christ Our Lord,* pp. 49-88, records several scattered attempts, other than translations from the French, which seem to have enjoyed little in the way of success or public notice. In 1875, for example, there was a two-volume translation of the seventeenth-century *Vita et doctrina Jesu Christi* by Avancinus (Leopold Guileilmi, Archduke of Austria), published by Burns and Oates. Father Coleridge edited a second edition in 1883. In 1897 appeared a work by James Duggan, priest of Maidstone, simply titled *The Life of Christ.* So far as I have been able to learn, German Catholic Lives by J. N. Sepp, P. J. Schegg, P. Naumann, and Joseph Grimm were never translated. The *Brit. Mus. Catalogue* contains no record of translation.

85. Appreciative remarks may be found in the *British Quarterly Review* 51 (April 1870) 535.

86. Constant Fouard, *The Christ the Son of God: A Life of Our Lord and Saviour Jesus Christ,* tr. George F. X. Griffith, with an Introduction by Cardinal Manning, 2 vols. (London: Longmans, Green & Co., 1892) xvi-xvii.

87. See the copyright page of *The Christ* (London: Longmans, Green & Co., 1908).

88. J. H. Didon, *Jesus Christ: Our Saviour's Person, Mission, and Spirit,* Amer. ed., trans. Bernard O'Reilly, 2 vols. (Philadelphia: The American Catholic Historical Book and News Publishing Co., 1891) xlv-xlviii.

89. Ibid., 1:84.

90. "A New Life of Christ," *London Quarterly Review* 77 (January 1892) 275-76.

91. Ibid.

92. See the notice in "Theology and Apologetics," *London Quarterly Review* 80 (April 1893) 160-61.

93. James Tissot, *The Life of our Saviour Jesus Christ,* Amer. ed., 3 vols. (New York: The Werner Co., 1903), 1:ix.

4 CAUSES AND EFFECTS
THE ORIGINS AND INFLUENCE
OF THE BRITISH STYLE

*There is no historical task which so reveals a man's true
self as the writing of a Life of Jesus.*

Albert Schweitzer

It should by now be apparent that during the late Victorian years
the Life of Christ became a recognized and widely read literary form.
After the early scandals of Strauss and Renan, the controversy over
Ecce Homo disclosed the need for an orthodox work and the elements
necessary to ensure appeal to a wide spectrum of readers. Less than a
decade later F. W. Farrar stepped into the void, drew the right elements together, and produced a definitive Victorian Life. His efforts
were rewarded with enormous success. His book not only sold in vast
numbers; it spawned a brood of imitations which flourished to the
very end of the Victorian age. For a full quarter-century Farrar's successors mirrored in differing ways the shape and features of his *Life of
Christ.*

From the standpoint of either the intellectual or popular historian,
the Lives are thus a phenomenon important enough to call for explanations. In what way, we need to ask, does this literature fit into the
landscape of the Victorian age? Beyond the motives of individual
authors, what larger causes and circumstances gave rise to Britain's
quest of the historical Jesus? How and why did Britain's Lives differ
from the German works of this era? Why did so many of them look
alike? What effect did the Lives in their turn have upon the culture
and churches which so eagerly welcomed them? To answer these questions our investigation will have to range more broadly than it has up
until now. We need to look at the Victorians' response to foreign biblical study and the way in which they developed their own. We need to
observe the interlocking roles of scholar, church, and academy. We
need to follow the struggle of the churches toward an acceptance of
higher criticism in the 1870s and the 1880s. And along the way, we
need to make some comparisons—especially with the German scene.
The comparison with Germany, in fact, provides a good place to start.

1. Biblical Study in Britain

As noted previously, the new, critical tradition in biblical study
arose in the context of Deism and the German Enlightenment.[1] Viewed
in one way, this was only part of a widespread intellectual change
which encouraged historians to train a critical eye on all of their

sources, whether ancient or recent. The revolution fell with acute force, however, upon biblical study since orthodox belief had always held the scriptures sacred and hence exempt from such questioning. The new spirit of inquiry denied this exemption. It was rejected in quiet ways by textual critics who traced the documentary history of the Bible as they would any other ancient text, and in more strident ways by radical critics like Reimarus, whose polemic against the gospels shocked faithful believers. As the restraints upon criticism broke away, German scholarship increasingly became a nursery of experiment, argument, and new interpretations. It bristled with academic dispute.

Schweitzer's *Quest* provides a graphic picture of the consequences this freedom brought to the study of the life of Jesus in Germany. Though Reimarus was for a time forgotten, Strauss's *Leben Jesu* jolted scholarship with a new wave of scepticism about the biblical sources. While Strauss was quarreling with the theological world over miracle and the theory of myth, Christian Weisse and Christian Wilke quietly proposed the theory of Mark's priority, a thesis which profoundly altered study of the gospels and through the century slowly won its way to a consensus. Around mid-century Bruno Bauer explored the option of total scepticism about the life of Jesus; but his views were countered by the "liberal Lives" of Theodore Keim, Daniel Schenkel, H. J. Holtzmann, Bernhard Weiss, and others. Their views were in turn attacked from two sides by the radical scepticism of Wrede and the eschatological school led by Johannes Weiss and Schweitzer himself. By the end of the century German scholarship seemed to have produced almost every possible interpretation of Jesus. In the process, boasted Schweitzer, biblical critics had accumulated a record of real intellectual progress, won slowly and through struggle.

The British scene, in contrast, presents almost none of this. There is little conflict, little dialogue among spokesmen, little real diversity. Almost every Life we have observed falls into one of two rather clearly marked classes. There are the rationalists and the orthodox. The freethinkers are a small group who fail in the larger market but keep to their task. They write for the small circle of independent minds— the doubters and deniers who stand outside the churches and apart from the mainstream of public opinion. They write with conviction, but their ideas are derivative—chiefly from the continent. They are neither read by the folk on the street nor answered by spokesmen for orthodoxy. Their books do not really change; they repeat the same arguments, and present the same humanitarian freethinker of Nazareth. They engage in no real dialogue with the orthodox, whose Lives, for their part, manifest a similar uniformity. Farrar and Geikie and Edersheim write from within the fold of belief; their aim is to instruct and reassure; and their audience is the many, not the few. Their books do not really differ from one another. They are, in their style, as predictable as are the rationalists. To read them is at times to feel as if one is passing through a museum gallery of reproductions: there is the same Jesus, the same orthodox deity, drawn again and again by different hands. The lights and shadows may vary; the image in the foreground is the same—so repetitive, in fact, that it raises questions. How can this curious uniformity be explained? We know that in Britain the orthodox tended to ignore freethought, partly because rationalist Lives seemed to borrow from the continent. The puzzling factor is that the British writers also refuse to engage in any serious discussion with the continent. Despite the presence of a formidable tradition of criticism in Germany, Britain's Lives travel a private path, careful to avoid any but the most oblique collision with continental critics. What are the causes of this curious policy? What are the circumstances which allowed a Farrar, a Geikie, an Edersheim to write his Life without really facing the questions raised by a Strauss, a Christian Weisse, or a Bruno Bauer?

Some fifty years earlier, in the 1820s, the explanation might well have been ignorance. British divinity then was in most quarters unaware of German developments and could hardly have attended to them with the seriousness they deserved.[2] Theologians and leaders of opinion who had made the acquaintance of German scholarship were accustomed either to revile it or to confess that they found it frankly incomprehensible.[3] When Hugh James Rose delivered his Cambridge sermons of 1825 on the state of Protestantism in Germany, his text came, rather ominously, from Isaiah 47:10: "Thy wisdom and thy knowledge, it hath perverted thee."[4] The Germans were at first defended by E. B. Pusey, who had studied under Eichhorn and made the acquaintance of both Schleiermacher and Strauss, but soon he too changed his mind. The few divines who had studied on the continent either turned against the views of their German professors as did Pusey, or kept to themselves, as did Connop Thirlwall, a lonely tower scholar who in any case accepted the German historical methods only in very moderate form.[5]

The British universities were no more cosmopolitan. The preparation of theological students at Oxford, Cambridge, Edinburgh, and Dublin offered no comparison to the rigorous instruction in Semitics and textual studies available in the leading German schools, such as Göttingen, Tübingen, and Berlin. Except among Congregationalists, the nonconformist theological academies were even weaker than the established schools.[6] In Catholic institutions instruction in criticism was, of course, not an option. Oxford and Cambridge before mid-century stood badly in need of academic reform, not least in theology, where the governing ideal was the gentleman cleric versed in classics rather than the pulpiteer steeped in the biblical languages.[7] The university circumstance is significant; we shall return to it later. In the meantime, the arrival of Strauss's *Leben Jesu* in Britain did little to improve things. While it disclosed to some how little the British knew of German scholarship, others thought it proved they already knew too much. We need only recall the critic from the *Edinburgh Review* who found Strauss "beyond the visible, diurnal sphere of English comprehension" to observe that the *Leben Jesu* created no enthusiasm for the German "neologians." Nor could one get encouragement from spokesmen like William Palmer, who sounded the alarm about covert Straussians in the Sterling Club.[8]

This climate of uneasy but determined isolation began to break up toward mid-century. Although both Palmer and the *Edinburgh* critic wrote in the 1840s, the same decade saw the growth of more informed opinions. Palmer may have swept Strauss and very conservative Germans into the same indictment, but others began to make distinctions. J. R. Beard's *Voices of the Church,* meant as a reply to Strauss, contained extracts from Neander and Julius Müller, who argued strongly against the *Leben Jesu.* We have already had occasion to mention T. & T. Clark of Edinburgh, the Scottish firm which as early as 1835 had begun translation of more moderate German works and published them in its "Biblical Cabinet." The trend gained impetus in the 1850s with the advent of Clark's "Foreign Theological Library," a major, long-term enterprise which presented the best of Germany's conservative theologians in English. In the 1830s the leading journals still hesitated to take on German works: the *Quarterly* did not review Strauss; F. C. Baur's great works went untranslated and virtually unnoticed.[9] At mid-century this picture began to change. Translations, lectures, reviews were with each year opening a bit more of German scholarship to English readers. By 1860 reviews of the latest continental works, especially conservative ones, were a regular feature of the High Church *Literary Churchman,* of intelligent nonconformist reviews like the *London* and *British Quarterlies,* and even of conservative organs like the *British and Foreign Evangelical Review.* Certainly by the time the churches entered the last quarter of the century, the age of isolation was past.

From 1860 onward, the era during which most of the successful Lives were written, their shape cannot be explained by the insulation of British divinity from the continent. The contrast between the earlier and later eras can be quickly perceived by anyone who cares to examine an older harmony or devotional Life, likely to be written as if Strauss and German criticism never existed, and compare it with Ellicott's *Historical Lectures* of 1859 or Farrar's *Life*, where the notes and bibliography were thick with German sources.

Much more important than a mere knowledge of the Germans, however, was the way in which one came to learn of them. Before it came into English, German criticism was usually filtered by the publishers and editors. Reassuring books were translated; sceptical ones laid aside. The effect of this has already been noted; for all practical purposes the only German works which the British read for themselves were from very conservative critics. In the entire list of T. & T. Clark's Foreign Theological Library, it is difficult to find the translation of a single German author who does not belong either to a mediating school of theology or to that group of German evangelical scholars whose views of scripture bordered on Fundamentalism. Thus one can find in the Library Hengstenberg but not Karl Hase; Delitzsch and Keil but not Wellhausen; Dorner but not Schleiermacher; Lange and Ebrard but not Strauss; Olshausen, Stier, Zahn, and Bernhard Weiss, but not Schweitzer, Wrede, or Johannes Weiss.[10]

We observed as well how frustration with this conservative monopoly of translations prompted a few of the more unconventional thinkers in Britain to establish the Theological Translation Fund, which sought to translate the more adventurous German works.[11] This venture achieved neither the output nor circulation of Clark's series. Moreover, selective translations were accompanied by equally selective assessments. With the help of publishers like Clark and favorably disposed critics in the religious press, Germany's conservative critics and theologians were represented as voices of reassurance from the very wilderness of doubt. In both Old and New Testament studies there were a few German names that could be recited among the soldiers of orthodoxy. Early in the century there had been Hengstenberg, the fierce controversialist and opponent of Strauss; in the middle years there were the Old Testament scholars Keil and Delitzsch, milder men but learned in the extreme and devoted to old views of biblical inspiration and authority. Toward the end of the century there was the equally learned and capable Theodore Zahn of Erlangen, a student of the New Testament and Early Christian literature. When in 1893 the *London Quarterly* presented a review article on "The Canon of the New Testament," Zahn's *Geschichte des Neutestamentlichen Kanons* received first priority:

> The great work of Professor Zahn of Erlangen, which we place at the head of our list, belongs to the conservative school, which has by no means died out in Germany, but, indeed, shows many signs of rejuvenescence. The destructive tendency has expended itself and the process of re-edification is making good progress.[12]

Even more effective, however, were the inclinations of the press and religious leadership in Britain to celebrate the "demise" of Germany's more destructive schools of criticism. The very nature of academic discussion in Germany combined with an accident of chronology to make this strategy workable. In New Testament study the strongest, most sceptical attacks on the scriptures had been launched early in the century—by Strauss first and then by Ferdinand Christian Baur and the "Tübingen school." Chiefly on the strength of Baur's vast erudition, the Tübingen critics proposed a rearrangement of the New Testament canon no less drastic than that which Julius Wellhausen was later to propose for the Old. First advanced in the 1830s, Baur's theory broke new ground, but then was disputed and modified as the century wore on. In the same way, Strauss put forward his theory of myth with great boldness in the 1830s. In subsequent decades the force of sustained attacks compelled him to alter some of his judgments. When his new Life appeared in 1864, he openly admitted that on some points he had gone too far. Schweitzer later was to deplore these concessions as the case of a brilliant but harassed man overestimating his opponents. Yet the principle Strauss followed, the rule of revision in the face of convincing criticism, is a perennial ideal of scholarship; it was one of the more admirable (if not omnipresent) features of German inquiry during the age.

British observers were nevertheless inclined to take another view of the situation. To them such changes did not signal progress, but error, confusion, and uncertainty. German criticism could not be very formidable, they argued, for it was always changing its mind. What Tübingen solemnly asserted in one year, Gottingen and Berlin might deny in the next. The career of Strauss provided a fitting example. In the *Leben Jesu* of 1835 he had rejected the spiritual Christ presented in the Fourth Gospel; in 1864 he seemed to withdraw his objections. His wavering soon became the target of witticism and ridicule. Of Strauss's position on the Fourth Gospel, Henry Wace wrote that he "doubts once more the doubts he had entertained of all his former doubts"—a clever rebuke which the *Guardian* quoted with approval.[13] Although the *Westminster Review* warned in its appraisal of the second Life that the shouts of a German decline were being uttered prematurely, other journals did not hesitate to seize upon Strauss's retreat from positions he had earlier taken with great conviction.[14] What better proof of the bankruptcy of liberal higher criticism than this amusing spectacle of vacillation and self-doubt!

The same reasoning was applied with obvious pleasure to Baur and the Tübingen school. Baur had held that the New Testament books showed the stress of competing factions within early Christianity. Certain writings like Matthew and James had emerged from Jewish Christianity, where followers of Christ continued to observe the rituals inherited from their old faith. Others, like the Gospel of John and the great Pauline epistles, arose later within the rising gentile faction, which opposed many of the old Jewish customs. Only in the late second century, with the rise of the Catholic church, were these conflicts resolved in a compromise, which came to expression in mediating books like Acts and Luke. Now it was crucial for this theory that some New Testament books be dated late, others early. Evidence to the contrary could damage it fatally; and as time passed, precisely that evidence seemed to appear. As Baur's successors pushed books like John, Luke, and Acts back to an earlier date, the Tübingen structure began to show cracks, and British observers seized their opportunity.

As early as the 1860s, when Baur's works were yet untranslated, British spokesmen were referring to the "discredited" Tübingen school. At Samuel Wilberforce's Oxford diocesan conference in 1866, says M. A. Crowther, Payne Smith applied this argument and "rejoiced that the rationalist school of German theology was being overthrown by a new generation, and attacked Ewald and Baur."[15] The High Church fortnightly *Literary Churchman,* which began in 1855 with the intent of keeping clergymen abreast of foreign developments, took comfort in the same argument; it made a regular practice of referring to the decline of Tübingen, pointed to internal disagreements in Germany, and applauded the work of conservatives like Keil, Delitzsch, and Hengstenberg.[16] Nonconformists were no different. As late as 1893, in the Congregationalist manifesto entitled *Faith and Criticism,* W. F. Adeney, who was by no means unappreciative of Baur's work, nonetheless wrote,

> The inherent historicity of the New Testament in its description of the age of the Apostles is also becoming more apparent. This is seen in the collapse of what is known as the Tübingen hypothesis. . . . To Baur we owe an incalculable debt of gratitude for teaching us to read our New Testament from the inside. . . . Nevertheless, his extravagant theories have been broken up and shattered. With the almost inevitable habit of an inventor, he has ridden his inventions too far until he has made imagination take the place of perception.[17]

This gratifying state of affairs was described at length in other works like Scottish Free Churchman James MacGregor's *Studies in the History of Christian Apologetics, New Testament and Post-Apostolic.*[18]

This filtered view of German criticism was not the only source of reassurance. By the 1860s there were signs that Britain was developing a school of conservative scholarship all its own. Among the Anglican critics who had expressed early doubts about Baur's theory was the writer of a commentary on Galatians (1865) who put his verdict thus: "I feel very confident that the historical views of the Tübingen school are too extravagant to obtain any wide or lasting hold on the mind of men."[19] The author of this remark was Joseph Barber Lightfoot, a man destined to play a large role in the development of a strong native tradition in British biblical study. Along with two other Cambridge scholars, B. F. Westcott and F. J. A. Hort, he devoted himself to a career-long study of the New Testament and early Christian history. For about thirty years between 1860 and 1890 this Cambridge trio carried out a program of study and writing which, in the words of a successor, "raised English theology . . . from a condition of intellectual nullity up to the level of the best German work, while they infused into it a characteristic English spirit of caution and sobriety."[20] As advocates at once of an orthodox theology and high standards of scholarship, they soon acquired an authoritative place in New Testament study. Against traditionalists who despised the Germans, they patiently pleaded their case for a legitimate, restrained, sober application of historical criticism to the biblical record. Eventually they were joined by William Sanday of Oxford and A. B. Bruce of the Scottish Free Churches. The Cambridge men were the prime figures, and their influence was great both within and outside of the Anglican communion.

The importance of the Cambridge three in holding back the sceptics was vividly demonstrated in the curious fate of the anonymous *Supernatural Religion*. When it first appeared in 1874 *Supernatural Religion* promised to be a very disturbing book. With a show of scholarship that suggested the vast erudition of the Germans, its author (retired India merchant W. R. Cassels) proceeded to challenge the traditional view of the New Testament sources. He discarded the supernatural, repudiated much of the gospel record, set aside the gospel of John, and denied the divinity of Jesus. To some it came as an impressive performance; the learned spirit of German scepticism seemed to have arrived definitively on British soil.[21] Lightfoot thought differently. He was goaded to action by a slight which the book delivered to his friend Westcott and by hints that the author was Connop Thirlwall, scholar-cleric of a previous era whom Lightfoot revered but who was now too frail and aged to defend himself. The reply appeared in a series of articles published by the *Contemporary Review* between December of 1875 and May of 1877. Lightfoot's tone was calm and judicious, his style almost colorless in its quiet sifting of fact, evidence, and conjecture. Still, it was not long before thoughtful observers recognized beneath the dispassionate surface of the articles a masterpiece of controversial literature. No critic in Britain could match Lightfoot's comprehensive grasp of New Testament literature and his wide-ranging knowledge of the early Christian world. His analysis of *Supernatural Religion* turned up weaknesses of every kind: errors of fact, slips in logic, tangles in philology, theses built on fragile conjecture. By the appearance of the last article, the ponderous scholarship of *Supernatural Religion* had been thoroughly dismantled. Publication of a third volume with answers to the critics salvaged nothing.[22]

After Lightfoot's critique *Supernatural Religion* became a discredited book.[23] With it, thought many, the majority of the sceptical higher critics had been disarmed. As late as 1900 James Stalker, author of one of the Lives, observed,

> The impression prevails in English-speaking countries that with the overthrow of the Tübingen theory on the Continent the criticism of the Gospels has practically come to a standstill, and that Bishop Lightfoot administered the *coup de grace* to all negative speculation on the Gospels in England.[24]

In fact, things were not so simple. *Supernatural Religion* was to an extent amateurism dressed in scholar's clothes; it should not have been mistaken for the work of a genuine higher critic. Lightfoot would have been quick to concede that easy victories could not be scored over against more accomplished German scholars. Yet the effect of this critique was to create an impression of orthodoxy liberated from siege and higher critics scattered in retreat.

Lightfoot's own later work contributed further to this impression. Like his Cambridge friends he never worked directly or at length on the biblical gospels; but he on occasion did address the topic, thus leaving an impression of reassurance drawn chiefly from his other work, which was not entirely justified. His greatest energies were spent on the history of early Christianity. He began work in the 1870s on a critical edition of the apostolic fathers, beginning with the study *Ignatius and Polycarp*. According to the Tübingen theory, a number of these writings had to be forgeries since they claimed to be from the first century yet showed no signs of the Jew-gentile conflict which then plagued the church. To show that the Apostolic writings were authentic would be to weaken seriously Baur's reconstruction. Lightfoot's great achievement in the *Apostolic Fathers,* finished in 1885, was to show that this was precisely the case. The Apostolic letters were definitely authentic; the Tübingen view had once again to be revised.[25]

Lightfoot's contributions to conservative criticism were the most substantial and enduring. In their day, however, the textual and historical studies of Westcott and Hort were just as widely appreciated. Their most lasting contribution was to be the critical edition of the New Testament, on which they worked diligently for years. Their judgment on historical questions, however, was as coveted and widely respected as their textual skill. Hort was, publicly at least, more reticent, less a spokesman than a symbol, but Westcott wrote and lectured on many topics, frequently defending a more traditional view of the scriptures against sceptical criticism. Nowhere was this more evident than on the vexing question of the gospel of John. We have seen how both German and British rationalists pressed the attack on the Fourth Gospel. Its account of Jesus, they insisted, was so different from that of the other three that it could not be regarded as either a valid historical record or authentically from the pen of St. John.[26] Westcott, however, came to its defense. He made a case for both the authenticity and historicity of the book in his *Introduction to the Study of the Gospels* (1860) and again in *The Gospel According to St. John* (1882). He was joined by Lightfoot as late as 1890, when the article "Internal Evidence for the Authenticity and Genuineness of St. John's Gospel" appeared in the *Expositor;* it was later reprinted with two further studies in *Biblical Essays* (1893).[27] Earlier the leading disciple of the Cambridge trio, William Sanday, had written a similar defense in *The Authorship and Historical Character of the Fourth Gospel* (1872).

With such works as these, then, the Cambridge three and their younger colleagues helped to deflect the force of sceptical criticism as it arrived in the British Isles. Their work tended to demonstrate that one need not apologize for his scholarship if it led to more traditional views. One could also reinforce the case by appealing to the defiant few traditionalists, who, even within Germany, held out against radical criticism. If still more support was needed, there was always the internal dissension in the camp of the sceptics, the disparity in their conclusions, the persistent shifts of their opinions. In the late Victorian years it was important to hold the sceptics at bay. Arguments and examples like these provided an effective shield, and it was crucial protection for those who intended to write Lives of Christ. It gave them reassurance and the right to proceed. We are not surprised, then, to learn that Farrar was a close friend of Westcott and a fervent admirer of his achievement.[28] As members of the "intensive" school of scholarship, Westcott and his friends provided the right complement to Farrar's "extensive" style.[29] Similarly Edersheim revered Lightfoot, studded his *Life and Times* with notes from Westcott's commentaries and *Introduction*, and often on the gospel of John appealed to "the results of his masterly criticism."[30] In the same vein Fairbairn spoke warmly of the results of their criticism, and Presbyterians like Stalker and Nicoll paid frequent tribute to Lightfoot's reassuring scholarship, Nicoll especially recalling with fondness his dismantling of *Supernatural Religion.*[31] To succeed, or even be born at all,

Britain's Lives required, and received, a womb of conservative biblical criticism which offered both shelter and nurture.

2. Biblical Study and the Universities

If all of this is so, we then need to push the inquiry a step further. If the prevailing form or style of biblical criticism helps to explain the Lives, what explains the prevailing form of biblical criticism? Why, for example, did Anglican, dissenter, and Scottish Presbyterian alike take such comfort in the apparent decline of Tübingen and the reversals in the mind of Strauss? Why is it so hard to find an Oxbridge don or Scottish divine willing to defend the views of Renan or the non-supernaturalist liberal Lives from Germany? Why is there no one to develop, or even defend, a theory of thoroughgoing eschatology, such as that of Weiss or Schweitzer? Or a theory of thoroughgoing scepticism in the manner of Bauer or Wrede? Wherever one looks, one finds scholars and leaders of opinion determined to resist any form of biblical study that threatens a rather conventional Christian orthodoxy. Is there a way to explain this?

Beginning from the German side of things, theological and philosophical factors call for consideration. From within the German context some have suggested that the explanation of the drive toward free biblical criticism is to be found in the peculiar theology of Lutheranism. Rudolph Bultmann, for example, insists that the great principle of justification by faith lies at the heart of it.[32] Luther's crucial religious insight was that no earthly thing—no ritual or artifact, no cleric or tradition or document—can be allowed to stand between man and God. Anything that pretends to intervene in this holy transaction becomes an idol. In the late Middle Ages a corrupt church had intruded on the conversation between God and man until Luther's defiant appeal to scripture shattered the system and ended the idolatry. But believers had no more been liberated from the church than, in the second stage of reform, they became enslaved again, this time to the dogmatic systems of Protestant theologians. Pietism once more freed the Christian spirit, only to restart the enslavement by resisting the advances of the Enlightenment and holding blindly to the untenable beliefs in miracle, prophecy, and infallible scripture. In the nineteenth century, the spirit of Luther again resurfaced among the scholars, for they realized that the principle of justification frees the mind of all idols, including the idol of scripture. To set apart any fact or document or historical event as beyond criticism is to rest one's faith upon a crutch; it is an appeal to the objective, a relapse into the idolatry of the medieval peasant who fixed his faith upon a writ of indulgence. The way of Luther, therefore, leads inexorably from Wittenberg to Göttingen, from the study of Squire George at the Wartburg to the study of Strauss at Tübingen. The scepticism of the critic is not only permitted; where human idols usurp the place of faith, it is commanded.

As long as we confine ourselves to individual critics, there is undoubtedly a measure of truth in this reasoning. If Bultmann and Harnack and others saw their own work in this light, it would be foolish to deny their claim. But while Luther's doctrine may have moved individual scholars, it is difficult to see how it will account for the entire German critical tradition. Scandinavia was wholly Lutheran in the nineteenth century, but it could show no record of criticism comparable to Germany's. Within the German lands, moreover, Lutheran voices were also among the staunchest opponents of free criticism, while a number of Reformed scholars, rooted in a theological tradition widely spread in Europe, practiced it vigorously. The appeal to Luther will provide a theological rationale, but not a historical explanation of the German circumstance.

This becomes even more apparent when we apply the converse of Bultmann's view to Great Britain. Justification by faith was hardly an unknown idea among English-speaking Protestants. Evangelical Anglicans, English Congregationalists and Baptists, and Scottish Presbyterians were all strongly imprinted with it, though the form was traceable to Calvin, not Luther. Yet in Britain these groups were no more open to higher criticism than any others.[33] As is clear in the case of *Ecce Homo*, it is characteristic of Britain that differences of theology and denomination seem to have little effect on the response to criticism. Catholics and Wesleyans, Congregationalists and High Churchmen, Evangelicals and Presbyterians converge in their defense of miracle, the divine Christ, and a most reluctant use of the critical method. This reticence is not distinctive of one theological tradition; it is common to all. If we are to explain the British style and its difference from the German, the appeal to a confessional theology will not take us very far.

What, then, of philosophy? Historians of thought point to the widespread influence of Hegel's idealism upon German culture in the nineteenth century. What appealed to religious historians and biblical critics of the age was Hegel's distinction between *Begriff,* an idea, and its imaginative or sensuous presentation, which he called *Vorstellung.* While an idea has permanence, its presentations, which may be found in myth, or art, or actual historical events, vary with a given time or place. Literature in any form may thus be a guide to truth. No matter how filled with myth, or legend, or embellished history, the Christian scriptures still serve as the vehicle for conceptual truth. Within this framework Hegelian scholars had no qualms about dissecting documents, sacred or secular. Under the guidance of Hegel, says Robert Grant,

> impartial objective research was to solve the riddles of history. The facts might be dissolved in source analysis; the all-important ideas would remain.[34]

Along these lines Strauss, for example, could comfortably argue that while the gospel accounts of Jesus were mostly myth, they conveyed a profound philosophical truth by presenting the idea of union between God and man. Philosophy can thus be seen providing the intellectual warrant for the freest criticism of the Bible.

In this reasoning there is once again a measure—even a substantial measure—of truth. Strauss, Baur, and others did find in Hegelian thinking a release from the constraints of traditional dogma, but we can no more trace the entire German critical tradition to Hegel than we can to Luther. Other thinkers, such as Harnack and Schweitzer, showed no special affection for Hegel yet pursued the same searching lines of inquiry, regardless of their effect on the traditional beliefs of the churches. In Britain too we can find an idealist strain of thinking which was derived in part from other sources but bore a close resemblance to Hegel's philosophy of spirit. Early on it led thinkers like Coleridge and his disciples, as well as some Broad Churchmen, to adopt freer views of the scriptures. It had the same effect later on, when idealism flowed into the Anglo-Catholic wing of the Church of England and gave rise to the *Lux Mundi* group. Yet even here, the ever-so-restrained, cautious steps toward criticism taken by these scholars can hardly be compared to the liberalism of a Harnack, who completely rejected miracles, or a Wrede who found in the gospels a fiction. There is a disengagement from traditional orthodoxy in the German critics which simply cannot be found in the British, who strove to blend their historical analyses comfortably with older patterns of thought. When we do find scepticism in Britain—among rationalists, a literary light like Matthew Arnold, or a Semitic scholar like Robertson Smith—it has very little to do with Hegelian idealism. In sum, Hegel will help, like Luther, to explain certain critics in both countries. He will not account for the course of an entire critical tradition in either.

That being so, we are compelled to leave the high road of ideas and travel the less elevated path of institutions. Can we find, in the structures within which scholars did their work, the factors which distinguish the German from the British style? Are there, among the social cords which fastened biblical study to the university and the universities to church and society, ties or connections which set criticism

on the continent apart from criticism in the Isles? It seems to me not
only that there are, but that these are clearly more basic to the differences than any principles of the theologians or philosophers.

If we again turn first to Germany, the clues to be drawn from the
nineteenth-century university in society suggest a scene of great cultural and political diversity. Despite a shared language, German lands
were through most of the century not a nation, but a weakly bound
confederation of states, duchies, kingdoms, and free cities, each with
a fair measure of civic autonomy. Even after mid-century, when
Bismarck forged the empire and Prussia became the ascendant power,
the imperial regime found it difficult to impose its will upon the
smaller states.[35] The sheer size of the German and Austrian lands reinforced this regionalism. Geographically German was spoken over a
stretch of Europe larger and more culturally varied than the domain
of the British Isles. Using the 1850s as a point of comparison, the Protestant populations of the two lands were about equal at 18,000,000.[36]
While in Britain this populace was drawn together by short distances
and ease of contact, however, German Protestants inhabited independent states spaced among an even larger Catholic population. The
Protestants, whose intellectual traditions make them of more interest
for this study, fell into four groups: Lutheran, Reformed, Evangelical
United (formed from the union of Lutheran and Reformed in Prussia
and elsewhere in 1817), and a smaller number of dissenting sects.
Ecclesiastically, German Protestantism was much more diverse than
even these differing theological strands suggest.

> The Protestant Church in Germany, owing to its close connection
> with, and subordination to, the state is cut up into as many sections as
> there are kingdoms, grand duchies, duchies, principalities, and free
> cities. Each . . . has its own ecclesiastical organization, with its separate
> polity, worship, and administration, perfectly independent of the
> others. . . . Territorially, then, there are actually no less than thirty-
> eight Protestant churches within the limits of the German Confedera-
> tion. So in Switzerland, each canton has its independent Reformed
> Church, without any official connection whatever with that of the
> neighboring canton.[37]

While linked by common history and common creeds, Germany's
Protestant churches tended, because of the political divisions, to be
regionally independent.

Now if we imagine a theological student set upon ministry in the
church of his duchy or kingdom, his aims would take him naturally to
the regional university. These institutions had a variety of origins
reaching back to the later Middle Ages. From the end of the seventeenth century, moreover, territorial sovereigns assumed the right to

found a university in their provinces, and whether from desire for prestige or real educational need many rulers had exercised the privilege.[38] By the 1850s there were more than twenty-six such institutions in the German Confederation, besides a number of seminaries with less than full university status.[39]

To describe these universities as regional, however, is to describe only their manner of origin and site of operation. Provinciality tended to vanish as one entered the gates. Except for certain chairs of theology which, if Protestant, had to be held by Protestants and if Catholic, by Catholics, the professorial appointments at most German universities were by this time remarkably free of sectarian restrictions. The same freedom was enjoyed by students. Expatriate Philip Schaff wrote to his American readers in 1857,

> You may find Lutherans, Reformed, Roman Catholics, Greeks, and even Jews, and many foreigners from all countries of Europe and America amongst the students. There they enter upon an unlimited field of independent study. . . .[40]

Nor was this the case of one or two strange faces in an otherwise homogeneous group. The German schools were as a rule large enough to exclude that. In the 1850s Berlin had nearly 200 professors and 2,000 students; Halle had an enrollment of 660; Leipzig, 800; Göttingen, 700, which was down because of political troubles from more than 1,400 in the 1830s.

The large and open enrollments may in part be read as the mirror image of something more basic. Since the age of Enlightenment, the principle of toleration, of free and open inquiry had won a crucial place in German higher learning. Already in the middle of the 1700s reformers at a few key institutions had laid the groundwork of the modern German university. Göttingen's founder and guiding spirit, Gerlach Adolph von Münchhausen determined that his fledgling academy should become a beacon of liberal learning, and revealingly, he found that this could happen only if he could ensure that "theology play a quiet role." To avoid acrimonious debate among Protestant sects, the university "forbade denunciation of teachers for heretical opinions." Münchhausen "sought further to guarantee peace by appointing doctrinally neutral professors of theology."[41] In Prussia, the University of Halle reached the peak of its eighteenth-century fame in the 1740s after a series of reforms which achieved, among other things, "a level of freedom in theological matters unequaled in Germany. Moreover, the force of its example propagated these innovations in other universities."[42] At Vienna, where university reforms were to become a leading model for changes in German lands, it was determined "to set up the institutions of study without exception as purely secular organizations by removing all remnants of ecclesiastical tendencies."[43] At Trier Nicholas von Hontheim, author of the Febronian attacks on papal authority and prochancellor of the university, unabashedly "introduced the philosophy of the Enlightenment into the curriculum and placed Göttingen graduates on the faculty."[44]

As the effects of these large decisions rippled out to lesser schools in smaller states, the result was cumulative. Theological discussion continued, but in a lower key. Only in exceptional cases—such as Strauss's *Leben Jesu*—did debates exhibit the dogmatic rancor or evangelical warmth of earlier ages. In fact there were some contemporary observers who even discerned a discouraging impact on theological study. Writing later in the century, J. Conrad of Halle noted that of those students who entered the theological faculties, "a very considerable portion never after entered upon any ecclesiastical office at all."[45]

Yet the reforms of these years did more than set up the philosophy of the Enlightenment as an alternative or rival to the theology of the churches. They began to carve the outline of a portentous change, the establishment of a new academic ideal. It went under the name of *Wissenschaft,* the scholar's vigorous, unceasing pursuit of scientific truth. The schools which pioneered along this new path as early as the 1750s were Halle, Göttingen, and Erlangen. "Significantly," writes Charles McClelland in the most recent survey of the German universities,

> all three were Protestant, largely state-funded and state-controlled, modernizing in outlook and curriculum. . . . Their secularizing tendencies (or at least their opposition to church orthodoxy as the guiding principle of the curriculum) helped nurture new ideas about the goals of higher education, and for the professoriate, about the search for truth, resulting in . . . a modern research ethic in scholarship.[46]

During the subsequent fifty years *Wissenschaft* provided the reigning ideal for these schools and many of their graduates. Other universities lagged behind, however, until in 1810 Frederick William III of Prussia made the decision that changed the nature of German higher learning. Reeling from defeat at the hands of Napoleon's armies, he determined that Prussia's recovery must begin with the mind. He called upon one of Germany's finer intellects, Wilhelm von Humboldt, for guidance and with him presided over the foundation of the University of Berlin. Humboldt made the university a virtual temple to the ideal of *Wissenschaft.*

> The creation of the University of Berlin, heralded by preliminary steps at Halle, Göttingen, and Jena, was a deliberate break with academic tradition. . . . The new University was intended primarily to develop

knowledge, secondarily and perhaps as a concession, to train the professional and the official classes . . . Humboldt conceived the salvation of
the German nation coming from the combination of teaching and
research, and time has proved him right.[47]

The innovations at Berlin soon became a paradigm, "with the result
that the medieval universities made all possible haste, one after
another, to modernize themselves in accordance with the Berlin idea."[48]
The consequences of this development were wide-ranging, but the
most instructive for our purposes were twofold. First, Berlin and *Wissenschaft* gave a sharp stimulus to the growth of a career professoriate. More than a mere association of colleagues, Germany's university professors soon took the form of an elite community, with admission granted only on the basis of demonstrated achievement in
research. In the vestibule of these cherished precincts stood the *Privat-
dozent,* known to every campus and spending his days and most of his
nights working to prove himself. Their plight and productivity has
been well described:

The docents are the recruits from among whom the professors are
ultimately obtained. . . . In its pre-World War I form it [the *Privat-
dozentur*] was a large group of persons who entered a severe and unpaid
novitiate in the hope of making an academic career. There could be no
better proof of the esteem in which the universities were held. The German student had won his doctorate on the basis of a thesis, presumably
showing some capacity to do original work. . . . He wanted to make a
career in scholarship or science. Did he get a university appointment
which at the crucial moment of his development made him comfortable
and overloaded him with teaching routine? Not at all. He got an
unsalaried license to teach, . . . offered a lecture course or two . . . and
. . . attached himself to a laboratory, a clinic, or a library, in order that
he might continue his productive work. The Privatdozenten formed the
nursery from which . . . the German university selected its *Extraordinarii* on the basis of teaching ability and scholarly productivity; from
the *Extraordinarii* of all Germany and German-speaking countries . . .
the *Ordinarii* were selected; at every stage the two factors counted; the
candidate must have been able to expound his subject, he must have
produced. It was a severe system . . . but in every field . . . it developed
a host of workers, a supply for the universities.[49]

As an institution, then, the new German university paid highest
tribute to the research ethic. The university existed not first of all to
build character or provide a haven and finishing school for the sons of
the aristocracy. It existed for the professor—both for his inquiries and
for the recruitment of new inquirers. The system of instruction thus
focused upon the lecture, which gave written and oral exposition of
the professor's studies. The lecture system, observed Schaff, is what
explains "the high standard of scholarship and the marvellous amount

of literary fertility, by which the university professors in Protestant
Germany surpass their colleagues in other countries."[50]

A second consequence of the Prussian example in Berlin was a new
birth of academic freedom. In the decades after 1810, the liberty of
the scholar acquired an almost sacred status. It was cherished as the
birthright of the academic mind. At first the freedom was total, but
when it was exercised in political affairs, German governments turned
repressive. Experience with the *Burschenschaft* movement and the
revolts of 1848 moved the ruling orders to limit severely the rights of
political dissent. Yet out of this there developed an interesting com-
pensation. Various observers have noticed that the German governments offered a kind of exchange: nearly complete freedom in intellectual matters in return for nearly total acquiescence in political matters.

> They [German professors] are supposed to have attained such a degree
> of intellectual and moral maturity as to be fully able to take care of
> themselves, except in political matters, in which the German govern-
> ments are as illiberal and intolerant, as they are liberal in allowing an
> almost unbounded freedom of thought and speech on every other
> subject.[51]

As the century wore on, the professoriate seemed to accept this bargain
even with a measure of enthusiasm; it staunchly supported the
empire.[52]

Churches could not be so pragmatic as the state. As German
biblical study and theology charted a more scientific course, the
religious establishment also sought ways to limit academic freedom.
Yet here there is a different story to tell. In the first place, it must be
noted that the German churches were already the most tolerant in
Europe.[53] Views that would have brought actions from the church or
state elsewhere were simply quarreled about in Germany. It was only
the most radical views, those of Strauss, Baur's Tübingen school, and
Wellhausen the Old Testament critic, that occasioned any more serious
actions. Only against Strauss, moreover, did the crusades ever come
close to achieving their end. Indeed Strauss was perhaps the only German critic to suffer real persecution, and many of his miseries were
self-inflicted. After the *Leben Jesu,* he was removed from Tübingen,
became *non grata* at Ludwigsburg, moved positionless to Stuttgart,
and was driven by public outcry from an appointment at Zürich. Yet
so deep was the tradition of academic freedom already planted that
Strauss was truly surprised at his fate and disillusioned when his colleagues repudiated him.[54]

The case of Strauss proved to be an exception.[55] Subsequent scholars
had few difficulties. When they did, they found a simple expedient;
they moved. The number of academies in the German Confederation

and the diversity of governments which controlled them offered a dignified, sometimes rewarding, route of escape from pressure. This happened even in cases where the problems and pressures were political. A political disturbance disrupted Göttingen in 1837, and when seven liberal professors, including the biblical Orientalist Ewald, were deposed, they "met with an enthusiastic sympathy all over Germany, and received honorable calls to other universities."[56] Ferdinand Christian Baur is said shortly before his death to have complained bitterly that the "Tübingen school" had been destroyed by ecclesiastical opposition; yet this was hardly a victory for persecution. His disciples simply transferred to other faculties, whence his views received an even wider hearing.[57] Again, while he was at Greifswald, Julius Wellhausen's *History of Israel* drew a fierce reaction from conservative voices; yet when he began to feel pressured, he simply transferred to the philosophical faculty at Halle as instructor in Semitic languages.[58]

It was thus a combination of factors—the effects of Enlightenment, the ideal of *Wissenschaft*, academic freedom, diversity of options, and mobility—that in terms of pure scholarship made the German universities the finest in Europe. Their ascendance in biblical study was no accident.

When we move across the waters to Great Britain, we encounter a rather different world. While its Protestant population roughly equaled Germany's, Britain came much nearer achieving a common national identity. Ireland had, of course, long been difficult to absorb. But Scotland and Wales, despite differences, formed with England a largely Protestant community. On matters of polity, liturgy, disabilities, and establishment, disputes between the parties and denominations of this Protestant world were frequent and often acrimonious. But as we saw with *Ecce Homo*, these differences tended to fade into irrelevance when discussion turned to rationalism or the new historical criticism. Prominent spokesmen were recognized and read across denominational lines. Methodists listened to Presbyterians, Presbyterians to Congregationalists.[59] Nonconformity as a whole did not hesitate to approve or discuss the works by Church of England divines.

In biblical criticism, attention to Anglican study was important for another reason. The level of scholarship elsewhere was not high. For nearly half a century after 1843 Scottish divinity struggled against the weakening effects of the Great Disruption.[60] The Congregationalist academies had been strong a century ago, and they survived to produce probably the best nonconformist scholarship of the Victorian era, but it was rarely of the first rank. The great emotional wave of the evangelical revival had taken the rigor from theological study.[61] Methodists and Baptists, inclined to flaunt their uneducated ministry, were only beginning to set up theological schools. In 1834 the plan for a Methodist seminary at Hoxton passed in Conference but over considerable opposition. Charles Spurgeon established a college for Baptist preachers but had to appoint a Congregationalist its first principal.[62] From these slender means and small beginnings no biblical scholar of repute could be expected till late in the century.

The burden of leadership in British criticism thus fell upon the two ancient English universities, Oxford and Cambridge.[63] They stood toward British learning, generally and in divinity, as Berlin and Göttingen, or Halle, did toward German scholarship. What ideal presided over these schools, and what sort of scholarship did it yield? Till well through the Victorian era, the English universities were clerically dominated, but university life could in no sense be described as narrowly religious. Nor was it rigorously intellectual. The aim of English higher learning might best be described as aristocratic and social. Long engaged in producing statesmen and clerics who guided the course of the nation, the ancient universities had committed themselves chiefly to the formation of a certain kind of character—the English gentleman. It was an old pattern, but in the early nineteenth century it received new stimulus from the example of Thomas Arnold at Rugby and the theory of writers like Newman. "The English universities and the endowed public schools," observed Abraham Flexner in the 1930s,

> formed a closed social and intellectual circle up to almost the last quarter of the nineteenth century. They were both organs of the Anglican Church; they were concerned with the production of a type—the English gentleman, a moral and social rather than an intellectual type. The revolution wrought by Dr. Arnold at Rugby made the formation of character the main object of a gentleman's education. That is still the center about which the public schools and the Oxford and Cambridge Colleges revolve.[64]

At Arnold's Rugby the premise of education was an undisguised elitism. He had been entrusted with some of the best of England's young men. Before they left for the university, it was his task to build in them a moral vision, a style of character, a sense of responsibility to the nation. His method was to reinvigorate the old pattern of a general education steeped in the classics. Such a regimen provided the graduate with discipline, skill in written and oral expression, and a fund of wisdom from antiquity which enabled him to move with ease at the highest levels of society.

At Oxford Arnold's student would have found the master's ideal jealously protected by men like the Oriel Provost Edward Copleston. Already in 1810, defending Oxford's commitment to the classics against criticism in the *Edinburgh Review,* he insisted that "while not directly qualifying a man for any particular employment, it enriches him intellectually and enables him to follow any calling he chooses 'with better grace and more elevated carriage.' "[65] Whatever its merits, this clearly was not a professional training focused intensively on one discipline and aiming at its mastery, the pushing back of its frontiers. Indeed, when Newman later lectured on the university and placed the classical ideal at the core of a liberal education, he explicitly repudiated professionalism: "This implies that its object is . . . the diffusion and extension of knowledge rather than the advancement." It was a view echoed later by Westcott: "Though the university cannot help begetting a few professors, its true function is the nurturing of citizens, of gentlemen, of Christians."[66] Even so, the practice did not always live up to the proclamation. The somnolence of the eighteenth century had not been entirely shaken at Oxford and Cambridge. In classics, the core of the program, standards were modest. Owen Chadwick quotes an amusing comment of Mark Pattison on the letters B.A.: "They are an evidence that a youth has been able to afford not only the money, but . . . the time, to live three years among gentlemen, doing nothing, as a gentleman should."[67]

On a more important level, however, the liberal ideal of Copleston and Newman, like Humboldt's *Wissenschaft,* had profound implications for university policy and practice. The subtle process of building character in the English schools worked by example and personal contact, and at Oxford or Cambridge it made the college rather than the university the focal point of instruction. The student, usually arriving from a public school whose relation with a given college ensured placement, typically became a Fellow with attachments—say to Oriel, or Balliol, or Merton—that would last through life. Within this system he contracted with tutors, in or outside of his own college, for the sort of intimate instruction, individually or in a small group, which was the hub of the system. In these tutorials lay the preparation which finally decided the fate of the student in examinations.

One key consequence of this was that the professor, the beacon of *Wissenschaft* in Germany, figured in England chiefly as a sidelight. He had a certain prestige, and he lectured. But he was not essential to either the training or fate of the student. The report of the Commission on University Reform at Oxford in 1852 was quick to notice the circumstance:

> In the first place there is little demand for professorial teaching. The influence of the Colleges has continually tended to limit the Studies of the University to subjects which can be taught by their own Fellows, and within their own walls. . . . It is not to be expected that young men, who

suppose their success in life to depend on success in these Examinations, will bestow or (as they think) waste time in attending Lectures which are in no way likely to promote their main object. Students . . . have had no sufficient motive for studying even History or Theology.[68]

What obtained in England, then, was precisely the reverse of the German configuration. Instead of the professor, whose public lectures exposed the students to the frontiers of his science, it was the tutor, England's equivalent of the Privatdocent, who served as the lynchpin of undergraduate instruction.

Whatever the cultural and collegial merits of this system (and they were not insignificant), it had certain scholarly disadvantages. It tended to cut the student off from the newest researches; and it worked a considerable hardship upon the tutors, who were usually junior faculty. Flexner described it thus:

> The recent undergraduate becomes . . . a tutor. He is financially and socially at ease. He is a member of the most charming society in the world, the peer of his elders. He has space, quiet, isolation, good food and drink, and long vacations. . . . He may, of course, work on. Equipped with the capacity and desire, assuredly he will and does, especially if a professorship is his goal. But he is under no great competitive pressure to do so . . . Indeed, is not the reverse likely to happen? For the tutorial fellow takes on a heavy teaching burden which he usually carries most conscientiously—carries, as a tutor remarked, till he is "used up."[69]

Whereas Germany's *Privatdozenten* pursued their researches as the only escape from poverty and insecurity to professional status, England's tutors found themselves often in the opposite position—secure, unmotivated, committed to other tasks. Certainly scholarship of high calibre emerged from some Oxford and Cambridge tutors; but as the commissioners noted, the system did not encourage it.

To all of this, theological study at the English universities was no exception. The clerical presence was pervasive, especially at Oxford. The two great religious revivals of recent history, led by Wesley and Newman, were traceable to Oxford men. If the Church has been called the Tory party at prayer, the universities might have been described as the Church in thought. Even before the years of the Oxford movement, theological developments at the universities held the interest of the nation. They were reported in the *Times* and discussed by statesmen and social leaders. Anglicans regarded the schools as their preserve. When in the 1850s Parliament considered the bill to admit dissenters, there was strong resistance.

Nonetheless the level of theological instruction was not high. In the eyes of the Commission, it did not impress:

Oxford still educates a large proportion of the Clergy; but learned theologians are very rare in the University, and, in consequence, they are still rarer elsewhere. No efficient means at present exist in the University for training Candidates for Holy Orders in those studies which belong peculiarly to their profession.[70]

Understandably so. For prospective clerics, as for others at Oxford, the reigning ideal was the gentleman parson, or statesman, or barrister, able to assume a role of leadership, in command of social or ecclesiastical obligations, but even among those likely to stay at the university as tutors, not the specialist at the leading edge of his discipline.

The conception and character of higher learning were not the only bridles upon frontier scholarship in biblical study. There were to a degree certain forcible restraints—censure, invoking of blasphemy laws, loss of prospect for advancement, even action in the ecclesiastical courts. Early in the century some of these heavier measures were employed in the Church's party quarrels between Evangelical and Tractarian. Toward mid-century this threat sometimes loomed over theological discussion and biblical study. One need only recall the damage done by William Palmer's charge of "Straussians" leveled at the members of the Sterling Club. Given the public nature of theological discussion in Victorian culture, the victims of this smear had to labor to clear their reputations. The claims were absurd, but indictment was almost as good as a conviction. In 1860, as is well known, the great controversy over *Essays and Reviews* brought two of its contributors to the ecclesiastical courts. In 1866 James Martineau, an excellent candidate, "was excluded from a professorship at University College, London because he was a Unitarian."[71] Even Farrar, whose achievements included not only *The Life of Christ* but countless devotional and instructional writings for the Church, may have been delayed on the road to preferment by reaction to his *Eternal Hope* (1870), which expressed doubts of eternal punishment.[72]

Taking the wide view, however, we must conclude that such threats did not really menace scholarship significantly. The arts of such repression were uncongenial to the Victorians. The Essayists of 1860 were the most outspoken in their attacks on tradition, and the action against them ultimately came to nothing.[73] The other, more subtle pressures were no doubt real, but scarcely crushing, for the fact of the matter is that in the main external threats were not needed. Most scholars restrained themselves. Imbued with the ideals of university leadership, of gentlemanly conduct, of responsibility to the religious life of the nation, they could think of nothing more repugnant than the pursuit of rash, unsettling theories, however persuasive their claim to truth. It was said that Seeley, a Cambridge man, published *Ecce Homo* anonymously out of concern for the religious feelings of his father. Like his colleagues in other disciplines, the biblical scholar at Oxford or Cambridge worked within a network of overlapping loyalties. There were ties to his pupils, his college, his university; ties to the Church and the religious sensibility of the populace. Placed only alongside these, not above them, were the claims of one's discipline. The gentleman scholar was regarded as a leader, and that entailed certain responsibilities. He must consider the effect of his ideas on the less informed mind of the masses. To be set free from other attachments and pursue truth in a void was unthinkable. What Berlin honored as devotion to *Wissenschaft* Oxford was apt to censure as irresponsible leadership. There was thus no need to police Victorian scholarship in biblical study. Its leaders followed a protocol of what we may call interior restraint. Coming upon a radical, or deeply unsettling notion, they were inclined not to advertise it, but to hold their assent and wait for disproof. In the meantime, it was injudicious to disturb the ordinary believer.

Almost to the very end of the century, the critics at Oxford and Cambridge took the lead in establishing Britain's approach to criticism. The Cambridge trio and the younger William Sanday of Oxford developed a solid, but cautious and reassuring style of criticism. The reason for this should now be perfectly clear: they were gentlemen scholars. Theirs was a sensibility which pursued the true, but with an instinctive conviction that it must also lead to the good. When they saw versions of the truth, such as the Tübingen theory, which seemed to lead away from the good, they paused or pushed on in the conviction that the error would in time be found. Their allegiances were several not single: not only to their discipline, but also to the faith and populace of the churches. Their careers illustrated this. Hort, who held more radical views, was slow to publish. Lightfoot left his beloved university, diminished his critical productivity, and perhaps shortened his life because his Church called him to be Bishop of Durham. Westcott too assumed a bishopric and devoted his later life to social and ecclesiastical matters which left little time for New Testament research.[74] Sanday spent all his days as a scholar, yet as will become clear in chapter five, he could be dislodged from conservative views only with the greatest of effort.

The influence of these examples, moreover, spread well beyond the Church of England. Quietly, Nonconformist and Scottish divines tended to mirror the pattern set by Anglican scholarship. This was partly out of deference. Till late in the century none of these other traditions produced critics as technically skilled as the Anglicans. It was partly from circumstance as well. Since they were preparing clergy in the theological schools of smaller churches with more intimate contexts, they felt even more keenly the leader's sense of responsibility.[75]

These attachments go a long way toward explaining an almost inescapable feature of theological discussion in the Victorian context. The manner, or style, in which new ideas were presented was crucial to their proper reception. Strauss and Renan were despised not just because of their ideas, but because they seemed to take delight in tearing down sacred things. The Essayists were cited by many for their defiance and ill manners. Colenso was similar; he left Hort dismayed "by the discouragement which the cause of progressive Old Testament criticism in England has sustained through the natural revulsion against the manner in which he has represented it."[76] As for rationalists like Thomas Scott and Edward Clodd, it was precisely because of their undisguised militance that they usually went unread. When conversely unconventional positions were presented with humility and reverence, as happened with *Ecce Homo,* they earned at least a hearing, and often much more.[77] The scholars who handled critical issues, says W. B. Glover, "were most unanimous in their sympathetic concern for the religious feeling of the masses of people."[78] Given their ideals and attachments, we find it hard to imagine their acting otherwise.

3. Crises and Resolutions

Not until the 1880s was Britain's tradition of gentlemanly scholarship truly put to the test. The examiner turned out to be Julius Wellhausen. Though it had precedents, his *History of Israel* was a revolutionary book. It had appeared in Germany in 1878, was expanded in 1883 and translated into English in 1885. Its tone was authoritative, and at times abrasive; it had the accent of the German and rather too little of the gentleman.[79] What it proposed was nothing less than a dismissal of the classic Christian reading of the Old Testament, and a profound reconstruction of Hebrew antiquity. For Wellhausen Abraham did not worship the one true God; the books of Moses were compiled by late editors; Genesis, laden with mythology, derived from several late sources; David did not write the Psalms; Solomon never knew the Proverbs; the prophets were the first monotheists; Wisdom literature went back no further than the age of exile. Beginning as a group of scattered nomadic clans, the Hebrews were polytheists who under the leadership of Moses began to worship Yahweh, the strongest of the gods. They conquered Palestine, set up a monarchy whose decay later provided the backdrop for the prophets' program of revival under the banner of monotheism, and then watched as foreign powers conquered and delivered the nation to exile. At that point the priests sought the revival of at least a religious community, and they produced the elaborate rituals and law codes supposedly dating from the time of Moses. In fact, they were the final gasp of Judaism, the residue of a last attempt to recover lost glories.

For Christianity, as for Judaism, the implications of this theory were shattering. If Wellhausen was correct, then the accepted notion of a sacred scripture which recorded the clear design of God at work from Adam to Ezra could no longer stand. The idea of an Old Testament filled with anticipations of Christ seemed suddenly dubious. Even the readings Jesus and Paul gave to the Hebrew scriptures began to look like errors. Wellhausen had driven a wedge squarely into the center of the British critic's multiple loyalties; he was forcing a choice between the claims of criticism and the claims of the religious community. Nor could there be, at this late date, any evasion of the issues. Earlier in the century, as New Testament criticism arrived, fortune favored the British school. When Strauss and Tübingen advanced their theories, higher criticism was unknown and unwanted. The new views were dismissed without discussion. With the advent of the Cambridge three in the 1860s and 70s, cautious criticism began to win a hearing. At precisely this time, the edges of dispute softened in Germany. Conservatives had with partial success upheld conventional beliefs, and more important, radicals themselves could be seen changing their minds. The leap to criticism then could be seen diminishing to a more natural step. But now that Wellhausen had intervened, all was changed. The gap between criticism and the churches, so recently shrunk to a mere crevice, opened again into a chasm.

There is not a single church on the British scene in the 1880s where the force of this new dilemma was not felt acutely. Among Anglicans Charles Gore provides an instance of the interior war between gentleman and scholar. Teaching the Bible to ordinands at Cuddesdon Seminary in 1880 he "did not conceal what he thought of the criticism of Genesis, and said, 'I hope someday to be able to say this publicly.' "[80] So too a canon of Manchester cathedral, addressing his bishop after an unusually bold sermon on the newer biblical study: "I think much the same as you, but I dare not say it. You would have been burnt for such a thing in the older days."[81] Among Scots and English Free Churchmen, the question of criticism, with Wellhausen clearly in the shadows, precipitated a major public struggle in almost every communion. In the Scottish Free Church it led to the celebrated heresy trial of Semitic scholar W. Robertson Smith, who outspokenly assumed the new approach.[82] It fueled the controversy among English Presbyterians which prevented the appointment of George Adam

Smith to their theological college.[83] It figured prominently as a back-drop to the "Down Grade" controversy which vexed English Baptists till a compromise statement was drafted under the guidance of the diplomatic John Clifford at a tense, crowded assembly of the Baptist Union in 1888.[84] It created agonies for Congregationalists who, despite a tradition of open inquiry, were shaken by R. F. Horton's *Inspiration and the Bible* (1888).[85] Though Methodists were spared a quarrel which swirled about a single personality, the same stresses, strains, and disagreements may be read throughout the 1880s from the pages of the *Methodist Recorder,* the *Methodist Magazine,* and the *London Quarterly.*[86]

Scholars in all of these traditions found the business of speaking in defense of criticism deeply troubling to their souls, in large part because it was so exceedingly difficult to show how, even if legitimate, it could do any actual good for the churches. Precisely because their professional ideals embraced more than the Germans' total loyalty to *Wissenschaft,* they found themselves torn. Wellhausen's reconstruction of Israel's history was compelling. If valid, it threw into disarray the long-accepted religious reading of the Old Testament, which saw in it types, or anticipations, of Christ. Yet if the Old Testament was to be still the church's book, how should one now interpret it? [87] Critics groped, but found no answers. It was crucial in Victorian society that the public be brought along, not too far behind the leading edge of the scholars, but the arguments were very technical. As Glover says, "Any attempt at popularization lost the force of very cogent philological arguments which were essential parts of the critical framework."[88] Nor can we find in these decades a creative and recognized theologian able to incorporate the new view into received Christian dogma.

Without an effective popular voice, then, those sympathetic to Wellhausen found it difficult to defend him. Their position invited attack; and they received it, particularly, says Chadwick, from those most involved with the masses: preachers and teachers. "Several of the most famous preachers in England—Liddon, Spurgeon, Joseph Parker of the City Temple—were among stern opponents of what had happened."[89] Spokesmen like these were quick to press the critics with just the charge one might have guessed: violation of the gentlemanly ideal. The formal charge against Robertson Smith alleged that his writings "by their ill-considered and unguarded setting forth of speculations of a critical kind, tend to awaken doubt, especially in the case of students."[90] Even Robertson Nicoll, whose Life has been noticed and whose journal *Expositor* fostered intelligent discussion of criticism, was led to remark at one point that criticism "should dawn on

the church as gently as the sunlight, and I am not at all sure but that
heretics ought to be burnt. I mean the fellows who make a big row and
split their churches."[91] In the aftermath of *Lux Mundi,* the famous
1889 Anglican High Church manifesto which sought to join criticism
and idealist philosophy, at least one contributor felt that he and his
colleagues should have been more careful.[92] Unquestionably Wellhausen delivered a jolt amid the passage to criticism; he left the churches
nursing new abrasions and anxieties.

Nevertheless, the carriage did not slow down. The interesting thing,
in view of all this, is that the churches not only moved steadily to
accept criticism, but they moved with surprising speed. In just over a
decade from 1880 to about 1893 the majority of scholars and a fair
portion of educated laity in each of the British churches came round to
a critical view of the scriptures, at least in principle. There was of
course the usual variance from church to church and region to region.
Rural parishes and congregations moved more slowly. Congregationalists, with a share of learned pastors, preceded Baptists, who numbered many uneducated members and clergy. Presbyterians preceded
Methodists for somewhat the same reasons. Yet even here there were
unexpected advances. Primitive Methodists came from probably the
least educated sectors of Victorian society, but when A. S. Peake took
charge of ministerial training at Hartley College, criticism filtered in,
and without disturbance. Unlike the bitter falling-out in America
between Fundamentalists and liberals, Britain escaped titanic and divisive
theological struggles. Denominations remained intact. Quarrels
occurred but were resolved; religious life steadily went on. Glover has
observed the ease of the transition:

> The late start that Old Testament criticism got in England is the more
> remarkable in view of the swift progress that it made after 1880.
> Remarking on the "extraordinarily rapid" progress of the decade pre-
> ceding 1892, Sanday rightly observed that the rate was "the utmost that
> can be at once sound and salutary."[93]

Chadwick has agreed, and he locates the transition during precisely
the same decade.[94]

As a matter of fact, this transition to criticism, the acquiescence in
the new approach, seems almost too smooth. Historians like Glover
and Chadwick who record it fail to note how puzzling this phenomenon at first sight appears. Nearly all of the clues drawn from Victorian
society would lead us to expect just the sort of great and acrimonious
struggle that fractured the American churches. Theologians and critics
worked in a very public context, where their views were monitored by
the religious community through pulpit and press. The religious com-

munity, regardless of denomination, was marked by a most traditional orthodox theology. There were lingering suspicions of the entire critical enterprise, inherited from the days of Strauss and the Tübingen menace. Even the best spokesmen for criticism could manage to make only a defensive case for it, insisting that it need not do harm to belief.[95] The defense, moreover, rested on technical considerations, which in the case of Wellhausen's theory, were difficult to get across at a popular level. The clear advantage belonged to the popular preachers like Liddon and Parker and Spurgeon who brought the full weight of their prestige and oratory against the critics. Creative theological solutions were nowhere to be found.

Given these discouraging circumstances, we are still left with a final question: how is it that the transition to criticism came so easily? Despite a path strewn with hazards, the churches managed in the 1880s and 90s to move with speed and without disaster to a full acceptance of higher criticism. How did it happen? The answer, we can only conclude, is to be found in the one favoring circumstance that tended to remove all obstacles: the widespread and successful image of criticism created by those authors who wrote Lives of Christ. It was on the very eve of the 1880s and during that decade that the Lives enjoyed their greatest popularity with Britain's religious readers. Anyone who read of Wellhausen and his doubts about the Old Testament had an equal opportunity to open a Life of Christ and read its reassurances about the New. Rationalists aside, the Lives were positive books, reaffirming, inspiring, engaging; and whatever their methods, which to be sure were often subcritical, they were perceived by their audience as the products of criticism—with a difference. Readers had no difficulty discerning in them the sort of constructive religious scholarship that dry defenses of Wellhausen could never be. The use of the historical approach, as we noted in several of the best Lives, brought to the story of Christ a freshness, a dramatic force, a narrative vividness, and a glimpse of exotic scenes that the Victorian reader associated with fiction often enough, but rarely with the biblical story. When woven from these strands the story of Christ produced an effect both fresh and inspiring. And if this was so, then criticism need not be accepted as a grudging concession to the scholars; it could be embraced as a source of edification and instruction, a stimulant to the religious life.

That this sentiment was widespread among ordinary readers is a conclusion we are almost forced to draw from the extraordinary and sustained popularity of the Lives during the years that stretched from the appearance of Farrar's work to the end of the century. Scholars and spokesmen testified explicitly to the very same disposition. Judgments from every band of the religious spectrum can be adduced to show that while Wellhausen unsettled, the Lives of Christ reassured. Here, for example, is A. B. Bruce, one of Scotland's leading critics in the 1880s and 90s:

> It must suffice to state the final result of the long and laborious inquiry into Christian origins. We now know that the Gospels are in the main history, not fiction. We have an intimate acquaintance with the man Jesus Christ, as He walked and worked in the world. We know approximately the very words He spoke, and what He taught concerning God, man, Himself, the Kingdom of God and its righteousness.[96]

Congregationalist A. M. Fairbairn shared his view:

> The most distinctive and determinative element in modern theology is what we may term a new feeling for Christ. . . . It is certainly not too much to say, He is today more studied and better known as He was and as He lived than at any period between now and the first age of the Church.[97]

Elsewhere he added, "We may say that more recent Lives [of Christ] are distinguished by a growing sense of being on firm historical ground."[98]

As the turn of the century came nearer, other prominently placed spokesmen echoed this opinion. Among Anglicans men of no less stature than Charles Gore, E. W. Benson, and W. H. Fremantle had come to see the positive effects of gospel criticism and began to extend the endorsement to the troubling area of Old Testament study as well.[99] W. F. Adeney, New Testament critic in Edinburgh, added his voice:

> The effect of the most searching and ruthless inquiry is that the central Figure of all history and all religion stands out with a new clearness and outline, and at the same time with commanding majesty, nay, with the awfulness of true Divinity, so that we are constrained to exclaim with Thomas, "My Lord and My God."[100]

With endorsements like these leading the way, the inexpert layman could be excused if he put aside his anxieties about Wellhausen, who after all posed a threat only to the less crucial Old Testament, and opened his Bible at last to the critics.

The impact of the Lives of Jesus on Victorian society and religious sensibilities may without overstatement be said to have been deep and, in certain realms of discussion, decisive. Quite apart from their influence on devotional sentiment, by which "the human Christ became more real to the world,"[101] they came to play a pivotal role in the process by which Christianity in Britain reconciled itself to the enterprise of biblical higher criticism. If during the unsettled decade of the 1880s the debate over criticism had become exclusively a debate over Wellhausen, the British churches could hardly have gone over to the cause of the scholars with so little pain. Indeed, some of the churches, like American Fundamentalists, may never have made the shift at all. Critics themselves—whether it was Westcott, or Sanday, or Driver, or Bruce—could do little more than offer a defensive argument, justifying the principle of criticism with little (save for small technical advances) to show of the benefits to be derived from its practice. Nor in Britain could the scholars go their own way, as in Germany; they had to bring at least a consensus of religious opinion along with them. What was needed, therefore, was a demonstration of the virtues in criticism; and that demonstration came to be provided by the Lives of Christ. In the last quarter of the Victorian era they stood out as the most visible and publicly comprehensible exhibit of the benefits which newer historical scholarship offered the religious community. They provided a bridge of reassurance over which the churches passed undamaged—though not unshaken—to the acceptance of biblical higher criticism.

NOTES

1. See above, p. 9

2. There is room for debate on this point. Older scholars like V. F. Storr, *The Development of English Theology,* 4, and G. M. Young, *Portrait of an Age,* 74, as well as more recent students like Chadwick, *Victorian Church,* 1:532 and Drummond and Bulloch, *Church in Victorian Scotland,* 240-65, argue the position that in the first half of the century British thought, whether Anglican, dissenting, or Scottish, knew little of what was happening in Germany. Some recent assessments, such as Merton A. Christenson, "Taylor of Norwich and the Higher Criticism," *Journal of the History of Ideas* 20 (April 1959) 179-94; Walter Ralls in an indirect manner in his article "The Papal Aggression of 1850: A Study in Victorian Anti-Catholicism," *Church History* 43 (June 1974) 248 and n. 19, and John L. Speller, "Alexander Nicoll and the Study of German Biblical Criticism in Early Nineteenth-Century Oxford," *Journal of Ecclesiastical History* 30 (October 1979) 451-59, have challenged this view without however altering it substantially. The subject is in need of some distinctions and more precise study, some of which have been provided by M. A. Crowther in her *Church Embattled,* particularly chaps. 2 and 3: "The Threat from Germany," and "Germany and the Broad Church."

3. The effect of this was noticed as late as 1853 by William Cureton of the British Museum staff, whom Crowther, *Church Embattled,* 55, quotes as follows: "German criticism and German research upon all subjects connected with theology are generally most censured and most reviled by those who are the least acquainted with them. We believe that the indiscriminate condemnation of almost all work of theological research in Germany by some professors and tutors in our universities, and perhaps, indeed, by some of the Bishops of our Church, who are unable to read a line of the original writings, and condemn only from hearsay, or second-hand information, is not only highly unjust, but, in this country, has been, and is, injurious to the cause of impartial research, by which alone truth can be elucidated and upheld."

4. Hugh James Rose, *The State of the Protestant Religion in Germany* (Cambridge: n. p., 1825) 4. See also Crowther, *Church Embattled,* 55. On the response of the Scottish clergy to German neology, see Drummond and Bulloch, *Church in Victorian Scotland,* 240-65.

5. Thirlwall earned a certain early infamy for a translation of Friedrich Schleiermacher's commentary on Luke, but as Chadwick notes, *Victorian Church,* 2:79, he joined the unanimous declaration of the bishops in 1861 against the writers responsible for *Essays and Reviews.*

6. That Congregationalists awakened more quickly, and with less anguish, to the need for theological adjustment to criticism is evident in the Samuel Davidson controversy, which took place in 1856. Davidson was removed from his post at Lancashire College for unsound views on the Pentateuch, but by a rather small two-vote majority of the college committee; see Chadwick, *Victorian Church,* 1:407. Drummond and Bulloch, *Church in Victorian Scotland,* 248-49, note that though it was proposed as early as 1839 to appoint a chair of

Biblical Criticism at each of the Scottish universities, the idea met stiff resistance. Edinburgh acquired one in 1847; but Aberdeen, Glasgow, and St. Andrews did not have them until the 1860s.

7. On the need for university reforms, particularly at Oxford and Cambridge, see the graphic remarks of G. M. Trevelyan, *British History in the Nineteenth Century and After, 1782-1919,* 2d ed. (1922; New York: Harper Torchbooks, 1966) 26-27, 355-56. Trevelyan concedes that university education in the years after 1825 was considerably better than in the worst years of the previous century, but this was hardly something to boast of. Only after the mid-century reforms, on which more will be said below, did real quality return to scholarship at both schools. Theological training was certainly no exception to the generally depressed state of learning; see Crowther, *Church Embattled,* 224-30.

8. See above, pp. 28-29.

9. Baur's ideas found an English presentation in rationalist R. W. Mackay's *Tübingen School and its Antecedents* (Hertford: n.p., 1863) in the early 1860s. His works, most notably the important *Church History of the First Three Centuries,* were not translated till the 1870s, the latter being published by the Theological Translation Fund in 1878.

10. T. & T. Clark Publishers, *T. & T. Clark's Catalogue* (Edinburgh, 1974) 57.

11. See above, p. 113.

12. "The Canon of the New Testament," *London Quarterly Review* 80 (July 1893) 261.

13. The comment appeared in Wace's *The Gospel and its Witnesses* (London: John Murray, 1883), which the *Guardian,* 1692, reviewed in 1883.

14. Even Peter Bayne, an intelligent, broad-minded critic who fully appreciated the importance of Strauss's criticism, confessed disappointment in the second Life. See "Strauss' New Life of Christ," *Fortnightly Review* 4 (March 15, 1866) 319.

15. *Church Embattled,* 212.

16. Ibid., 60.

17. W. F. Adeney, "The New Testament," in W. H. Bennett, et al., *Faith and Criticism: Essays by Congregationalists,* 3d ed. (London: Sampson Low, Marston & Co., Ltd., 1893) 65. A statement of very similar convictions came from A. M. Fairbairn in 1892: "I believe we have passed through a period of great critical activity as regards the New Testament, with most decided gain to Positive Christianity and evangelical truth. Fifty years ago negative criticism was just beginning. Twenty-five years ago the tide began to turn. The hard and doctrinaire principles of the Tübingen school seemed at first to carry all before them, but a more strictly historical school, both in Germany and in England, has arisen and supersedes the Tübingen, and we may now expect the most important and constructive results . . . . the clear gain is this, we know the New Testament as it was never known before," Selbie, *Life,* 226.

18. See the notice of this work in "Theology and Apologetics," *London Quarterly Review* 79 (January 1893) 372-73, where this feature in particular is mentioned. In a similar vein was A. B. Bruce, "F. C. Baur and his Theory of the Origins of Christianity and the New Testament" (Present Day Tracts, #38: London, 1885). This latter treatise provides a revealing exhibit of the connection between institutional structures and scholarship which we shall explore later in this chapter. John Dickie, *Fifty Years,* 88, observes that Bruce's chair at Glasgow, entitled "New Testament and Apologetics," was established under this peculiar combined title because of the threat posed by Baur and the need for an orthodox defense of the New Testament.

19. J. B. Lightfoot, preface to *The Epistles of St. Paul: A Revised Text with an Introduction* (n.p., 1865), quoted in Chadwick, *Victorian Church,* 2:70.

20. Hastings Rashdall, *Principles and Precepts,* ed. H. D. A. Major and F. L. Cross (Oxford: Basil Blackwell, 1927) 164. Similar testimonies may be found in Young, *Portrait of an Age,* 74; W. F. Howard, *The Romance of New Testament Scholarship* (London: Epworth Press, 1949) 55-83; and Neill, *Interpretation,* 32-60.

21. Chadwick notes that one of the book's most enthusiastic admirers was John Morley, in the *Fortnightly Review,* 16:504; see *Victorian Church,* 2:70.

22. The author of *Supernatural Religion* later revised his work to meet certain of Lightfoot's criticisms, but he was unsuccessful. In 1889 Westcott wrote to Hort: "S. R.'s correction of his blunders was, I think, the worst point about him. It may be of interest to know on what critical basis he formed his judgment, but his later defence of it has, I think, no interest whatever." Westcott to Hort, 9 January 1889, Arthur Westcott, *Life and Letters of Brooke Foss Westcott,* 2 vols. (London: Macmillan and Co., Limited, 1903), 2:60.

23. It is of course possible to read more drama into this battle of books than was actually the case. Both Neill, *Interpretation,* 36-37, and the editors of a Lightfoot memorial refer to the comments of the Dean of Lichfield, who had followed the controversy closely and was told in the early eighties by a well-known bookseller: "When the book *Supernatural Religion* appeared, it had an extraordinary reception. It was emphatically praised by the Reviewers, and its sale was so rapid that publishers could hardly produce it, in its successive editions, fast enough to meet the demand. But before the series of Dr. Lightfoot's articles was even approaching completion, the book was already a glut in the second-hand market." See George Eden and F. C. MacDonald, eds., *Lightfoot of Durham: Memories and Appreciations* (Cambridge: University Press, 1933) 9-10. Neill, *Interpretation,* 36, is incorrect in referring to the author as *J. A.* Cassels.

24. James Stalker, "Our Present Knowledge of the Life of Christ," *Contemporary Review* 77 (January 1900) 130. Stalker himself was by no means of the same opinion. He went on to state that this was in fact "a very innocent view of the state of scholarship."

25. This is treated in depth by Neill, *Interpretation,* 55; see also Dickie, *Fifty Years,* 86, where Lightfoot's work, along with Westcott's *History of the Canon,* is seen as furnishing the chief answer in Britain to Tübingen.

26. For this argument see E. A. Abbott's entry under "Gospels" in the *Encyclopedia Britannica,* 9th ed., vol. 10.

27. These were "External Evidence for the Authenticity and Genuineness of St. John's Gospel" and "Internal Evidence . . . Additional Notes," in J. B. Lightfoot, *Biblical Essays* (London: Macmillan & Co., 1893) 44-198. Incidentally, Lightfoot also singled out the disagreements of continental critics and their retreat from more radical views as a victory for traditional beliefs. After reviewing several of the leading negative critics of John he states: "we cannot fail to be struck with two facts: (1) the variety of their opinions; (2) their gradual retrogression from the extreme position taken up at first. The pressure of facts has compelled them to abandon one position after another, and to approximate more and more closely to the traditional view," *Biblical Essays,* 51.

28. On Westcott and Farrar see Joseph Clayton, *Leaders of the Church 1800-1900: Bishop Westcott* (London: A. R. Mowbray & Co., 1906) 34.

29. See above, p. 80.

30. See Edersheim, *Life and Times,* 1:463, n. 2, and the notes throughout.

31. Nicoll, *Church's One Foundation,* 65-66; see also Stalker, "Our Present Knowledge," 124-32; and Fairbairn, *Place of Christ,* 4.

32. Rudolph Bultmann, "New Testament and Mythology," in *Kerygma and Myth: A Theological Debate,* ed. Hans Werner Bartsch (1953; New York: Harper Torchbooks, 1961) 3-4. Harnack adopted a similar approach in *What is Christianity?,* tr. T. B. Saunders (London: Williams and Norgate, 1901) 278. According to Frederic Lichtenberger, *History of German Theology in the Nineteenth Century,* tr. and ed. W. Hastie (Edinburgh: T. & T. Clark, 1889) 18, intimations of this position can be found early on in the views of Wilhelm De Wette.

33. The two scholars who did venture into more radical paths of criticism, Samuel Davidson (a Congregationalist) in 1856 and William Robertson Smith (Scottish Free Church) in the 1870s and 1880s, were both removed from their posts. See Chadwick, *Victorian Church,* 1:407, and Glover, *Evangelical Nonconformists,* 117-29.

34. *Bible in the Church,* 31.

35. Discussions of the peculiar confederate character of the German Empire may be found in any number of modern European or national German histories, such as Charles Breunig, *The Age of Revolution and Reaction: 1789-1850* (New York: W. W. Norton, 1970) 180-87, 223-27, 230-51; and Norman Rich, *The Age of Nationalism and Reform,* 2d ed. (New York: W. W. Norton, 1977) 119-44, 216-27. A classic work is Hajo Holborn, *A History of Modern Germany,* vols. 2 and 3: *1648-1945* (New York: A. A. Knopf, 1959).

36. England and Scotland numbered roughly 18,000,000; Germany, not including German-speaking Austria, had a population of nearly 38,000,000. See Chadwick, *Victorian Church,* 2:218 on England; Philip Schaff, *Germany, Its Universities, Theology, and Religion* (Philadelphia: Lindsay & Blakiston, 1857) 129 for the German figures.

37. Schaff, *Germany,* 130-31.

38. Ibid., 32.

39. Ibid., 29-31.

40. Ibid., 50.

41. Charles E. McClelland, *State, Society, and University in Germany, 1700-1914* (Cambridge: University Press, 1980) 39.

42. Steven Turner, "University Reformers and Professorial Scholarship in Germany, 1760-1806," in Lawrence Stone, ed., *The University in Society,* vol. 2: *Europe, Scotland and the United States from the Sixteenth to the Twentieth Century* (Princeton: Princeton University Press, 1974) 504. See also Friedrich Paulsen, *The German Universities and University Study,* tr. Frank Thilly and William Elwang (New York: Charles Scribner's Sons, 1906) 44-50.

43. McClelland, *State, Society and University,* 73.

44. Ibid., 74.

45. *The German Universities for the Last Fifty Years* (Glasgow: David Bryce & Son, 1885) 80.

46. McClelland, *State, Society, and University,* 58.

47. Abraham Flexner, *Universities: American, English, German* (New York: Oxford University Press, 1930) 312.

48. Ibid., 316; see also Paulsen, *German Universities,* 48-55.

49. Flexner, *Universities,* 325-26. On the stimulus given to scholarly publication by German professors in the nineteenth century, see Turner, "University Reforms," 524, where he observes a significant change in the character of publications from the eighteenth to the nineteenth centuries.

50. Schaff, *Germany,* 47.

51. Ibid., 50-51; see also Crowther, *Church Embattled,* 45; Grant, *Bible in the Church,* 131.

52. McClelland, *State, Society and University,* 228-30, 288-89.

53. Schaff, *Germany,* 142, claims that in Prussia at least the influence of Enlightenment ideas was widespread among the middle and upper classes due chiefly to the favor of Frederick the Great.

54. See Harold Huston, "Some Factors in the Rise of Scientific New Testament Criticism," *Journal of Religion* 22 (January 1942) 89-95.

55. Ibid.

56. Schaff, *Germany,* 78.

57. W. G. Kümmel, *The New Testament,* 144.

58. Ibid., 281.

59. Glover, *Evangelical Nonconformists,* 140.

60. Chadwick, *Victorian Church,* 1:399; a more complete discussion of the weakened state of theological learning in Scotland during the early and mid-Victorian years can be found in Drummond and Bulloch, *Church in Victorian Scotland,* 240-65.

61. Chadwick, *Victorian Church,* 1:407.

62. Ibid., 376-77, 407.

63. Ibid., 257.

64. Flexner, *Universities,* 224; also Best, *Mid-Victorian Britain,* 150-51, 165.

65. Quoted in Robert McPherson, *Theory of Higher Education in Nineteenth-Century England* (Athens, Georgia: University of Georgia Press, 1959) 19; on Newman, see pp. 52-67. Martha McMackin Garland, *Cambridge Before Darwin: The Ideal of a Liberal Education, 1800-1860* (New York: Cambridge University Press, 1980), shows how pervasive this same ideal was at Cambridge till well into the mid-Victorian years.

66. Quoted in Chadwick, *Victorian Church,* 2:439-40.

67. Ibid, 2:442.

68. "Extracts from Report of her Majesty's Commissioners . . . Universities and Colleges at Oxford," in *The Universities in the Nineteenth Century,* ed. Michael Sanderson (London: Routledge & Kegan Paul, 1975) 95.

69. Flexner, *Universities,* 278.

70. "Extracts," 94.

71. Chadwick, *Victorian Church,* 1:395.

72. R. Farrar, *Life of Farrar,* 274.

73. See Chadwick, *Victorian Church,* 2:75-90, especially p. 83.

74. On Westcott's career, see *DNB,* s.v. "Westcott, Brooke Foss."

75. On this see especially Glover, *Evangelical Nonconformists,* 257; also pp. 145-46 and 60-112, where the reluctance of A. B. Davidson, Old Testament scholar at New College, Edinburgh, to publish his critical views furnishes a vivid illustration of this sensitivity among the Scots.

76. Quoted in Fenton Arthur Hort, *Life and Letters of Fenton John Anthony Hort,* 2 vols. (London: Macmillan, 1896), 2:312.

77. On this see my "Reception of *Ecce Homo,*" *Historical Magazine of the Protestant Episcopal Church* 46 (March 1977) 63-84.

78. *Evangelical Nonconformists,* 145-46.

79. Chadwick, *Victorian Church,* 2:59.

80. Ibid., 2:98.

81. Ibid.

82. Glover, *Evangelical Nonconformists,* 110-29.

83. Ibid., 200-03.

84. Ibid., 162-76.

85. Ibid., 176-86.

86. Ibid., 205-13.

87. On the importance of typology in a wide range of Victorian cultural endeavors see George Landow, *Victorian Types, Victorian Shadows* (London: Routledge & Kegan Paul, 1980) 15-63; on the lack of a constructive theology capable of incorporating the results of criticism, see Glover, *Evangelical Nonconformists,* 251-55.

88. *Evangelical Nonconformists,* 133.

89. Chadwick, *Victorian Church,* 2:106; later in the century these opponents gained some support from the gifted Assyriologist A. H. Sayce. His *"Higher Criticism" and the Verdict of the Monuments* (London: Christian Knowledge Society, 1894); his pamphlet *Archaeology and Criticism* (London: Francis Griffiths, 1909); and a later book *Monument Facts and Higher Critical Fancies* (London: Religious Tract Society, 1904) were products of an eccentric personal crusade designed to show how archaeology proved the Bible and disproved the higher critics. An examination of Sayce and his impact may be found in Barbara J. MacHaffie, " 'Monument Facts and Higher Critical Fancies': Archaeology and the Popularization of Biblical Criticism in Nineteenth Century Britain," *Church History* 50 (September 1981) 316-28.

90. Quoted in Glover, *Evangelical Nonconformists,* 120.

91. Darlow, *Nicoll,* 160.

92. Chadwick, *Victorian Church,* 2:106.

93. Glover, *Evangelical Nonconformists,* 110.

94. Chadwick, *Victorian Church,* 2:74.

95. Glover, *Evangelical Nonconformists,* 110; for an instance of this defensive case for criticism see R. F. Horton, *Inspiration and the Bible: An Inquiry,* 2d. ed. (London: T. Fisher Unwin, 1888), preface et passim. He argued, as did a number of others like A. S. Peake, that acceptance of criticism would help to purge those crudities and contradictions in the scriptures which made Christians vulnerable to attack from the sceptics; preface to First Edition, x-xi.

96. A. B. Bruce, "Christ in Modern Theology," *Contemporary Review* 63 (May 1893) 690.

97. Fairbairn, *Place of Christ,* 4.

98. Ibid., 286.

99. Consider, for example, Gore's remarks in "The Holy Spirit and Inspiration," in Gore ed., *Lux Mundi* (London: John Murray, 1889) 249: "At this stage," he wrote, the gospel records are "not so historical as to be absolutely without error, but historical in the general sense so as to be trustworthy." For Benson's attitude see A. C. Benson, *Life of Edward White Benson,* 2 vols.

(London: Macmillan and Co., 1900), 2:684-85, where there is a quote from *Fishers of Men:* "The Church of the present and of the coming day is bringing her sheaves home with her from the once faithlessly dreaded harvests of criticism." Fremantle's similar views may be found in his essay contributed to F. W. Farrar, ed., *The Bible and the Child* (London: James Clarke & Co., 1897) 107.

100. W. F. Adeney, in Farrar, *Bible and Child*, 85.

101. Chadwick, *Victorian Church*, 2:110.

5 A PARTING OF WAYS:
SCHOLARSHIP AND
POPULAR LIVES, 1900-1910

*The study of the life of Jesus is the snare in which
the theology of our time is destined to be taken
and destroyed.*

David Friedrich Strauss

"No characteristic of the theology of the second half of the nineteenth century has been more outstanding than its preoccupation with
the life of Christ." So wrote James Stalker in 1900 at the outset of a
retrospective essay on the course of gospel study throughout the late
Victorian Age.[1] The timing of the article was significant. It appeared
at precisely the turn of the century—in the *Contemporary Review* for
January, 1900; and the verdict Stalker reached as he looked back on
more than five decades of inquiry would have been difficult to dispute. By 1900 the life of Christ had spawned a literature greater than
that devoted to perhaps any other sacred subject, and there was little
hint that in the new century the flow of such works was likely to cease.
We have noticed that Stalker himself was a chief contributor to this
enterprise, publishing a Life which was among the largest of popular
successes.[2] As he assessed the situation after an interval of more than
twenty years since his own book, he gave an apt and revealing summation of the literature:

> Most of the lives of Christ—especially those published in English—have
> simply told the story in detail, from the idyllic scenes of the holy child-
> hood, through the labors and conflicts of the public ministry, to the
> tragedy of the crucifixion, taking occasion by the way perhaps to
> discuss, with more or less of fulness, the problem of miracles and the
> mode of teaching by parables.[3]

That this was indeed the pattern of most British Lives is evident from
the register of works that made an appearance in chapter three. Most
simply told the story, working from the premises of orthodox theology, trusting to the historicity of the gospels, and drawing freely from
books of travel, personal journeys to the Holy Land, and scholarship
on Jewish customs and social life.

The latest works, those which appeared at, or just after the turn of
the century, seemed moreover to signal no great departure from the
classic pattern. We may cite as a key instance William Sanday's article
on "Jesus Christ," contributed to volume two (1899) of Hastings'
Dictionary of the Bible.[4] Long enough to stand independently, "Jesus
Christ" was later printed and bound as a separate work under the title
Outlines of the Life of Christ.

Sanday's was a significant Life for several reasons. A younger man than any of the Cambridge three, he had gradually acquired the leadership of the moderately critical school as the senior men took up other ecclesiastical tasks; except for the aging Westcott, he was by 1899 Britain's foremost New Testament scholar. His judgments carried a mark of authority recognized well beyond the limits of the Church of England. His scholarship indicated that there could be no turning back from the embrace of the critics. The transition had been made with reluctance by many; but once in place, it could not be undone. A sensitive critic, Sanday made no attempt to defend what now seemed indefensible. His study of the gospels compelled him to give up passages dear to traditional piety. The troublesome infancy narratives and genealogies of Matthew and Luke were relegated to a chapter on "Supplemental Matter," where it was made clear that the larger record of the gospels did not stand or fall with these inferior and inaccurate traditions.[5] Jesus in Sanday's view shared the primitive beliefs of his day about the cosmos, beliefs the mind of modernity is compelled to declare erroneous. Some miracles were exaggerated, while others had been drawn up in imitation of Old Testament narratives and prophecies.[6] The passages surrounding the institution of the Eucharist were unclear and disclosed "lacunae in our knowledge." Duplicate narratives, such as the feedings of the thousands, were very likely duplicate traditions of the same event, not accounts of several events. Though others before him had made some of these concessions, Sanday made more. Beyond that, there was in the style of the *Outlines* a certain restraint, a conscious scholarly distance from the topic. The *Outlines* was written in a measured, judicious, even conciliatory manner; it had inhibitions one could not find in the free-flowing narratives of Farrar and Edersheim.

Yet in keeping with the British style, Sanday carried his doubt and dissections only up to a certain point. For all of his conciliatory tone, his concessions had a way of turning up only on peripheral matters. Where the crucial issues of orthodox theology and critical certitude came into play, the *Outlines,* like its predecessors, once again reassured. And in the process it managed to reproduce with few changes the portrait of Christ which half a century of conservative biblical study had made thoroughly familiar to church and populace. "Even if we make to negative criticism larger concessions than we have a right to make," Sanday insisted,

> there will still remain in the Gospel picture ineffaceable features which presuppose and demand that estimate of the Person of Christ which we alone call in the strict sense Christian.[7]

By this he meant the miraculous, yet fully human Christ, the Son of God incarnate in flesh, whom the gospels presented faithfully as a teacher and savior for all mankind. With a few amendments, the view of Sanday was the view of Lightfoot and Farrar and the conventional piety of several decades earlier. It was evidence, in fact, that after nearly a half century of acquaintance with criticism little had really changed. Sanday was convinced that after the siege engines of the critics had done their work on the gospels, a few of the outworks might have to be abandoned, but the citadel was quite secure. The evangelists—John as well as the synoptics—gave an essentially reliable history of Jesus, of his ministry which lasted over a period of at least two years, of his teaching and claim to be Messiah in a sense never really understood by the Jews of his day, and of his rejection, his death, his miraculous resurrection and sacrifice for the sins of men.[8]

Sanday's posture was shared by others like G. H. Gilbert, whose *Student's Life of Jesus* appeared in 1896. Despite its title the *Student's Life* was not designed only for the young or uninformed; it touched, with similar verdicts, on the issues raised by Sanday. Other noteworthy contributions included George Matheson's picturesque devotional volumes, *Studies in the Portrait of Christ* (1899), W. J. Dawson's *The Man Christ Jesus* (1901; new edition 1904), and J. H. Rigg's *Scenes and Studies in the Ministry of our Lord* (1902).[9] Through none were professional critics in the mold of Sanday, each of these authors worked from similar orthodox assumptions and presented a Jesus who mirrored the traditional faith of middle-class believers. In working with the gospels they felt themselves still to be within the realm of authentic history. In the 1880s and 90s this confidence reassured the public and played a key role in the transition made by the churches to an acceptance of higher criticism. In 1900 there was no sign that this confidence had waned. A Methodist critic, surveying the most recent attempts, recorded the prevailing view:

> The close study of the gospels can only deepen the impression of their historical trustworthiness; while a loving and patient scrutiny of the portrait of Jesus will both create and confirm loyalty to the conviction of the Christian Church, which through all ages has adored and exalted Jesus as the true Son of God.[10]

Among orthodox believers there seemed good reason to be cheerful. For nearly a generation in Britain, longer elsewhere, biblical critics had enjoyed the license to dig, yet in the case of the gospels the excavation had only led, again and again, to historical bedrock. It was true that Old Testament study had not gone as well, particularly since Wellhausen's work on the Pentateuch. Yet precisely for that reason, it was crucial to learn from the newest Lives that the churches' faith in the New Testament records was much better placed. People found comfort in learning that the life of Christ, at least, stood on firm historical ground. Things were not as they seemed, however. When observers wrote buoyantly about the state of gospel criticism in 1900, they could not have known that they were inscribing a memorial to the end of an era. The comment above might in fact be taken as the epitaph on an age of confidence that was shortly to disappear. Within the space of a decade the scholar who had regarded the gospels chiefly as history and educated himself on the Lives of Farrar and Geikie and Edersheim was to find his confidence assailed repeatedly by a new generation of far more sceptical New Testament critics. He would find also that biblical science itself had become more complex; that the ranks of older scholars who believed as he did were thinning rapidly due to death or defection; that the mood of theologians was turning hostile; and that in a short time scepticism would reach the point where the very existence of Jesus would be denied and seriously debated. Finally, he would discover that the culture as a whole had evolved habits and forms uncongenial to the religious literature so widely read in earlier years; that the leisure and occasions for retelling the story of Christ had diminished; that new authors could not hope to command the wide public attention that came so easily to *Ecce Homo* or Farrar and his disciples. Between 1900 and 1910 the currents of society and scholarship which blended so well to produce the successful Lives of earlier generations began now to pull apart. The effect of this separation was to leave study of the life of Christ a very different thing from what it formerly had been.

These large changes in post-Victorian thought and culture need closer scrutiny. How did new theological and critical trends affect those who wrote Lives? How did cultural shifts affect those who read them? After 1900 there were still those in the churches and academies who insisted upon working in the same fashion as the older authors, but the slow evolution of society and a sudden scepticism among the critics began to bring on changes that none could for long fail to recognize. Chief among these was the fact that a Life of Christ which satisfied both scholar and populace became exceedingly difficult to write. Increasingly after 1900, the technical critic of the gospels was to travel one route; the popular writer of devotion was to take another. In a curious way, and under new forms, the old division between harmonist and devotionalist began to reassert itself. The age when a single writer could hope to win both the interest of the ordinary reader and the approval of the critical scholar—the age of Seeley and Farrar, of Fairbairn's *Studies* and Edersheim's *Life and Times*—began to slip off the horizon.

1. Scholars and Scepticism

The first ominous signal of the new era was the *Encyclopaedia Biblica*, a multi-volume summation of the century's work in biblical study edited by A. Sutherland Black and the eccentric Anglican Old Testament scholar, T. K. Cheyne.[11] Quite unlike Hastings's *Dictionary*, published slightly before it, the *Encyclopaedia* bore liberal markings. It was dedicated to the memory of W. Robertson Smith, the most controversial of all British critics, several of whose articles appeared in updated form in its pages. It had too a more international flavor, with contributions from figures like Wellhausen, Schürer and Adolph Harnack on key subjects. Despite this, volume one, "A to D," caused little stir. W. T. Davison of the conservative *London Quarterly* was positively gratified with the result. "Every student," he wrote of both the *Encyclopaedia* and Hastings's *Dictionary*, "must gratefully acknowledge how much toil, study, patient planning, and minute, watchful, untiring care has gone to the preparation of these invaluable works."[12]

This was in 1900. In 1901 volume two appeared and sent a shock of alarm and dismay through the ranks of traditional orthodoxy. Among several disturbing articles, the rock of greatest offense was the entry by Paul Schmiedel of Zurich under "Gospels." This was a superb and lengthy sketch of where gospel research stood at the end of the century. It provided analyses of the Johannine problem, the tangled synoptic question, and the theory of Marcan priority as well as lucid, succinct discussions of date, provenance, and historicity of the sources. At the end of each section, however, lay a stark negative conclusion. Jesus' discourses had been set in artificial contexts; pivotal sayings like the Lord's prayer were recorded in dubious fashion; miracles grew by extension from parables or, as Strauss said, from the example of Old Testament accounts; John was unhistorical; and even the synoptics could only rarely be trusted. "The chronological framework," argued Schmiedel,

> must be classed among the most untrustworthy elements in the gospels. Not only are the data often quite vague—a defect for which we could not blame the evangelists if they had no precise information; often it is impossible to have any confidence, when Mt. so frequently says "then" (*tote*), "on that day" (*en ekeinē tē hēmera*) or the like or when Mk. says "straightway" (*euthus*), the event really followed on what immediately precedes it in the narrative.[13]

This sort of rigorous doubt might have been disturbing enough to the preacher or theologian, but it was disastrous to anyone who hoped to embark, in the older fashion, on a Life of Christ. How was one even to begin if the sources had been pulverized into a heap of fragments utterly without connection?

After coming near to total scepticism, Schmiedel fell back on nine synoptic "pillar" passages, only one of which exceeded two verses in length and all of which fit ill with the Christ of traditional orthodoxy.[14] Mark 10:17, 18, for example, where Jesus seemed to say he was neither good nor God, was one of the chosen fragments. These passages, Schmiedel insisted,

> might be called the foundation-pillars for a truly scientific life of Jesus. . . . they . . . prove that he really did exist, and that the gospels contain at least some absolutely trustworthy facts concerning him. If passages of this kind were wholly wanting in them it would be impossible to prove to a sceptic that any historic value whatever was to be assigned to the gospels; he would be in a position to declare the picture of Jesus contained in them to be purely a work of phantasy, and could remove the person of Jesus from the field of history.[15]

Here, plainly, was scepticism on an alarming scale. If this was how one purchased certitude about Jesus, there could be little doubt it had come at an enormous price.

Schmiedel's article quickly became notorious for its attack on the gospels, and more conservative spokesmen fought back. Davison of the *London Quarterly* hastened a retreat from his earlier approval of the *Encyclopaedia*:

> It is the trustworthiness of the narratives, at least in their main outlines, which forms the chief practical issue for most Christians, and it has long been made clear to careful observers that much current "criticism," whilst professedly busy with its own work of determining date and authorship, had virtually prejudged the whole question of credibility, and would not accept the gospel story at any price.[16]

To hand back the mere fact of Jesus after biblical science had drained his life of all sequence, his personality and teaching of all substance was, in Davidson's view, not unlike conceding defeat and calling it victory. Had Schmiedel's article appeared alone, it might not have caused so much alarm, but in the *Encyclopaedia* it carried the editorial blessing of a prominent figure in the Church of England. That it took a place alongside entries from orthodox Christian scholars throughout the nation was more than even broad-minded men found palatable. It violated the code of the gentleman-scholar.

Nor was Schmiedel the only stumbling block. There were other disturbing articles by the well-known scourge of traditionalists E. A. Abbott and by, of all men, A. B. Bruce, long honored as the Scottish Presbyterian complement of the Cambridge three. Though not so sceptical as Schmiedel, Bruce confessed in the article on "Jesus" that even the synoptics by no means "possess a uniform degree of historic probability."[17] He offended even more by silence than by his speech. His portrait emphasized strongly the ethical side of Christ, his splendid teachings and supreme moral example, but included little on his miracles or divinity and virtually nothing on such theologically significant matters as atonement and resurrection. The following typified Bruce's hedging, half-hearted, evasive manner:

> There is one thing about which we may have comfortable certainty. Whether miraculous or not, whether the works of a mere man, or of one who is a man and more, these healing acts are a revelation of the love of Jesus, a manifestation of his "enthusiasm of humanity."[18]

Such tactics could not pass the scrutiny of more conservative minds; Davison for one deeply regretted that the new scepticism had been "emphasized by the eloquent silence of Dr. Bruce."[19]

Presbyterian W. Robertson Nicoll, by no means an unthinking conservative, was also dissatisfied. In his own widely read *British Weekly* he wrote grimly of the new situation:

> For many years the Church of Christ in this country, and particularly in Scotland, has been agitated by disputes over the Old Testament. They are not over, but the end is in sight. Now the New Testament is once more thrown into the furnace, and with it the Christian religion itself. It was inevitable . . . we have in the new volume of the *Encyclopaedia Biblica* a thoroughgoing criticism applied to the New Testament. . . . It is of no avail to lift up hands in horror. The critics have to be met. If they are not frankly encountered the door of faith will be closed on multitudes.[20]

Like Davison, Nicoll singled out the articles by Schmiedel and Bruce. In connection with the former he claimed that the *Encyclopaedia* embodies "a deliberate attempt to obliterate Christ."[21] Of Bruce he was more reluctant to speak, as the article had appeared after the great Scottish critic had died. Still there was no mistaking Nicoll's keen disappointment. "If the article had been unsigned there would have been little difficulty in concluding that the author had abandoned the supernatural element in the life of Jesus."[22] The memory of Bruce's once-fervent orthodoxy opposed such a conclusion, but the movement of his mind seemed clear. "Those who followed Dr. Bruce's career must have marked with deep regret his gradual descent to naturalism."[23]

The *Encyclopaedia* was not the sole source of disturbing new views. Nicoll's review also embraced Alexander Robinson's *Saviour in the Newer Light* (1895), Cheyne's "Few Things Needful" in the *Expositor* for April, 1901, and the United Free Churchman James Moffatt's *Historical New Testament*.[24] What annoyed Nicoll about each of these

three was that their criticism emanated "from the bosom of the orthodox Church."[25] Moffatt, for example, had reasoned that "unconscious
affinities and conscious prejudices" so affected the evangelists as to
cast serious doubt on the historical value of their narratives. To this
Nicoll replied,

> It is obvious that if this is admitted the conception of a personal relation
> and a personal debt to the Lord Jesus Christ, in which the essence of
> Christianity has been supposed to lie, becomes practically impossible.
> We do not know enough of Christ historically. Our ignorance of His life
> is too complete for any possible relation to Him.[26]

Quite apart from theological snares in the new views, however, what
lay beyond dispute was their devastating effect on the enterprise of
writing a Life of Jesus, at least as it had been carried on in the previous century. It was natural enough to attempt a Life from the four
gospels regarded as in the main reliable; it was still possible from the
three synoptics, supposing there was reason to doubt John; but it was
futile even to venture such a task on the basis of the nine "pillar" texts
which the scepticism of a Schmiedel left to impoverished biographers.

Davison and Nicoll were not alone in their protests; they were joined
by others whose views were conservative in no blind or unthinking
way.[27] Nevertheless, the very sources of opposition, popular journalists like Nicoll and spokesmen like Davison, slightly out of their field,
disclosed that orthodoxy was coming into danger on another flank.[28]
The ranks of authoritative moderate criticism were thinning rapidly at
the top. Twenty-five years earlier one might have looked to Lightfoot
or Westcott for a knowledgeable orthodox reply to the sceptics, but in
just over a decade death had seized each of the Cambridge three:
Lightfoot in 1889, Hort in 1892, and the venerable Westcott in 1901,
the very year of the *Encyclopaedia*. The distinguished Methodist
critic, W. F. Moulton, had died two years before the close of the century, and among the Scots Bruce died in 1900, though clearly his views
had by this time shifted to a point where it was just as well if he were
no longer around to voice them. After more than two decades of
ascendance, moderate criticism found itself suddenly leaderless.

Among younger gospel critics with a tie to orthodoxy H. B. Swete
and William Sanday were the most likely successors to the Cambridge
three, but to know their scholarly styles was to know that this could
never be. Swete did succeed Westcott after a fashion, assuming the
Regius Professorship of Divinity at Cambridge upon the latter's elevation to the see of Durham.[29] As an academic and university officer he
was an able man, who managed to prove wrong those who doubted
the wisdom of his appointment. But Westcott had been bigger than his

offices, a man of strong, sympathetic mind, with national stature and a reputation as a first-rank textual critic and biblical expositor. Swete on the other hand was shy, fastidious, and reserved—a meticulous scholar who sensed complexity where his predecessor found broad, reassuring truths. Oxford's Sanday, as we shall see shortly, was of similar temperament; vacillating and cautious as a critic, he did not find it easy to lead a campaign, or to achieve that difficult union of assertive faith and credible scholarship which marked the Cambridge three.[30] In the course of his attack on the *Encyclopaedia,* Robertson Nicoll looked back wistfully to the days of Lightfoot's "terrible answer" to *Supernatural Religion* and regretted that his work had been "practically ignored by the new critics."[31] He may also have looked back because he knew he would find no Lightfoot in the present, because Sanday, Swete, and the orthodox of the new generation were only too ready to retreat from positions earlier taken, to revise, qualify, and, as the century progressed, bow to the verdicts of the Germans. The critic who perhaps came closest to filling the empty place was F. C. Burkitt of Cambridge, but he was still a younger man whose books were just beginning to appear after 1900 and who, in any case, was the first to admit that the tangled questions of gospel history admitted of no simple solutions, orthodox or otherwise.[32]

The example of Burkitt, moreover, reminds us not to make too much of persons. He if anyone was a thorough critic cast in the mold of Lightfoot; if authoritative conclusions were to be found, Burkitt was patient and thorough enough to reach them; but with each year biblical study had been growing more complex, turning into a science very different from what it had been a generation before. Synoptic study in particular had become so tangled that where the patience of the Cambridge critics once led to reasonably definitive verdicts, the industry of a Burkitt or Sanday led only to ever larger questions. Already in 1898, when Armitage Robinson spoke to the Church Congress on the synoptic problem, he made the situation quite clear: "in England," he wrote, "so far as published work is concerned, we are at the very beginning—the foundations have not yet been laid."[33] His thoughts were proved right during the following decade at Oxford, where William Sanday's seminar full of gifted young New Testament critics required several years of work on the intricate relations of Mark, "Q," and the two other evangelists before it yielded in 1911 the still quite undefinitive *Oxford Studies in the Synoptic Problem.*[34] Clearly the discipline was drifting steadily toward the specialist, the monographer, and the fastidious student who set aside large issues to become master of small ones.

Further evidence of this shift to minutiae and finer studies can be found in the rise of the specialized theological journal. In earlier years religious reviews like the *British* or *London Quarterly,* the *Church Quarterly* or *Dublin Review* took up a wide variety of subjects from literature, travel, and politics to theology and biblical criticism. The secular literary reviews like the *Edinburgh* and the *Quarterly* recipro-cated by speaking just as freely on religious and theological topics. By the end of the century this had begun to change. The secular press became more hesitant to take up the difficult technical questions of New Testament criticism or theological thought; on the religious side these matters were taken up in a new forum, the professional academic journal. Among the earliest successful publications of this sort was the *Expositor,* begun in 1875 for the purpose of providing pastors with the results of the most recent exegetical and textual study.[35] Then at the turn of the century came several periodicals of the more strictly scientific sort: the *Journal of Theological Studies* in 1899; the *Hibbert Journal* in 1902; the *Review of Theology and Philosophy* in 1905.[36] The *Hibbert* made the listing of new works in the theological sub-disciplines a regular feature, and for ready reference classified each new entry according to a numbered code. Narrow in scope, these organs were clearly designed for the specialist; they took up texts and studies, allowed room for discussion of earlier contributions, and in general made it their purpose not to advocate so much as to inform and inquire.

In a sense this change was by no means peculiar to the study of sacred literature. G. M. Trevelyan in his wise and memorable essay *Clio, A Muse* was able to detect the same slow transition from literature to specialized science in all historical study as practiced in the Victorian age.[37] As the century progressed, the day of the colorful and splendid literary historians—of Carlyle and Froude, Macaulay, Lecky and Green—began to fade. In their place came an ever-growing army of lesser but often more precise students, the academicians whose monument was to be found not in epic narratives, but in the greyer grandeur of the *Cambridge Modern History.*[38] The quarrel over the merits of these two styles, which continues under various forms to our own day, may here be left aside. In the biblical sciences of the late nineteenth century, it is hard to avoid the conclusion that such a shift was both inevitable and necessary. Yet however that may be, one thing is certain: it did not augur well for synthesis and comprehension, the processes so essential to the writing of a full-scale Life of Christ.

If historians were creating problems on one side, theologians after 1900 were beginning to raise them on another. Just as scholarship verged on pronouncing the biography of Jesus unattainable, theology was beginning to call it unnecessary. The first of several schools which took an unfavorable view of the older Lives of Christ can be traced to earlier decades, when new ideas took root at Oxford among younger men under the tutelage of the neo-Hegelian philosopher T. H. Green. Green, who held the Whyte Professorship of Moral Philosophy from 1878 to his early death in 1882, was not a very public figure. His style was cryptic and unengaging, and his religious views departed measurably from orthodox belief. Yet his deep concern for ethical questions and his religious vision left a lasting impression on those who came under his sway. His influence was particularly strong in the case of the young Anglo-Catholic clerics—J. R. Illingworth, H. Scott Holland, and others—who later became identified as the *Lux Mundi* group. His impact on young liberals like Hastings Rashdall was scarcely less significant.[39] "He it was," said Holland of his mentor, "who shook us all free from the bondage of cramping philosophies and sent us out once again on the high pilgrimage toward Ideal Truth."[40] Holland's phrasing was apt. As in Hegel so in Green and his Oxford disciples, the philosophical stance was idealist. In reaction against the growing appeal of agnosticism and scientific naturalism, Green contended that ideas were fully as real as physical objects; that the world is finally explicable only in terms of mind, or spirit, not matter; that God and the human soul, as the highest entities in this ideal order, are of utmost and eternal importance. It followed from all of this that the value of physical facts and of mere historical events was secondary; they were less important in themselves than as vehicles for the transport of ideas. By means of external events certain ideal truths are conveyed from God to man, or from one man to the next.

The implication of this for life-of-Jesus research was not far to seek. Green's views tended to exercise the same effect on his disciples as Hegel's did upon Strauss and Baur. Since concept mattered more than event, the idea of a Christ, of a divine man bringing together both God and his creatures, was far more crucial than the accidental circumstance of history which suggested it. It was useless on these terms to inquire about the social and cultural background of Jesus' life as writers of Lives had done with such care and energy. To guess at the color of his robes, to seek out the customs of his people was mere antiquarianism—interesting perhaps, but of little relevance to real religion. Indeed, it was questionable to Green whether the so-called historical evangelists—the synoptics—were even to be preferred to the Fourth:

> More, probably, than two generations after St. Paul had gone to his rest, there arose a disciple, whose very name we know not (for he sought not his own glory and preferred to hide it under the repute of

another), who gave that final spiritual interpretation to the person of
Christ, which has for ever taken it out of the region of history and of the
doubts that surround all past events, to fix it in the purified conscience
as the immanent God.[41]

Here for the idealists was the vital element of faith. Even if by
some remarkable feat of historical reconstruction we could surmount
"the doubts that surround the past" and know for certain Christ's
life and times, that would all be of less value than the pure spirituality
of St. John. Elsewhere Green put his case in the form of a dilemma.
"There is an inner contradiction in that conception of faith which
makes it a state of mind involving peace with God and love towards all
men, and at the same time makes its object that historical work of
Christ of which our knowledge depends on evidence of uncertain
origin and value."[42]

It should not be supposed that all, or even any, of Green's disciples
pressed the dilemma this far. Henry Scott Holland for one certainly
did not.[43] Yet as a style of thought, a new spirit, the stress on eternal
idea as opposed to historical fact became an attractive option; as it
did, it undermined the rationale for Lives of Jesus. On the principles
of the new philosophy, which virtually removed Christ from the plane
of history, the older Lives simply had no purpose.

Idealism had gained a public face as early as 1889, when it became
evident that it had served as the inspiration of the *Lux Mundi* manifesto. In the following two decades, and particularly after 1900, it
continued to draw the interest of a number of thoughtful minds.[44] Its
attractiveness as a system capable of releasing believers from the perils
of historical science was by then unmistakable. In some cases it provided a warrant for those who pressed for a distinction between the
"Jesus of history" and the "Christ of faith."[45]

Alongside the scepticism among New Testament critics, the decline
of the moderate school, the problems of specialization, and new theological questioning, there must be placed still another set of factors
hostile to Lives of Christ. Scholarship on the continent, now more
than ever observed in Britain, had itself taken dramatic new turns,
several of them directly counter to interest in the historical Jesus. Of
the new movements perhaps the least antagonistic was the theology of
Albrecht Ritschl, which had acquired a formidable circle of German
advocates that by the end of the century included Adolph Harnack,
Wilhelm Herrmann, Heinrich Weinel, and Hans Wendt. The position of the Ritschlians on the life of Christ was somewhat ambivalent.
Most of them followed Harnack in casting out the Fourth Gospel and
leaning heavily on the synoptics, where they were prepared to find
much more of a historical distillate than critics like Schmiedel allowed.

At this point, however, theological considerations intervened. For Ritschl's followers it was the teaching of Jesus, rather than his life, that held the key to Christian experience. The imperishable kernel of the gospel was not the record of Jesus' days as he grew from infancy to maturity and embarked on a course of teaching and healing till his opponents turned on him and secured his death. These factors were secondary to his role as supreme prophet, the revealer of the will of God. As with all prophets, it is the mind, the teaching of the master that we treasure, not the accidental details of his life. Since Jesus bore a certain divinely inspired attitude toward the world, his God, and his fellow man, that is what people should seek to re-create in their own lives if they are to be his disciples. "Jesus," as Harnack put it in his widely read *What is Christianity?*, "desired no other attachment to Himself, than what is contained in the keeping of his commandments."[46]

The effect of these views on the older sort of research into the life of Christ was not encouraging. If the teaching, the mind of the master, was what counted, the life of Christ was no more important to the Christian than the life of Plato to the Platonist. To know the thought of the master—his ideas—as left in his proverbs or discourses was quite sufficient.

Although Ritschl seems never to have acquired a wide following in Britain, critics like Harnack often figured prominently in theological discussion. James Stalker felt in 1900 that the movement was already beginning to affect studies of the life of Christ in Britain.[47] Ritschl acquired a very sympathetic interpreter in the respected Congregationalist theologian A. E. Garvie. His *Ritschlian Theology* (1899) gave a considerably more favorable estimate of the school than did the two Scotsmen who wrote on the subject: James Orr in an 1897 work of the same title and James Denney in *Studies in Theology* (1894). That Garvie appreciated the Ritschlian approach was even more evident from a series of essays he contributed to the *Expositor* and later published separately as *Studies in the Inner Life of Christ* (1907).[48]

This latter work is of special interest as it demonstrates vividly the effect of the Ritschlian presuppositions when applied to Lives of Jesus. What Garvie chose to trace was not the course of external events in Jesus' life, but the shaping of a unique—indeed uniquely divine—personality. In Jesus, he contended, men have found a mind perfect in consciousness of God, in moral sensitivity, and in surrender to the will of the Father. His unity with God was matched, moreover, by his sympathy with man, a bond so complete as to bring about reconciliation between the Maker and his creatures.

It is by no legal fiction that the iniquities of us all were laid upon Him, that He was reckoned among transgressors, and that God made Him to be sin for us. It was by an organic union, a vital self-identification, a tender devoted sympathy with the race, that He made its sin, guilt, shame and curse vicariously His own.[49]

Obviously even to get this far one must concede a certain minimum historical core to the gospels. The words, or logia, of Christ, for example, were important to Garvie, and he defended them vigorously against the thoroughgoing scepticism of Schmiedel. Yet the larger web of historical sequence—the threads of miracles, meetings with disciples, clashes with opponents, and journeys to Jerusalem which formed the staple of former Lives—he allowed to fade far into the background. The materials from which Farrar and Geikie had built long descriptive chapters he dismissed quickly in his preface, and with a hint of impatience.

It is the mind, heart, and will of Jesus as revealed in his words and works that the writer seeks to understand; enough is being written about the scenery, the upholstery, and drapery of the life of Jesus; an exaggerated importance is attached to a knowledge of contemporary custom and costume; even the ideas and ideals of His environment, important as a knowledge of these is, do not explain Jesus.[50]

Where the views of Ritschl had left their mark, the life of Christ obviously was not a subject wholly without interest; but there could be no doubt that the nature of the inquiry was sharply changed.

Another continental figure who deserves mention is France's brilliant Abbé A. F. Loisy. Although (or perhaps because) he was suspect in the Catholic communion even before the turn of the century, his work had won a measure of attention in Britain.[51] His response to Harnack in *L'Évangile et l'église* (1902) was translated into English within a year, and while hardly reassuring to fellow Catholics, it established him at once as a penetrating and significant student of dogma and its development. While his reputation rose in Protestant circles, he set to work on intensive studies in the gospels. *Le Quatrième Évangile* (1903) placed him clearly in the camp of those sceptical of the historicity of St. John. "The Christ of the synoptics," he wrote, "is historic, but he is not God; the Johannine Christ is divine, but he is not historic."[52] Bold as it was, such an assertion at least seemed reassuring in regard to the first three evangelists. But when he began to interrogate the synoptics in detail, Loisy's earlier confidence here too began to fade. In *Les Évangiles synoptiques* (1905-1906) numerous incidents in the gospel narratives thought to be historic succumbed to his cross-examination. By 1910, when *Jesus et la tradition évangelique* appeared, this scepticism had gone even further; here he declared from the outset "We must now renounce writing the Life of Jesus. All critics agree in recognizing that the materials are insufficient for such an enterprise."[53] Loisy did think there was historical material in the gospels, but the Jesus he reached, as a kind of residue after the acids of scepticism had done their work, was a distant, enigmatic figure. Part ethical advisor, part apocalyptic seer, he bore little resemblance to the Jesus of most British Lives. The nearest thing to him, according to one critic, was the unbalanced Christ of Ernest Renan.[54]

Loisy was too individual a thinker to acquire a school of disciples in either Britain or his own country, but his studies added yet another formidable name to the list of critics increasingly doubtful about the historic quality of the gospels. Moreover, if in France Loisy was somewhat a lonely figure, Germany by the end of the century presented an entirely different prospect. Here the chorus of negative opinion grew stronger and more strident with each passing year. We have already noted the attack on the evangelists led by the Swiss critic Schmiedel; we have seen too the shift from Christ's life to his teaching initiated by the Ritschlians. As the decade wore on, similar questions began to issue from newer scholars and other schools. Paul Wernle's analysis of the evangelical record, entitled *Die Quellen des Lebens Jesu* (1905), set down bluntly the verdict that was becoming a commonplace: "On the basis of . . . the oldest sources we can write no biography, no so-called Life of Jesus."[55] Such doubts were in turn reinforced by spokesmen such as Otto Pfliederer of the *Religionsgeschichtlicheschule*. In *The Early Christian Conception of Christ* Pfliederer further weakened trust in the evangelists by stressing their tendency, like other ancients, to shape history according to religious myths.[56]

Even so, in Germany the severest blow was yet to fall. The theory of "consistent eschatology," according to which Jesus was viewed as a first-century visionary, wholly immersed in Jewish apocalyptic thought, had been in the field since its striking formulation in Johannes Weiss's monograph of 1892 on the preaching of Jesus.[57] The argument was slow to persuade on the continent, and almost unknown in Britain, until it acquired the powerful advocacy of Albert Schweitzer. In 1901 Schweitzer had published *Das Messianitäts- und Leidensgeheimnis: Eine Skizze des Lebens Jesu,* a work which in more thorough fashion made Weiss's original case for Jesus as apocalyptic visionary. This book was followed in 1906 by *Von Reimarus zu Wrede,* the monumental survey which won Schweitzer enduring fame as a theologian and appeared in English as *The Quest of the Historical Jesus.* There could be little doubt of the *Quest*'s epic proportions. In its pages Schweitzer ranged over more than a century of biblical study, brilliantly ordering his material, placing key figures like Strauss and Bruno Bauer, charting both breakthroughs and blind paths, and forcibly pressing his case for apocalyptic. The book was almost as rich in energy, sarcasm, and colorful style as it was in lucid analysis and grasp of its subject. It appealed to more than the specialist.

Although the *Quest* was not translated until 1910, the best critics in Britain recognized immediately the importance of Schweitzer, even while they disagreed with his thesis. William Sanday made it a point to disseminate Schweitzer's views as he had those of other Germans; and F. C. Burkitt of Cambridge was responsible for the translation.[58]

The bearing of Schweitzer on life-of-Jesus inquiry in Britain was twofold, and in neither way very reassuring. In the first place the chief contention of the eschatological school was that Jesus belonged almost inextricably to his own times. Schweitzer was convinced that if one looked honestly at the gospels, without importing the more congenial notions developed by later theology, one would find Jesus a very foreign figure indeed. The first-century Jesus believed in miracles, demons, and prophecy in a sense much more literal than even quite conservative modern Christians were likely to allow. He believed in the immediate end of the world during his lifetime; he came later to think that his own death would usher in this world cataclysm; and he taught no enduring moral code, but an *"Interims-ethik"*—an ethic of the moment—to be observed while men waited passively for the great act of God at the apocalypse. However we turn him, argued Schweitzer, Jesus is a figure almost inscrutable to the modern mind, whether Christian or not. His world, his times were so different as to make most modern interpretations of him arbitrary and useless.

If historical criticism had shown anything about Jesus, ran the *Quest's* persuasive conclusion, it had demonstrated that

> He will not be a Jesus Christ to whom the religion of the present can ascribe, according to its long-cherished custom, its own thoughts and ideas, as it did with the Jesus of its own making. Nor will He be a figure which can be made by a popular historical treatment so sympathetic and universally intelligible to the multitude. The historical Jesus will be to our time a stranger and an enigma.[59]

Schweitzer made his case most brilliantly against the authors of "liberal" Lives, who sought to re-create Jesus in terms of the ethical ideals and anti-supernaturalist bias of the later nineteenth century; but his arguments applied with equal force against the orthodox, supernaturalist Jesus who dominated Britain's Lives. Both were creations of later theology and modern sentiment; neither resembled the brooding apocalyptic seer who was the Jesus of history. On Schweitzer's terms, most all of the literature devoted with such scholarly energy, loving sentiment, and sincere piety to the life of Jesus was an exercise in futility.

Of course one could quarrel with Schweitzer's verdict, and at first in Britain many did. In his work on *The Kingdom of God in the Teaching of Jesus*, Norman Perrin has shown how at the Oxford Congress of 1908 the leading British critics without exception sought either to deny the influence of apocalyptic on the mind of Jesus, or to show that if he had used apocalyptic language, he did so in a sense other than that understood by his contemporaries.[60] But even assuming one could make progress on this unpromising front, apologists for the older Lives still faced the attack upon the sources, which Schweitzer did nothing to weaken. On the contrary, it was Schweitzer who insisted that scepticism be carried to the last refuge of the apologists: the gospel of Mark. In the face of continued assaults on the credibility of the evangelists, conservative spokesmen turned more and more to the Second Gospel. Since most critics very nearly agreed that this was the earliest account, Mark could be regarded as the historical kernel, the one point of certitude from which a Life of Christ might emerge. In Britain this conviction seems to have figured in the design of two newer Lives, which confined themselves strictly to the earliest source: W. H. Bennett's *Life of Christ According to St. Mark* (1907), and J. M. Thompson's *Jesus According to St. Mark*.[61] To Schweitzer this was at best a temporary refuge. For the purpose of discerning an extended sequence of historical events, Mark was no better than any other gospel. Here, as on so many matters, Schweitzer made his case with uncommon candor. "Formerly," he wrote in the shrewd imagery that enlivens the *Quest*,

> it was possible to book through-tickets at the supplementary-psychological-knowledge office which enabled those travelling in the interests of Life-of-Jesus construction to use express trains, thus avoiding the inconvenience of having to stop at every little station, change, and run the risk of missing their connexion. This ticket office is now closed. There is a station at the end of each section of the narrative, and the connexions are not guaranteed.
>
> The fact is, it is not simply that there is no very obvious psychological connexion between the sections; in almost every case there is a positive break in the connexion. And there is a great deal in the Marcan narrative which is inexplicable and even self-contradictory.[62]

According to Schweitzer what could be known about the external sequence of events in Jesus' life was very little indeed: the faint record of no more than a few months' preaching and the week prior to his execution. It was hardly surprising that a recent historian could refer to the effect of the *Quest* and similar works as reducing the Gospel of Mark to tatters.[63]

Not everyone was prepared to carry scepticism as far as Schweitzer did, of course, but by the end of the decade there could be little dispute: uncertainty about the life of Christ was growing. In 1906, the year of the *Quest*, there were certainly more doubters than in 1900. One sign of the new sceptical era, in Britain as on the continent, was a new theological issue. The distinction between the Jesus of history and what was variously called the Christ of theology, faith, dogma, or religion pressed itself to the foreground of discussion in the first decade of the new century. It is impossible to say who was the first to conceive this distinction or even raise it to prominence. In a certain sense it was implicit in all Lives of Christ, so far as they were an attempt to peel away centuries of dogma and discover the first-century Jesus. In another sense it was the perennial problem of faith and history, which reached as far back as Gotthold Lessing.[64] How could a first-century prophet, whom we know at all only through the fragile probabilities of historical science, nonetheless be the vehicle of eternal truths?

In Victorian Britain T. H. Green was certainly one of the earlier thinkers to come upon this antinomy when, as we have seen, he spoke of the "inner contradiction in that conception of faith which makes it a state of mind involving peace with God and at the same time makes its object that historical work of Christ of which our knowledge depends on evidence of uncertain origin and value."[65] To Edwin Hatch, author of the impressive and unfairly forgotten Hibbert Lectures on *The Influence of Greek Ideas and Usages on the Christian Church* (1888), the contradiction appeared in a different form—as the contrast between the simple Galilean peasant who delivered the sermon on the mount and the divinized, eternal Christ of official Christian theology.[66] In the mainstream of religious thought, however, this antinomy was seldom perceived. For most writers of Lives it had little force. They would surely have recognized that historians deal with the probabilities of historical evidence. But as Fairbairn was insisting as late as 1894, the probabilities seemed only to confirm what men already knew by faith: that the life of Jesus was substantially as the gospels and the theology of the church had delivered it.

In the newer, more critical climate evident after 1900, this confidence began to dissolve. Historians like Schweitzer were prepared to deny all—or nearly all—that believers had long affirmed. Faith and historical inquiry were beginning to pull in opposite directions. The Jesus of historical science was looking less and less like the Christ of the gospels and the church.

In response to this new situation, the thoughtful observer could choose from among three basic alternatives. One could argue first that the critics had failed in their aim; that the historical Jesus had never been convincingly disentangled from the Christ of the church; and that the two should therefore remain together. This was the position adopted by Scottish theologian D. W. Forrest in the Kerr Lectures for 1897 and published as *The Christ of History and of Experience.* The aim of this long theological essay, which stressed Jesus' moral unique-ness, was "to show that the union of the historical with the spiritual in the Christian Faith does not make of it an incongruous amalgam, that the same union pervades the entire moral life of man, and that the historical element in Christianity is of such a nature as renders it capable of exceptional verification."[67] This was in effect a reaffirma-tion of the orthodox view, implicit in the older Lives, according to which the evangelists were regarded as trustworthy historians whose theology was identical to that which the orthodox church has drawn from their writings. The position found able defenders throughout all of the decade after 1900.[68]

Others were not convinced by this reasoning, however, and insisted that the only valid course was to abandon altogether the theological constructs of traditional faith and turn unencumbered by dogma to the Jesus of history. Jesus in this view turned out to be the simple Galilean who taught love for God and neighbor and knew nothing of Greek metaphysics, who had no interest in abstractions like atone-ment and justification, and who neither claimed to be God nor rose from the dead. It was essentially the view of Hatch, as well as Harnack and other Ritschlians. When expressed in print, it was often accom-panied by language contemptuous of Greek speculation. Consider, for example, the following excerpt from an article in the *Hibbert Journal,* where a good deal of this discussion was carried on:

> We have to choose to-day between the metaphysical speculations of the un-Christian Christianity of the fourth century, "rooted in Hellenism," with their ghastly legacies of sophistication, unreason, and unnatural-ness, and the pure, natural morality of the Sermon on the Mount, taught lovingly and tenderly to Syrian peasants by Him whose yoke was easy and burden light.[69]

The crucial thing about opting for the Jesus of history, however, was the assumption that he could in fact be discovered. Hatch and others like him shared with Harnack and the Ritschlians the assumption that a good deal of Jesus' teaching, as well as certain central features of his life, could be known with certainty. After Schmiedel and Schweitzer, however, it was precisely this assumption that came increasingly under attack. Very little could be known about Jesus, said Schmiedel; and what little could be known, continued Schweitzer, Weiss, and others, suggested a figure very different from the moralizing Galilean so beloved by Hatch, Harnack, and others in search of the Jesus of history.

The profoundly disturbing effect of the new scepticism was given graphic expression by one observer writing in 1908:

> The very rapidity and success of historical research has produced in some minds a feeling of insecurity like that of people living in a district which is being undermined. They never know when next the ground is going to give under their feet. They would like to feel sure that the objective occurrence of the facts of the gospel in history is not a necessary condition of Christian belief or morality. These, they say, are beyond the reach of textual criticism and historical research.[70]

Pressured by the critics, the group alluded to here took refuge in still a third alternative: the Christ of faith without the Jesus of history. This to some appeared the only way to make faith secure from the relentless advance of historical critics. If Christ were once and for all lifted from the plane of mere events, if he were worshipped not as a historical figure whose status was precarious at best, but as an ideal, as a religious symbol; then believers would be free to welcome the advances of the critics. There would be no need to tremble at the footsteps of historians.

We can find a clear, straightforward statement of this position in an article contributed by the American A. O. Lovejoy to the *Hibbert Journal* for January, 1907:

> What the time really calls for, in other words, is the general proclamation of the dissolution of this ancient and entangling alliance between Christianity and detailed history. For though both conservative and radical critics, alike unable to point to any piece of clinching external evidence upon the now most debated matters of biblical history, must content themselves with involved conclusions drawn from internal evidences, the fact shows all the more plainly that just those incidents to which theology has attached the greatest dogmatic weight have been removed from the sphere of the clearly ascertainable to that of the problematical.[71]

Later he added,

> Christianity, in a word, ought no longer to let itself be involved in obscure and uncertain issues of historical detail, but it ought still . . . to proclaim the worth of personal and racial experience under the form of time, and the divineness of the historic order. . . . This will necessarily always imply an interest in the great sequences of past history, . . . But it will not make the historian—what in Christianity he has hitherto been—the keeper of the Ark of the Covenant.[72]

Lovejoy and those[73] who adopted a similar position were careful not to put their case against the historical Jesus too harshly. But it was clear that on such assumptions the energetic study of Jesus' life and times became a matter of somewhat less than vital importance.

By 1909 the question had generated such interest and such a variety of opinions that the editors of the *Hibbert Journal* devoted a special supplement to the topic. *Jesus or Christ?* appeared at the end of the year and drew to its pages an international array of scholars; among them the Scandinavian Nathan Söderbloom, the Swiss Schmiedel, the German Heinrich Weinel, American B. W. Bacon, and a set of British thinkers that included A. E. Garvie, George Tyrell, R. J. Campbell, Henry Scott Holland, Oliver Lodge, and Joseph Estlin Carpenter.[74] We need not here discuss the varying interpretations offered by such a formidable gathering of critics; the collection of essays as a whole may rather stand as testimony to the urgency of a problem created in good part by the new scepticism of gospel critics. Nor did the discussion end with the *Hibbert* supplement. There was a response to the special volume by Loisy in the April, 1910 number of the *Hibbert,* as well as a full-length contribution by Unitarian J. Estlin Carpenter, whose *The Historical Jesus and the Theological Christ* appeared in 1912.[75]

Whatever the routes traveled in answer to this theological question, one thing was increasingly clear. In the space of a mere decade Britain had witnessed a stunning reversal of opinion on the life of Christ. Whereas A. M. Fairbairn spoke in 1894 of "a growing sense of being on firm historical ground," ten years later it was becoming difficult to find a maker of opinion who had not begun to yield to the sceptics.[76] The Congregationalist P. T. Forsyth, in this as in other ways ahead of his time, had begun to make the move even before the turn of the century when he wrote that the gospels provide "a record too scanty for an imitable ideal, but enough for the focus of a spiritual force."[77] Writing from his peculiar Neo-platonist standpoint W. R. Inge, later to be Dean of St. Paul's, secured himself against the sceptics in *Contentio Veritatis* (1902):

> Religion . . . never speaks in the past tense. It is concerned only with what is, not with what was. History as history is not its business . . . . Events or aspects of events, which relate *only* to the past, may be left to historians. Phenomena or aspects of phenomena, which relate only to the material world, may be left to men of science. Errors in history, or errors in science, do not save or damn.[78]

On these terms Inge had little difficulty, when the time came, sacrificing the life of Christ:

Of Paul's divine Master no biography can ever be written. We have a vivid impression of a unique, effulgent personality. We have a considerable body of sayings . . . , and, for the rest, whatever royal robes and tributes of devotion the Church of A.D. 70-100 thought most fitting for its king.[79]

We could also turn to Percy Gardner:

It will probably always remain an impossibility to set forth even a brief narrative of the Founder's life which history can accept as demonstrated fact. Even the chronological skeleton of such a life cannot be sketched with certainty;[80]

or to Free Church theologian H. R. Mackintosh:

To a considerable extent the investigation of the life of Jesus, in recent times, has been stultified by a radical error in method; the error of supposing that the Gospels are biographies in the modern sense. It is true biography involves much more than a precise system of dates based on careful inquiry into the relation of different episodes to each other, yet it is totally inconceivable apart from some such chronological framework. We have only to glance at the Synoptics to perceive that they have not been composed on this plan.[81]

There is no need to multiply references.[82] Seventy years after his humiliation, in Britain as well as in Germany, Strauss, the most famous of the sceptics, had extracted his revenge. Even in conservative circles, study of the life of Christ had permanently been changed.

Even at this, questioning did not cease. In Britain, America, and on the continent, scepticism reached its final stage in theory of the "Christ-myth," which acquired prominent spokesmen in all three lands between 1900 and 1910. Quite simply, proponents of the "Christ-myth" argued that in fact Jesus never existed. Once criticism of the gospels had begun in earnest, it was perhaps inevitable that such a school arise. But the task of defending this remarkable conclusion fell chiefly upon Arthur Drews of Karlsruhe in Germany, W. B. Smith of Tulane University in America, an assortment of Dutch scholars,[83] and in Britain upon a man never more at his best than in controversy, the formidable Scottish rationalist John Mackinnon Robertson. A good measure of the movement's inspiration came from the newly developed sciences of anthropology and comparative religion. Drews, Robertson, and Smith were captivated by mythical parallels to Christian ideas which turned up in the studies of Near Eastern scholars like Hermann Gunkel and students of primitive religion like E. B. Tylor and James Frazer. The existence of blood sacrifices, redeemer myths, and divine visitations in so many primitive religions led them to suppose that Christianity might be the product of similar speculation. The gospels need not have been the record of historical events; they might just as easily have emerged from a set of primitive cultic rites no different in nature from those found in any of the countless other mystery religions that littered the face of the Roman world. So far from being a historic personage, Jesus looked very much like a mythical figure who assumed importance because he embodied certain ancient Mediterranean notions about atonement and divinity.

Robertson in Britain had been among the first to adduce Christian-pagan parallels in two large works, *Christianity and Mythology* (1900) and *Pagan Christs* (1903), but at first he saw no reason to deny altogether Jesus' existence. Only later in the decade, as he read Smith's *The Pre-Christian Jesus* (1906) and Drews's *Das Christusmythe*—English translation, *The Christ Myth* (1910)—did his opinions begin to change.[84] By 1916, when *The Historical Jesus* appeared, he was prepared not only to welcome the work of destructive critics like Schmiedel and Loisy but to declare that even they were too timid. His own position he stated in typically outspoken fashion:

> No fundamental difficulty remains when we recognize that the whole Gospel record is the composite result of a process of making a life history for a God. The command of the Messiah to Peter to keep silence as to his Messianic character is quite intelligible as providing at once the claim by Jesus and an explanation of the fact that no such Messianic movement was historically recorded. The blank enigma of the early "popular" evangel is solved when we realize that there had been no such evangel; that the cult had really grown out of the ancient sacramental rite; that the growing movement had to evolve a quasi-biography when the God of the rite was to be developed into a Messiah; and that the Judaism of the old Messianic idea had to be transmuted into a universalism when the cult came to a Gentile growth.[85]

Beyond this scepticism could not go.

Needless to say, the "Christ-myth" school did not go without opposition, even from other radical critics.[86] Loisy was disposed to regard the whole movement as superficial.[87] In Britain Robertson met his match in fellow rationalist F. C. Conybeare, whose *Historical Christ* of 1914 bitterly assailed the artificiality and overblown scholarship of its leading spokesmen.[88] But this is to go beyond our period. What we need notice is simply that by 1910, the year Drews's chief work came into English, the mere existence of Jesus was a topic of serious discussion. That the denial of his existence was a rather groundless supposition time and further scholarship would clearly show. That it could be debated at all, however, was a measure of how far sceptical criticism had traveled and how unfavorable for the typical Victorian Life of Christ the critical climate had at last become.

2. Cultural Changes

The growth of scepticism among scholars was therefore a decisive factor counting against the older study of the life of Jesus after 1900. The doubt of the critics acted as an acid upon the New Testament sources, dissolving old certitudes and removing from the sphere of history facts once commonly accepted as part of the authentic record of Jesus. Yet crucial as they were, the shifts of scholarship and religious thought were not the only forces combining near the close of the century to affect the fate of the Victorian Lives. British society had also been changing—in ways that left nearly as profound an impact upon those who read Lives as the rise of scepticism had upon those who wrote them. We cannot understand what happened to study of Jesus in the new century without also taking some note of these larger social and cultural changes, particularly as they touched upon the book trade, upon popular reading and recreational habits, and upon the underlying religious character of the nation.

There can be no question, in the first place, that the British publishing industry had made great strides throughout the latter years of the Victorian era. We noted earlier that whereas in 1850 the chief problem was that books were too few and too expensive, the intervening years had brought a minor economic revolution in the book trade.[89] By 1900, says Richard Altick, cheap literature of every kind, quality, and physical format had become a part of the Victorian scene.[90] Books once available only through the circulating libraries were now to be purchased for small, easily payable prices. We noticed earlier how the unfortunate alliance between publisher and circulating library, which conspired for so long to keep the price of newly written books artificially high, had come to an end.[91] Immediately as it did, the price of first-edition novels, for example, tumbled to 6*s.* and 5*s.*, and reprints to as low as 3*s.* 6*d.* or 2*s.* 6*d.*[92] The "penny dreadful," once monopolized by stories of crime and sentimental escapism, began to display authors of higher quality, among them Dickens and Macaulay. The Penny Novelist abridgements of W. T. Stead and the Penny Library of George Newnes made an array of first-rank novelists available at the very cheapest prices. The success of these enterprises was considerable.

For the religious author, however, all of this was a mixed blessing. It must be remembered that deeply religious men, like John Cassell and W. H. Smith, had been among the pioneers in the cheap book movement. For a time in the seventies and early eighties their publications, weighted heavily toward religious and morally uplifting topics, formed the only alternatives for the serious ordinary reader, who could not afford the expensive good literature and was not interested in the penny dreadful. Such readers might have been quite satisfied to choose one of the religious or educational pieces sold in such vast quantities by a firm like Cassell. Unless one lived near enough to a circulating library and could afford a subscription, there was actually little choice. Better to sit down with Cassell's *Biblical Illustrator,* or the cheap edition of Farrar's *Life of Christ,* neither of which, certainly, was bad literature, than to read nothing at all.

The victory of the cheap book movement changed this situation dramatically. After 1890 and especially 1900, the same reader could find at a nearby bookseller any number of authors from good to great—Dickens, Poe or Scott, Macaulay or Shakespeare—at a mere pittance a volume. For the average reader this was in every respect an unquestionable advance; for Lives of Christ, however, it was stiff competition. Anyone who wished to read a good book could now look in several directions.

Such was only the alternative offered by "good" or "classic" literature. As soon as we expand our gaze to embrace second- and third-rank material, the strength of the competition becomes almost overwhelming. Popular fiction had of course always held a sizable share of the Victorian market. By the end of the century, however, statistics show that it had crept to a position of almost complete dominance. Richard Altick's figures, taken from the free libraries of two rather large cities, are significant:

> At Sheffield in the period 1856-57, prose fiction accounted for almost half of the combined circulation of the consulting and lending departments. At Liverpool in 1867-68, out of 565,000 books called for, 189,800 were fiction. But this was nothing compared with what was to come: by the 1890's most free libraries reported that between 65 per cent and 90 per cent of the books circulated were classified as fiction.[93]

Serious nonfiction was clearly having a hard go of it by 1900. To this must be added one further statistic. If we are to speak of a decline in popular interest, few kinds of literature suffered a more visible falling-off than religious books. Drawing upon recently gathered figures, Patrick Scott of Edinburgh has shown that between 1859 and 1899 the number of religious books published in relation to the national total dropped steadily till, by the end of the century, they accounted for less than 10 per cent of all books printed. The precise figures are 31.1 per cent in 1859, 23.3 in 1869, 17.1 in 1879, 12.7 in 1889, and 9.2 in 1899.[94] The figures then were unknown, but the fact was something with which writers of Lives at the end of the century would have had to reckon. In prior decades the popularity of Farrar, Geikie, Edersheim, and others had defied the trend. After 1900 the author who could strike a similar success was becoming rare indeed.

The publishing industry, however, was not an entity to itself; it reflected, inevitably, not only the reading habits of the populace, but their broader social, intellectual, and recreational habits as well. In the interval between 1860 and the turn of the century these too underwent a process of change. A new freedom, even a new frivolity, had slowly been making its way into the old Victorian scene. We had occasion earlier to speak of the peculiar ethos of the mid-Victorian years. Whether it came from utilitarian philosophers or Evangelical preachers, the guiding principle of the middle class was sober self-improvement. The popularity of Samuel Smiles and *Self-Help* was no accident. When, as was most often the case on the Sabbath, one had the leisure to read, it would have been frivolous in the eyes of many to waste much time on popular fiction—the sort of literature whose chief benefit took the form of thoughtless, momentary diversion. One assumed that reading had better purposes; it was a means to knowledge, a badge of respectability, and a path to social advancement. Of course it would be a mistake to press this generalization, like any other, too far. On occasions—indeed many more occasions than the popular caricature would allow—the mid-Victorians read for sheer pleasure. But if students of Victorian attitudes like Walter Houghton are correct, the graver, more earnest side of mind always remained uppermost.[95] Only as the century progressed did the restrictions dissolve. There could be little doubt that the novel was less a taboo in 1890 than it had been in 1850, or that more people read for pure, pointless diversion in 1900 than in 1860.

Amy Cruse, in *After the Victorians,* has provided a vivid, engaging sketch of the kind of publication that emerged to meet this need as it developed in the mid-eighties and thereafter. Conjuring up fictional Mr. Smith, an old-style, serious, book-loving gentleman, she reports his reaction to a curious new periodical called *Tit-Bits,* which seemed to be in the hands of every reader in London. Upon inspecting the paper, Mr. Smith found it to be filled with brief snatches of the oddest and most irrelevant information, all under headings like "Curiosities of the Post Office," "The Incomes of Archbishops," "The Inventor of the Tricycle"—these tossed together without a trace of coherence or organization. When he further noticed that it was chiefly younger people who formed the readership of this paper, it suddenly occurred to him that the Education Act of 1870 was the villain:

> That brought him to the realization that an immense new class of readers, which would increase year by year, had been created, readers who had very little literary judgment and were ready to accept anything that was judiciously forced upon their notice, provided that it did not require any uncomfortable activity of the brain. He felt that he could not sufficiently admire the astuteness of those persons who had, in the very nick of time, provided exactly the literature that would suit this new public.[96]

This quaint, slightly patronizing portrait furnishes evidence of what indeed was happening to the Victorian common reader later on in the century. Reading was more than ever becoming a diversionary pastime, a means of entertainment and escape. The new state of affairs was reflected not only in *Tit-Bits,* but in its equally popular successors which inventive publishers poured on to the market, beginning with *Comic Cuts* and *Pearson's Weekly* in 1890 and proceeding to *Forget-Me-Not, Home Chat, Home Notes, Golden Penny, Sunday Companion,* and many others.[97] In this new market, where readers' attention-spans were gauged in minutes rather than hours, Lives of Christ could only appear as less attractive fare than they had been a generation before.

Among the papers on the above list, the *Sunday Companion* has a curious ring about it. A generation before, the Sunday companion in many Victorian middle-class homes would have been Bunyan, the Bible, or a religious book on the order of a Life of Christ. By the 1890s it might quite literally have been the *Sunday Companion,* a sheet whose occasional smatterings of religious news in no way interfered with its chief purpose of being a secular odds-and-ends paper. In this we have the hint of yet another fundamental change creeping upon late Victorian society. If people sat down less often with serious religious books on the Sabbath, it was not only because their habits in reading had changed; Sunday had changed, too. In many a mid-Victorian home the Sabbath was, by desire or default, the day set aside for serious, instructive, and usually religious reading. As Amy Cruse, Owen Chadwick, and others have pointed out, the devout middle-class family of 1860 would have found it natural to spend Sunday afternoon or evening in a reading circle or preoccupied with a set of sermons—in part because it was difficult to do anything else.[98] The custodians of social values—Evangelicals and dissenters chiefly—had managed to close off almost all other avenues of recreation. The great Sabbath agitation of the 1850s, which issued in the closing of the Crystal Palace on Sundays in 1853 and the overwhelming 1856 defeat in Commons of the proposal to open the British Museum and National Gallery on Sunday, proved the strength of the Evangelical-dissenter axis.

The hardship all of this worked on the poor was unquestionably severe. To such families, cramped in the ugliest corners of ugly cities, the Sabbath restriction on travel, commerce, and recreation could make their day of rest almost as unbearable as their days of labor. To those in the middle class who did not welcome them out of conviction, the taboos were at the least an annoyance. But on the writers and publishers of religious books such as the Lives of Christ the circumstances conferred a curious advantage. It left the populace with no alternative but to read; and on Sunday, more often than not, that meant to read religion.

By the end of the century, however, the Sabbath bonds had begun to loosen. Not only did popular fiction and papers like *Tit-Bits* cut into time formerly given to "heavier" reading; reading itself received competition from the new freedom to engage in sports and other outdoor recreations. The Sunday Observance Prosecution Act of 1871 worked to discourage private prosecutions of Sabbath-breakers permitted under the Ancient Observance Act of 1677. The British Museum, National Gallery, and selected other public institutions were opened by the 1890s.[99] The bicycle, automobile, and swifter, better-routed trains provided access to parts of the country once too remote to visit in the space of a single Sunday. In view of all this, it is hardly surprising that some of the old religious ties began to dissolve and churchmen began to resent the new opportunities for pleasure. "Christian parents," said the chairman of the Congregational Union in 1894, "no longer forbid their children to read novels or learn dancing; some of them accompany their sons and daughters to the theatre and the concert; in many Christian homes billiards and cards are allowed, and both in occupation and amusement the line that once divided the world from the Church is tending to disappear."[100] The speaker had no reason to confine himself only to the Sabbath, for the new recreational habits were affecting all of church life.

In January of 1904 the *Hibbert Journal* printed a symposium of articles by four prestigious authors under the title "The Alleged Indifference of Laymen to Religion."[101] The four offered various explanations: too much "ecclesiasticism," said Oliver Lodge; too much rationalism and sacerdotalism, thought Sir Edward Russell; too much orthodoxy and ossification, according to J. H. Muirhead; too glaring a contradiction between Christian ideals and the commercialism of contemporary Christian society, suggested L. P. Jacks. Several of the contributors pointed to the new recreations and the ease and attraction of weekend travel. Though their diagnoses differed, none questioned the fact of the disease.[102] It was clear enough that the end-of-the-century Victorians, whose parents or grandparents preferred to read as they passed a sober Sabbath, had come to a point where they cared greatly for neither reading, too much sobriety, nor the Sabbath.

Yet the deliberations of the *Hibbert* symposium hint at something far deeper, something more hidden than a slight shift in a few social customs. During the closing years of the nineteenth century a great cultural, intellectual, and social change was passing over the life of the people. The phenomenon which we call today secularization, though we have yet clearly to define or understand it, was filtering steadily through every level of British society. There are no simple explanations for this trend in Britain, any more than there are for secularization as it has occurred elsewhere in western Europe and America. There can be no doubt that by the close of the Victorian era Britain was less obviously a religious country than it had been a half-century before. The statistical studies of church membership and attendance cited by Owen Chadwick have yielded a rather exact date for the beginning of at least one phase of this decline in both Church and Chapel. The pivotal date, says Chadwick, was 1886:

> Until the last fifteen years of the century, the churches succeeded marvellously in their endeavors to keep pace with the rising population. After 1886, though the leaders of most churches had just as powerful a feeling of advance, the figures show that the churches failed markedly to keep pace with the rise in people; and more, that in towns where the population was still rising, the number of attendants at church began to decline.[103]

This last fact emerged with discouraging clarity from Richard Mudie-Smith's religious census of London in 1902. Here there was solid evidence that even relatively speaking the churches had failed to hold their ground. "So far from keeping pace," writes Chadwick, "they declined. They declined not only in relation to the rising population, but absolutely. And the established church lost more than any other denomination."[104]

Even more disheartening to religious leaders was the evidence that secularization had come at last to the middle classes. The workingmen, as K. S. Inglis has convincingly stated, were hardly lost to the Victorian churches, for the simple reason that they had never belonged in the first place.[105] Active, practicing members of the churches had long come chiefly from the middle layer of British society, and there were some contemporary observers quite aware of this.[106] The new fact of losses among this group came as a sobering revelation. Among those who noticed, none pointed out the new situation with more realism than C. F. G. Masterman, himself a participant in the London census of 1902 and a man who took no pleasure in what he saw:

> I think there can be no doubt that apart from any questions of future revival, present belief in religion, as a conception of life dependent upon supernatural sanctions or as a revelation of a purpose and meaning beyond the actual business of the day, is slowly but steadily fading from the modern city race.[107]

Later on he added,

> Among the Middle Classes—the centre and historical support of Eng-
> land's Protestant creed—the drift away is acknowledged by all to be
> conspicuous—by friend as well as by enemy. The country is here follow-
> ing the town; and amongst the industrial people the prophecy of Taine
> thirty years ago would appear to be fulfilling itself today: "By an insen-
> sible and slow backward movement, the great rural mass, like the great
> urban mass, is gradually going back to Paganism."[108]

For our own purposes, it must be remembered that secularization was
a very general trend, to which there was a host of assorted exceptions.
The process moved slower in Scotland than in England, in the country, as Masterman noted, than in the city; it took a different form
among Catholics than among Protestants, and affected some religious
practices more quickly than others. Yet it is hard to avoid the conclusion that the shift to the secular was at work in each of the behavioral
shifts we have noted here—in attitudes toward reading, recreation,
and Sunday. All of these changes created a social terrain less inviting
than that which lay before writers of Lives a generation earlier.
Although precise statistics are lacking,[109] it seems more than coin-
cidental that after 1885 virtually none of the newer lives could claim a
public success equal to those of Farrar, Geikie, Stalker, or even Fairbairn, the last of which at the turn of the century was already twenty
years old.

3. Diverging Paths

What we have observed thus far, then, are two sets of changes at
work in British society as it moved out of the Victorian era and into
the twentieth century. Both the scepticism of scholars and the secularization of the populace fell as a double blow of discouragement upon
study of the life of Christ as it had formerly been understood. But
what did this mean in more concrete terms? Despite the wishes of
some critics, it certainly did not bring a complete end to the enterprise
of sketching the life of Jesus. That would have been impossible. No
cultural change, however broad or widely felt, proceeds without those
who swim against the tide. So long as there remained believers unconvinced by the new criticism and unaffected by the new secularism,
there was sufficient reason for some to write of Christ in the traditional fashion, regardless of the spirit of the times. Within the
churches the story of Jesus' life still found, as it continues to find, new
tellers with little regard for the objections of the learned or indiffer-
ent. No more in Britain than elsewhere in Western Christendom did
the churches succumb totally to the pressures of modernity. What the
new situation did bring about, however, was something very much like

a parting of ways. After 1900 it became increasingly difficult for any writer to achieve that rare union of popular appeal and respectable scholarship which had been the mark of the best among the earlier Lives. By 1910 it was virtually impossible.

Earlier in this study there emerged certain earmarks, or key features, which were more or less to reappear in all of the Lives which dominated the remainder of the century. They were theologically orthodox, and they adopted the premises of Britain's moderate biblical criticism. They were further marked by a stress on the human Jesus, by a style crafted for a popular audience, and by an appeal to the romance of ancient Palestine. The first two characteristics enabled these Lives to pass the test of scholars; the last three enabled them to reach out toward a larger audience. This pattern remained substantially intact till about 1900. After that date, however, the circumstances of the new century made it exceedingly difficult for a writer to satisfy at once the demand of critics who had become more sceptical as their science became more complex, and a populace which had become less interested in religion. In the new situation authors who ventured upon Lives were forced, almost in spite of themselves, to choose an audience. To opt for a thorough scientific study was certainly to win the respect of scholars; but it was also to sacrifice the interests of a larger audience, less patient than ever with books that demanded too much time or technical understanding. To opt for a devotional Life, or a work in the older style of Farrar and Geikie, was to recapture some of this audience and achieve still a measure of popularity; but it virtually compelled one to sacrifice the claim to respect from serious critics.

"The theologians of every country," wrote Adolph Harnack in the preface to the English edition of his *Wesen des Christentums (What is Christianity?)* in 1900, "only half discharge their duties if they think it enough to treat of the Gospel in the recondite language of learning and bury it in scholarly folios."[110] Ideally speaking, the great Berlin scholar was no doubt correct; but after 1900 serious students of the gospels in Britain were finding this an ideal easier to state than achieve. We can observe the dilemma in the fate of several critics who stood at this difficult fork in the road, chose different paths, and came upon just those consequences one might have expected, given the new state of affairs.

David Smith of Magee College, Londonderry, was a Scottish Free Church scholar and former pupil of A. B. Bruce. Though aware of the unfavorable critical winds, he kept to the old ways and in 1905 published *The Days of His Flesh,* a work very much in the tradition of Farrar, Geikie, and Edersheim. It was clear from the preface of this work that even the conservative scholar had by this time to make some concessions to the critics. Smith admitted that the evangelists suffered slips of memory, fell into anachronisms, editorialized, and at times rearranged rather large blocks of material. In spite of this he insisted that for the most part the gospels consisted undeniably of accurate reportage, that they gave a clearly discernible outline of Christ's life, and—untenable as it seemed to almost everyone else—that the Fourth Gospel was a valid, historical supplement to the first three.[111] In fact, Smith's verdict on the sources came down with a tone of confidence that made other critics wince in discomfort:

> It may be questioned whether any other history carries such credentials or is entitled to equal reliance. It contains indubitably a certain admixture of unreliable elements; but these are easily distinguished, and so far from discrediting the mass serve rather to approve its value.[112]

Upon this premise, *The Days of His Flesh* traced the youth and early ministry of Jesus, his seasons of success and opposition, his teaching and miracles, his trial, passion, death and resurrection. The theology was orthodox, the book learned and conservative, and there can be no doubt that in certain circles it found an audience receptive enough to require new editions to at least as late as 1911.[113] Since there are no available sales lists and there is nothing extraordinary in the press notices of the work, one must be careful not to draw too large a conclusion from the mere register of new editions. Editions in the Victorian and Edwardian era often varied greatly in total numbers. Even so, nine in six years was not a trifle. Without doubt, *The Days of His Flesh* was a popular Life.

Yet if the work of Smith made an impact on ordinary readers, it made no similar impression on the community of scholars. His stance on the sources was hardly that of the leading New Testament critics in 1905, and there were many who would have found his defense of John positively archaic. No longer was there a "Cambridge school" of critics to support these views. Even the *London Quarterly,* the oracle of Methodist conservatism, balked at such an obviously antiquated position:

> Mr. Smith expressly states that "the evangelistic history is worthy of all acceptation"; and so far are the words of Jesus from the being inextricably confused with the comments of the evangelists, that "one knows instinctively where Jesus ceases and the evangelist begins." The case is one where the logic of the heart points to the presence of some illicit process in the reasoning.[114]

This telepathic method of determining the words of Jesus was, to say the least, curious, but Smith never shifted his ground. Seven years later, he published *The Historical Jesus,* a work in which the entire critical movement of the previous decade came under severe attack. He pronounced both Moffat and Schmiedel unsound and rejected out of hand the idealism of T. H. Green, whose Christianity he called "a mere phantom." Sensing perhaps his estrangement from the growing consensus of the critics, he insisted that between the new attitudes and the orthodox tradition of the historic Jesus there could be no reconciliation. For Smith the axioms of the scholars and the creeds of the churches were at an impasse. One had no choice but to choose for the churches.[115]

Nor was the situation very different for T. R. Glover, the classical scholar, who attempted to avoid the smothering entanglements of biblical science in his *Jesus of History,* published just beyond our period in 1916. Glover was enough aware of source criticism to steer away from the Fourth Gospel and travel most often the path outlined by Mark. He preferred the liberal, humanitarian Jesus, and his life carried a minimum of supernaturalist theology, a maximum of ethical reinterpretation tinged with agnosticism. "Whoever he [Jesus] was, whatever he is, whatever our Christology," he concluded, "one fact stands out. It was his love of men and women and his faith in God that took him there."[116] The book was also written in a smooth, lucid style which no doubt made it appealing to educated, half-committed Christians with a distaste for dogma. As a contribution to scholarship, it was useless. Glover casually dismissed apocalyptic at a time when, even in more traditional circles, it was too late for such facile rejections. And a scholar who loosely defined the "Kingdom of Heaven" in the teaching of Jesus as "providence"[117] was somewhat embarrassingly out of his expertise.

A very different state of affairs obtained for the American Nathanael Schmidt, whose *Prophet of Nazareth,* published in London as well as New York, had appeared in 1905. Taking a stance similar to Glover's and increasingly popular in America, Schmidt argued in Ritschlian fashion that Jesus was the last and greatest of the Old Testament messengers of the Lord, a prophet of a new order of justice and love. To make his case the author found it necessary to make long excursive studies of the linguistic evidence, comparative analyses of the contemporary German schools of thought, and extended, tightly reasoned studies in the complex questions of the sources. The finished product was without doubt a credit to gospel scholarship, but as the *Spectator* pointed out, such a Life of Christ had little chance of escaping the narrow chambers of the universities:

Whether Professor Schmidt's conclusions will be categorically accepted
by scholars we have no means of foretelling; but what may be considered certain is that they will not be adopted by the general public,
who will not be at the pains to understand learned decisions, and who
will always regard the Bible for all practical purposes as having been
written in Elizabethan English.[118]

Clearly in the new era scholarship and society were going separate
ways. Smith and Glover, who wrote for the crowd, disowned much of
biblical scholarship. Schmidt conversed with the experts, but not with
anyone else.

    Another critic whose work reflected the new complexities was G. H.
Gilbert, whose *Student's Life,* as noted, appeared in 1896. An informed
critic who had earlier studied at Leipzig, Gilbert continued to take a
keen interest in the progress of gospel criticism after he had made his
first attempt. In 1912, when he was ready to try again, he began his
new work, *Jesus,* with a frank recognition of the new attitudes. "The
decade and a half since my *Student's Life of Jesus* was published has
witnessed a wide and important change among scholars in their estimate of the historical value of these various [gospel] sources. In that
change I have shared."[119] Of this there could be little doubt. *Jesus*
began with a thorough study of the New Testament sources, in which
John was virtually abandoned and the synoptics came in for stiff reassessment. Between this and a substantial section on "The Legendary
Jesus," Gilbert managed to devote about a third of his book to what
remained of the historical Jesus. The Christ of *Jesus* was a thinner,
more shadowy figure than the Christ of the *Student's Life.*

    The single figure on whom the new perplexities pressed most severely,
however, was undoubtedly Oxford's William Sanday, author of the
highly regarded Hastings's *Dictionary* article on "Jesus Christ" and
perhaps the foremost gospel critic in Britain at the turn of the century.
Nowhere is the force of the new movements more clearly discernible
than in the disintegration of confidence which marked Sanday's scholarly career. When in 1899 his *Dictionary* article appeared, critics
spoke approvingly and called for a longer, definitive Life from the
same pen. Sanday obliged with the promise that such a comprehensive
work would soon be forthcoming. Then delays occurred. Instead of a
complete Life, the *Dictionary* article was reprinted in 1904, with Sanday stating in preface that "the writer is engaged upon a larger work
on the same subject, which is not likely to appear for some years."[120]
In 1907 came *The Life of Christ in Recent Research,* where the striking theory of apocalyptic was noted with the confession that "I am
coming to think . . . that we shall have to take more account of this
region than perhaps we have done . . . I confess that a good many

things appear to me otherwise than they did."[121] When in the following year a new edition of the *Outlines* appeared with only slight alterations, Sanday felt obliged to make apologies:

> A generous critic . . . reminded the writer of the obligation which he has assumed by the promise of a larger work on the Life of Christ . . . . The writer . . . is most anxious to fulfil his promise; but he has permitted himself to engage in these apparent digressions, at once as a help towards digesting his materials, and also that he may by these means make his larger work more compact and concentrated when the time for it comes.[122]

Christology and Personality (1911) began with what had now become a familiar refrain: "I hope this is the last of the preliminary studies which I found myself compelled to make in approaching the larger task which lies before me of writing, or attempting to write, what is commonly called a Life of Christ."[123] Even while he was promising his Life, Sanday seemed to be moving steadily away from his goal, not closer to it. Under pressure exerted by the arguments of the American B. W. Bacon, he eventually yielded his cherished position on the Fourth Gospel, conceding that it was neither historical nor authentic.[124] He found himself wavering on Schweitzer's eschatology, uncertain of earlier certitudes, and acutely aware that some problems of gospel study would require years of patient and careful research. In the end Sanday never did write his definitive Life; it is arguable that by 1910 he *could* not have written it. For the serious scholar it had at the moment become an almost impossible task.

Even if Sanday had managed to complete his definitive Life, it is worth wondering how eagerly it would then have been read by anyone outside the handful of critics who had his grasp of the complexities of gospel study. If by some rare feat of literary skill he could have distilled a clear result from the discussions of the scholars and passed it along in a form attractive to common readers, would they have cared? G. M. Young, the noted Victorian scholar of an earlier generation, was sure that by this time they would not:

> Religion, conceived as a concerted system of ideas, aspirations, and practices to be imposed on society, was losing its place in the English world, and the Oxford scholars about Sanday who were to settle the documents of the faith with an exactness and integrity which Germany could not have outmatched, delivered their results to a generation which ceased for the most part to be interested in the faith or the documents.[125]

There is a trace of exaggeration in this remark—but perhaps not more than a trace. One thing at any rate is certain. The era of popular Lives of Christ, which saw reassuring wisdom disseminated from conservative scholars to a grateful populace, had quite suddenly come to an end. After 1900 the scholar could provide little wisdom of a sort the ordinary reader could easily grasp; and he certainly could offer no reassurance. The era of the typical Victorian Life of Christ—of Farrar and Geikie, of Stalker, Fairbairn, and Edersheim—had drawn to a close.

NOTES

1. "Our Present Knowledge of the Life of Christ," 124.

2. This was his *Life of Jesus Christ,* published in 1879; see above, pp. 98-99.

3. Stalker, "Our Present Knowledge," 124.

4. Hastings's *Dictionary of the Bible,* ed. James Hastings, et al. (Edinburgh: T. & T. Clark, 1899).

5. William Sanday, *Outlines of the Life of Christ,* Amer. ed. (New York: Charles Scribner's Sons, 1908) 191-209.

6. Ibid., 105.

7. Ibid., 214.

8. On Sanday's view of the reliability of the Fourth Gospel, see ibid., 140; on his view of Jesus as a spiritualized Messiah, 91-101; on the resurrection, 170-86.

9. For still others see Ayres, *Jesus Christ our Lord.* Dawson's work illustrates vividly how writers of Lives to the very close of the century could be captured by the spell of Palestinian romance. In the preface to *The Man Christ Jesus,* Amer. ed. (titled *The Life of Christ*) (Philadelphia: George W. Jacobs & Co., 1901) vi, he wrote of the trip he, like so many others, had made to Palestine: "Here the plan of the book took final outline and its general principles were settled. Living for a time—alas! too brief—in the very scenes where Jesus moved, sailing on his own lake, beholding not alone the outlines of scenery which He beheld . . ., it was as though a new Gospel were rapidly unfolded to the wondering eyes. An indescribable sense of familiarity pursued the mind in every aspect of these sacred scenes. . . . It is as though Jesus spoke afresh in a land where all things speak of Him."

10. R. Martin Pope, "Recent Studies in the Life and Teaching of Jesus," *London Quarterly Review* 94 (July 1900) 60; for the similar views of the highly respected Methodist critic W. F. Moulton, see Glover, *Evangelical Nonconformists,* 205-11.

11. The *Encyclopaedia Biblica,* Amer. ed. (New York: Macmillan & Co.), was published over a period of four years, from 1899 to 1903. Volume one, "A to D," appeared in 1889; "E to K" in 1901; "L to P" in 1902; "Q to Z" in 1903. On Cheyne and his eccentricities see *DNB,* s.v. "Cheyne, Thomas Kelly." William Sanday, in an Appendix entitled "The Position in 1903," which was placed at the back of his *Outlines,* 243, pointed to 1901 and the appearance of volume two of the *Encyclopaedia* as the turning point of British biblical criticism toward more radical views.

12. W. T. Davison, "The Progress of Biblical Criticism," *London Quarterly Review* 90 (January 1900) 7. The article was later published separately under the same title by Charles H. Kelly, London.

13. Paul Schmiedel, "Gospels," *Encyclopaedia Biblica,* 2, col. 1873.

14. This is quite understandable under the critical principles Schmiedel employed. Assuming that much in the gospel narratives might have been altered or embellished to accommodate the needs of the early Christian com-

munities, he asked what sort of passage would provide indisputable evidence of a historical figure not created or colored by those who authored the documents. His method of answering was to seek passages that ran counter to the image of Jesus which the early church sought to present. Having slipped past the embellishing hands of the evangelists, such passages could be assumed to bear the stamp of authentic reminiscence.

15. Schmiedel, "Gospels," col. 1881. Other "pillar" passages were Mk. 3:21; Mk. 13:32; Mk. 15:34; and Mt. 12:31, 32.

16. W. T. Davison, "Christ and Modern Criticism," *London Quarterly Review* 95 (April 1901) 296. Further on, p. 298, Davison spoke sarcastically of Schmiedel as the writer "chosen by Canon Cheyne to tell Englishmen 'the true truth' concerning the Gospels."

17. A. B. Bruce, "Jesus," *Encyclopaedia Biblica,* 2. col. 2435.

18. Ibid., col. 2446.

19. Davison, "Christ and Modern Criticism," 293.

20. W. Robertson Nicoll, "Christ and the Newer Criticism," reprinted from the *British Weekly* in *Church's One Foundation,* 21.

21. Ibid., 30-31.

22. Ibid., 35.

23. Ibid., 36.

24. Moffatt's work was published by T. & T. Clark of Edinburgh in 1901.

25. Nicoll, *Church's One Foundation,* 22.

26. Ibid., 46.

27. See for example the review of the *Encylopaedia* entitled "Biblical Study," *Spectator,* 2 August 1902.

28. Davison wrote frequently for the *London Quarterly,* but most of his other published work lay in the field of either Old Testament study or devotional literature. For his published works see *Brit. Mus. Catalogue,* s.v. "Davison, William Theophilus."

29. On Swete's career see *DNB,* s.v. "Swete, Henry Barclay."

30. On Sanday's personality and career see *DNB,* s.v. "Sanday, William" and below, pp. 198-99.

31. Nicoll, *Church's One Foundation,* 65-66, 86-87.

32. Among the Scots both James Orr (1844-1913) and James Denney (1856-1917) made a formidable case for conservative positions, but each was first of all a systematic theologian, not an accomplished biblical critic. Their common failure to develop a sensitivity to the problems created by historical criticism was the most serious failing of two otherwise incisive theological minds. On both see Reardon, *Coleridge to Gore,* 426-29.

33. Quoted in Neill, *Interpretation,* 117.

34. Sanday's seminar had been meeting since 1894, yet a mere perusal of the *Oxford Studies* will show that the group by 1911 was very far from agreement

or final statements. In the preface Sanday found "conclusions" too strong a word to describe the results and followed it with "or steps toward conclusions"; William Sanday, "Introductory," *Oxford Studies in the Synoptic Problem,* ed. William Sanday (Oxford: University Press, 1911) xxiii. The testimonies to the complexities of gospel study and the many unsolved problems are legion in the decade after 1900. See for example A. E. Garvie, *The Inner Life of Christ,* Amer. ed. (New York: George H. Doran Co., n.d.) vii and especially the summaries of the state of gospel criticism that appeared throughout the decade in various Oxford and Cambridge symposia. Among these are W. C. Allen, "Modern Criticism and the New Testament," in *Contentio Veritatis: Essays by Six Oxford Tutors* (New York: E. P. Dutton, 1902) 206-42; Frederick Henry Chase, "The Gospels in the Light of Historical Criticism," in *Essays on Some Theological Problems of the Day,* ed. H. B. Swete (London: Macmillan and Co., 1905) 371-419; and Henry Latimer Jackson, "The Present State of the Synoptic Problem," in *Cambridge Biblical Essays,* ed. H. B. Swete (London: Macmillan and Co., 1909) 421-60.

35. On the role of the *Expositor* in late Victorian biblical study see Glover, *Evangelical Nonconformists,* 29.

36. The *Journal of Theological Studies* was founded jointly by the divinity faculties of Oxford and Cambridge; see Chadwick, *Victorian Church,* 2:452. There was a much earlier attempt at a journal of this sort, the *Journal of Classical and Sacred Theology* (1854-59), which despite a heavy investment of labor on the part of Lightfoot proved abortive. The reason for its demise—a lack of contributors—is significant as further evidence of the progress made by Victorian biblical scholarship during the last third of the century. See Eden and MacDonald, *Lightfoot of Durham,* Appendix C, 174-75.

37. G. M. Trevelyan, "Clio, A Muse," in *Clio, A Muse and Other Essays Literary and Pedestrian* (London: Longmans, Green and Co., 1914) 1-55.

38. A clear contemporary description of this change may be found in Chase, "Gospels in the Light of Historical Criticism," 373: "The study of history has now become a science, both in regard to its aim and in regard to its method. An historian of the old school was content to glean from his authorities a picturesque, or a majestic, or an instructive story. . . . The historian of to-day [1905], on the other hand, is primarily a student pledged to the work of research. His method is precise. He conscientiously collects his authorities; he analyses them; he compares them; he weighs them in the balances of his critical judgment."

39. Reardon, *Coleridge to Gore,* 305 n. 4.

40. Quoted in ibid., 305.

41. Thomas Hill Green, *Works,* ed. R. L. Nettleship, 2d ed. (London: Longmans, Green & Co., 1886-90), vol. 3, *Miscellanies & Memoir,* 242.

42. Ibid., 260.

43. See, for example, his article "The Jesus of History and the Christ of Religion," in *Jesus or Christ?* The Hibbert Journal Supplement 1909 (London: Williams & Norgate, 1909) 121-35.

44. See Reardon, *Coleridge to Gore,* 318, and the 1902 manifesto entitled *Personal Idealism: Philosophical Essays by Eight Members of the University of Oxford,* ed. Henry Sturt (London: Macmillan & Co., 1902).

45. See below, pp. 182-86.

46. Harnack, *What is Christianity?*, tr. T. B. Saunders (London: Williams and Norgate, 1901) 135.

47. "Our Present Knowledge of the Life of Christ," 125. W. R. Inge in *Protestantism* (London: Ernest Benn Ltd., 1927) was of the opinion that Ritschl's ideas did not greatly affect the liberal theologians of Great Britain. One prominent nonconformist whose stance resembled somewhat that of Ritschl and Harnack was the eminent Baptist John Clifford; see his *Ultimate Problems of Christianity* (London: Kingsgate Press, 1906).

48. This work was a long time in the making. The initial eight studies were written more than twenty years earlier, while Garvie was at work in the slums of Glasgow. They were expanded to ten and published in the *Expositor* serially during 1902 and finally put into a bound volume in 1907. See Garvie, *Studies in the Inner Life,* v.

49. Garvie, *Studies,* 122-23.

50. Ibid., vi.

51. Particularly after the appearance of *L'Évangile et l'église,* trans by Christopher Home as *The Gospel and the Church* (London: Isbister & Co., 1903), in 1902, the British theological press took notice of him. Percy Gardner began his review of *L'Évangile* in the *Hibbert Journal* 1 (April 1903) 602 as follows: "The name of the Abbé Loisy is little known in England at present. Certainly it ought to be better known." In the following years Loisy did become better known and formed the subject of a number of books and reviews. See "Romanus," "The Abbé Loisy as a Theologian," *Hibbert Journal* 2 (October 1903) 142-46; Percy Gardner, "M. Alfred Loisy's Type of Catholicism," *Hibbert Journal* 3 (October 1904) 126-38; and discussions of this last article by "Romanus" and Baron von Hügel in the *Hibbert Journal* 3 (January 1905) 376-80; (April 1905) 599-602. Non-Catholic assessments include W. T. Davison, "M. Loisy and the Vatican," *London Quarterly Review* 101 (April 1904) 288-307; and the *Contemporary Review* for March 1903, which carried translations of large extracts from *L'Évangile.* T. A. Lacey's *The Historic Christ* (London: Longmans & Co., 1905) was a defense of orthodoxy against the presuppositions of Loisy.

52. Translation mine. "Le Christ des Synoptiques est historique, mais il n'est pas Dieu; le Christ johannique est divin, mais il n'est pas historique." Though taken from the *Simples Réflexions sur le décret Lamentabili et sur l'encyclique Pascendi* (Ceffonds, 1908), 158, these words present in summary form the verdict of *Le Quatrième Évangile.*

53. For convenience I have adopted J. M. Robertson's rendering of this passage from the untranslated *Jesus et la tradition* as it appears in his *The Historical Jesus* (London: Watts & Co., 1916) 143. Chapters 15-18 of this

work present a criticism of Loisy from the even more radical standpoint of the rationalist "Christ-myth" school. See below pp. 186-87.

54. Robertson, *Historical Jesus*, 143.

55. Quoted and translated in ibid., 143. A translation of Wernle's *Die Quellen* into English appeared in 1907 as *The Sources of our Knowledge of the Life of Jesus*, trans. E. Lummis (London: Philip Green, 1907).

56. "It is to the great and abiding credit of the scientific theology of the nineteenth century that it has learned to distinguish between the Christ of Faith and the man Jesus of history, two entities which have been identified by ecclesiastical dogma. By means of careful and toilsome critical investigation it has been shown how the dogma of the God-man gradually took form, precipitated as it were from the intermingling of religious ideas of various origin with the reminiscences of the early Church concerning the life of her Master": Otto Pfliederer, *The Early Christian Conception of Christ: Its Significance and Value in the History of Religion* (London: Williams and Norgate, 1905) 7.

57. See the discussion of Norman Perrin in *Kingdom of God*, 16-23.

58. See William Sanday, *The Life of Christ in Recent Research* (New York: Oxford University Press, 1907), especially chaps. 2-7; F. C. Burkitt, preface to Schweitzer, *Quest*, v-vii.

59. Schweitzer, *Quest*, 398-99.

60. Perrin, *Kingdom of God*, 39-45.

61. Thompson's Life was published by Methuen & Co., London in 1909; Bennett's had first appeared serially in the *Expositor*. *The Contemporary Review* in its listing of "Current Theological Books," 97 (February 1910) 18, referred to Bennett's narrowly defined study with the revealing comment that it was "a sign of critical times."

62. Schweitzer, *Quest*, 333-34.

63. Horton Davies, *The Ecumenical Century, 1900-1956*, vol. 5 of *Worship and Theology in England* (Princeton: Princeton University Press, 1965) 179.

64. On this see Henry Chadwick's introduction to *Lessing's Theological Writings* (London: Adam & Charles Black, 1956).

65. See above, p. 176. The idea of a distinction between Christ in dogma and Christ in history was implicit from the start in the very enterprise of writing a life of Jesus. Strauss begins with it on the first page of the *Leben Jesu*, and it appears, as we saw, in the preface to Seeley's *Ecce Homo*, as well as other works that discussed problems of method. But as a fully articulated subject of theological dispute, it did not come to center stage until late in the century. In Germany, Ritschl, Wilhelm Herrmann, Pfliederer (see above, n. 56), and Harnack all wrestled with this issue, and in 1896 it provoked Martin Kähler's invigorating *Der sogenannte historische Jesus und der geschichtliche, biblische Christus* (Leipzig: A. Seichert, 1892), which was to be prophetic of much in twentieth-century theology.

66. The importance of these lectures could be read in the rare tribute Hatch received of an almost immediate translation into German and a publication, with additions, under the auspices of Harnack; see Neill, *Interpretation,* 137-38.

67. David W. Forrest, *The Christ of History and of Experience,* The Kerr Lectures for 1897 (Edinburgh: T. & T. Clark, 1897) 6.

68. Two of the more interesting were G. K. Chesterton, "Jesus or Christ: A Reply to Mr. Roberts," *Hibbert Journal* 7 (October 1909) 746-66; and Henry Scott Holland, "The Jesus of History and the Christ of Religion," in *Jesus or Christ?,* 121-35.

69. Arthur Harrington, "The Historical Jesus and the Christ of Experience," *Hibbert Journal* 3 (July 1905) 802; see also the article which began much of the discussion in the *Hibbert,* W. A. Pickard-Cambridge, "The Christ of Dogma and of Experience," *Hibbert Journal* 3 (January 1905) 253-70.

70. Dugald Macfadyen, "Faith and History," *London Quarterly Review* 110 (October 1908) 251.

71. A. O. Lovejoy, "The Entangling Alliance of Religion and History," *Hibbert Journal* 5 (January 1907) 270-71.

72. Ibid., 276.

73. One of the boldest exponents of this view was Paul Schmiedel, whose first claim to infamy in Britain was, as we have seen, his *Encyclopaedia* article on the gospels. In *Jesus in Modern Criticism,* tr. Maurice A. Carney (London: A. C. Black, 1907), he insisted that it would make no difference to his Christian faith if historians were to conclude that Jesus had in fact never lived.

74. Although the topic had been debated in the *Hibbert* since the article by Pickard-Cambridge (see n. 69 above), the supplement appeared in response to an article by the Rev. R. Roberts, formerly a Congregationalist pastor. Rev. Roberts's "Jesus or Christ: An Appeal for Consistency" appeared in the *Hibbert* for January, 1909 and was reprinted at the back of the special supplement, pp. 270-82.

75. See Alfred Loisy, "Remarques sur le Volume 'Jesus ou le Christ,' " *Hibbert Journal* 8 (April 1910) 473-97. An English translation was appended. Another work on the subject was J. Warschauer, *Jesus or Christ?* (London: James Clark & Co., 1909).

76. It should not be supposed, however, that more traditional views no longer found advocates. Toward the end of the decade there was a reappearance, in somewhat chastened form, of the view that the gospels could be traced back to eyewitness accounts. The spokesmen included Sir William Ramsay in two articles written in critique of Harnack for the *Expositor* (December 1906 and May 1907); George Salmon, who in his posthumous *Human Element in the Gospels* (London: John Murray, 1907) 274, wrote, "The more I study the Gospels the more convinced I am that we have in them contemporaneous history; that is to say, that we have in them the stories told

of Jesus immediately after His death, and which had been circulated and . . . put in writing while He was yet alive." This and a very similar passage from the idealist J. R. Illingsworth, *The Doctrine of the Trinity* (London: Methuen & Co., 1907) 37, were quoted with approval by yet another opponent of the new scepticism, C. F. Nolloth, *The Person of Our Lord and Recent Thought* (London: Macmillan and Co., 1908) 63-64 and n. 1.

77. P. T. Forsyth, "Revelation and the Person of Christ," in *Faith and Criticism*, 124.

78. W. R. Inge, "The Person of Christ," in *Contentio Veritatis*, 90.

79. W. R. Inge, "St. Paul," *Quarterly Review* 220 (January 1914) 45.

80. Percy Gardner, *A Historic View of the New Testament* (London: Adam and Charles Black, 1901) 74.

81. H. R. Mackintosh, *The Doctrine of the Person of Jesus Christ* (New York: Charles Scribner's Sons, 1912) 6-7.

82. For quite similar statements see "Romanus," "The Historical Jesus and the Christ of Experience," *Hibbert Journal* 3 (April 1905) 577; J. Estlin Carpenter, *The Historical Jesus and the Theological Christ* (Boston: American Unitarian Association, 1912) 14-16; and especially Jackson, "Synoptic Problem," 459, where he writes, "It has been pointed out that there are few persons of antiquity for whom we have as much to go on as in the case of Jesus. The admission must nevertheless be made that the reports which have come down to us of His life and ministry are singularly meagre. With the abandonment of harmonizing methods and greater or less reserve in the case of 'John', it is not likely that there will ever be another 'Life of Christ,' along the lines of a once famous work; a well-known author (Bousset) is perhaps on the right track when he treats of outward events in the career of Jesus in but a few pages."

83. The liberal Dutch critics were in part disciples of the penetrating German sceptic Bruno Bauer but managed to make their own original contribution to New Testament criticism as well. Though some of them antedated Drews, Robertson, and Smith by several decades, their influence on other lands, limited by language, was never very great. Among the more important were Allard Pierson (1831-96), Abraham Dirk Loman (1823-97), Samuel Adrian Naber (1828-1913), and Gerardus Johann Bolland (1854-1922). Equally significant were Willem Christian van Manen (1842-1905) and Wilhelm Brandt (1855-1915), neither of whom, however, went to the same lengths as the most radical of the school. On the Dutch liberal movement see McCown, *Search*, 74-75.

84. In Britain a lesser advocate of "Christ-myth" views was Thomas Whittaker, whose *Origins of Christianity* (London: Watts & Co., 1904) was seen as giving support to Christ-myth views; see Robertson, *Historical Jesus*, 187 n. 4 and 189.

85. Robertson, *Historical Jesus*, 119.

86. In Germany, where the movement's importance seems to have been overestimated, there was an enormous literature of rebuttal. See McCown,

Search, 69-86. In Britain there was less of a stir, but replies came from H. J. Rossington, *Did Jesus Really Live?* (London, 1911); J. Estlin Carpenter, *The Historical Jesus,* 16-37; and T. J. Thorburn, *Jesus the Christ: Historical or Mythical? A Reply to Prof. Drews' "Die Christusmythe"* (Edinburgh: T. & T. Clark, 1912).

87. A verdict which stung Robertson severely; see his somewhat acrimonious reply in *Historical Jesus,* 141.

88. F. C. Conybeare, *The Historical Christ: or, an Investigation of the Views of Mr. J. M. Robertson, Dr. A. Drews, and Prof. W. B. Smith* (London: Watts & Co., 1914). Robertson responded in *The Literary Guide* and the "Preamble" to *The Historical Jesus,* xvii-xxiv.

89. See above, pp. 64-69.

90. Altick, *English Common Reader,* 312-17.

91. Ibid., 312.

92. Ibid., 313. The general decline in the price of books was a century-long process spurred by advances in the methods and machinery of printing, a decrease in the costs of the raw materials and manufacture necessary for paper, and the improvement in the means of distributing printed matter. On all of these see R. K. Webb, "The Victorian Reading Public," 214-16.

93. Altick, *English Common Reader,* 231.

94. Patrick Scott, "The Business of Belief," Appendix, 224.

95. Walter Houghton, *The Victorian Frame of Mind: 1830-1870* (New Haven: Yale University Press, 1957), especially chap. 10, "Earnestness." Altick, *English Common Reader,* deals with these matters in chaps. 4 and 5: "Religion" and "The Utilitarian Spirit"; and there is discussion of the work ethic and improvement in Asa Briggs, *Victorian People*, chap. 5, "Samuel Smiles and the Gospel of Work."

96. Amy Cruse, *After the Victorians* (1938; London: George Allen & Unwin, Ltd., 1971) 193. On *Tit-Bits* and the new, light literature for the masses see also Esmé Wingfield Stratford, *The Victorian Sunset* (New York: William Morrow & Co., 1932) 208. The effect of the Education Act of 1870, it should be remembered, is a matter of considerable debate. It is questionable whether the new class of thoughtless readers discovered by Cruse's Mr. Smith was actually the sudden creation of the 1870 measure. See particularly the important qualifications by R. K. Webb, "Victorian Reading Public," 211.

97. Cruse, *After the Victorians,* 195.

98. Cruse, *Victorians and Their Reading,* 216; Chadwick, *Victorian Church,* 1:455-68.

99. See Geoffrey Best, *Mid-Victorian Britain,* 173; also K. S. Inglis, *The Churches and the Working Classes in Victorian England* (London: Routledge & Kegan Paul, 1963) 75.

100. Inglis, *Churches and the Working Classes,* 75.

101. Oliver Lodge, Sir Edward Russell, J. H. Muirhead, L. P. Jacks, "The Alleged Indifference of Laymen to Religion," *Hibbert Journal* 2 (January 1904) 235-58.

102. Though Oliver Lodge had what we are accustomed to regard as a more recent insight: that the workingmen never were practicing members of the churches, and that if it was their indifference that formed the chief cause of concern, it was hardly a crisis of very recent origin. Although each of the analysts gathered by the *Hibbert* editors tended to look somewhat narrowly at theological and intellectual reasons for the new indifference, rather than the social and economic ones that come to mind today, intellectual forces among the populace should not be too readily discounted. Archbishop Benson late in the century was astonished when a circle of ladies seeking instruction were in doubt about the authenticity of John and about how much could be known with certainty about the life of Jesus. See Benson, *Life of Edward White Benson,* 2:299.

103. Chadwick, *Victorian Church,* 2:232; see also Esmé Wingfield Stratford, *The Victorian Aftermath* (New York: William Morrow & Co., 1934) 119-29, especially 126-29.

104. Chadwick, *Victorian Church,* 2:234.

105. Inglis, *Churches and the Working Classes,* passim.

106. Oliver Lodge, "The Alleged Indifference of Laymen, I," 235-41.

107. C. F. G. Masterman, *The Condition of England* (London: Methuen & Co., 1909) 266.

108. Ibid., 269-70.

109. The two world wars of our century have taken a toll on publishing records of the Victorian era. Among major nineteenth-century publishers, some let their records go for salvage during the war years, as was the case with T. & T. Clark; others, particularly if they were London-based, lost heavily during the blitz and in the fires on Paternoster Row. Such was the fate suffered, for example, by Cassell and Hodder and Stoughton. Letters to the author from T. & T. Clark, Edinburgh, 25 October 1974; Cassell & Company Ltd., 18 October 1974; and Hodder and Stoughton Ltd., 28 October 1974.

110. Adolph Harnack, preface to the English edition, *What is Christianity?* iii.

111. David Smith, *The Days of His Flesh: The Earthly Life of Our Lord and Saviour Jesus Christ,* 9th ed. (London: Hodder and Stoughton, 1911) xxv-xxxv.

112. Ibid., xlv.

113. The list printed at the front of the 9th edition, which appeared in 1911, shows new editions in 1905, 1906, 1907, 1909, 1910, and 1911.

114. See the notice of *The Days of His Flesh,* in the *London Quarterly Review* 105 (January 1906) 118.

115. David Smith, *The Historic Jesus* (London: Hodder and Stoughton, 1912) 3-21; on Green, see p. 19.

116. T. R. Glover, *The Jesus of History* (1916; London: Association Press, 1929) 178.

117. Ibid., 167.

118. See the review of *The Prophet of Nazareth* in the *Spectator,* 12 July 1906.

119. G. H. Gilbert, preface to *Jesus* (New York: Macmillan & Co., 1912) vii.

120. Sanday, "Prefatory Note," *Outlines,* vii.

121. Sanday, *The Life of Christ in Recent Research,* ix.

122. Sanday, "Preface to the Second Edition," *Outlines,* viii.

123. William Sanday, *Christologies Ancient and Modern* (Oxford: Clarendon Press, 1910) v.

124. See McCown, *Search,* 161.

125. Young, *Portrait of an Age,* 109.

INDEX

About the Author

A native of South Holland, Illinois, Daniel L. Pals attended the Dutch private schools of the Christian Reformed Church. He holds an A.B. degree from Calvin College in Michigan, a B.D. from Calvin Theological Seminary, and an M.A. and Ph.D. from the University of Chicago, where he studied under Martin E. Marty. At Chicago Professor Pals was a University Evans Scholar and German Academic Exchange Scholar. He served several years as editorial assistant for *Church History*.

Professor Pals has published "The Reception of *Ecce Homo*," in the *Historical Magazine of the Protestant Episcopal Church*. He also has published numerous reviews in *Religious Studies Review, Church History,* and *Foundations*.

Now chairperson of the Religion Department at the University of Miami, Coral Gables, Florida, Professor Pals has previously taught at Trinity College in Deerfield, Illinois, and Centre College, Danville, Kentucky.